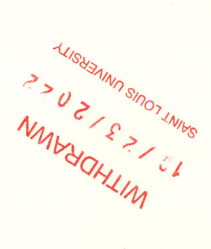

JAMES FENIMORE COOPER

Recent Titles in
Bibliographies and Indexes in American Literature

Joseph Conrad and American Writers: A Bibliographical Study of Affinities,
Influences, and Relations
Robert Secor and Debra Moddelmog, compilers

Melville's Classical Allusions: A Comprehensive Index and Glossary
Gail H. Coffler, compiler

An "Oliver Optic" Checklist: An Annotated Catalog-Index to the Series,
Nonseries Stories, and Magazine Publications of William Taylor Adams
Dolores B. Jones, compiler

Women in Southern Literature: An Index
Patricia Sweeney, compiler

Bibliography of the Little Golden Books
Dolores B. Jones, compiler

A Chronological Outline of American Literature
Samuel J. Rogal, compiler

Humor of the Old Southwest: An Annotated Bibliography of Primary and
Secondary Sources
Nancy Snell Griffith, compiler

Images of Poe's Works: A Comprehensive Descriptive Catalogue of Illustrations
Burton R. Pollin, compiler

Through the Pale Door: A Guide to and through the American Gothic
Frederick S. Frank

The Robert Lowell Papers at the Houghton Library, Harvard University
Patrick K. Miehe, compiler

Bernard Malamud: A Descriptive Bibliography
Rita N. Kosofsky

A Tale Type and Motif Index of Early U.S. Almanacs
J. Michael Stitt and Robert K. Dodge

Jerzy Kosinski: An Annotated Bibliography
Gloria L. Cronin and Blaine H. Hall

JAMES FENIMORE COOPER

An Annotated Bibliography of Criticism

Compiled by
ALAN FRANK DYER

Bibliographies and Indexes in American Literature,
Number 16

GREENWOOD PRESS
New York • Westport, Connecticut • London

Library of Congress Cataloging-in-Publication Data

Dyer, Alan Frank.
   James Fenimore Cooper : an annotated bibliography of criticism /
compiled by Alan Frank Dyer.
     p. cm.—(Bibliographies and indexes in American literature,
ISSN 0742-6860 ; no. 16)
   Includes bibliographical references and indexes.
   ISBN 0-313-27919-5 (alk. paper)
   1. Cooper, James Fenimore, 1789-1851—Bibliography.   I. Title.
II. Series.
Z8191.7.D9   1991
[PS1431]
016.813'2—dc20   91-27084

British Library Cataloguing in Publication Data is available.

Library of Congress Catalog Card Number: 91-27084
ISBN: 0-313-27919-5
ISSN: 0742-6860

First published in 1991

Greenwood Press, 88 Post Road West, Westport, CT 06881
An imprint of Greenwood Publishing Group, Inc.

Printed in the United States of America

The paper used in this book complies with the
Permanent Paper Standard issued by the National
Information Standards Organization (Z39.48-1984).

10 9 8 7 6 5 4 3 2 1

CONTENTS

PREFACE

The bibliography that follows is composed of 1943 reviews, journal articles, newspaper articles and editorials, dissertations, and books written between 1820 and 1990. While no pretense toward definitiveness is made, this compilation lists a majority of those sources available to the Cooper scholar.

Arrangement of the material into chapters is by broad subject category: Bibliography, Biography, General Studies, Frontier and Indian Novels, Literature of the Sea, Social and Political Writings, and Miscellaneous Publications. Each appropriate chapter is then subdivided into individual Cooper publications, with further divisions relating to material written before and after Cooper's death. Most of the fiction and non-fiction was easily placed under one of these broad chapter headings, although a few created problems. For instance, both *The Crater* and *Homeward Bound* are often listed with Cooper's sea fiction, but from a thematic point of view they seemed more closely tied to the social and political category and have been placed there.

Annotations are provided for most entries. While they are descriptive rather than critical in nature, references to other conflicting and supporting entries are often made. Those items that the compiler has not seen are so noted.

Although there was no concentrated effort to identify pertinent newspaper editorials and reviews, those that were discovered during the normal course of research have been included. In general, the newspaper name and date alone have been provided for nineteenth century citations. Page numbers are given only for the larger metropolitan dailies (e.g., *New York Times*, *Times* [London]).

Essays and reviews in foreign languages have been excluded, although occasional reference is made to the existence of European bibliographies dealing with Cooper.

INTRODUCTION

James Fenimore Cooper published his first novel, *Precaution*, in 1820. Although it was largely ignored by the reviewing media in the United States and abroad, one journal, the *Literary and Scientific Repository* (1920),[*] saw in it what future critics were to praise: Cooper's ability to write fiction that was truly American. *The Spy, The Pioneers, The Pilot, The Last of the Mohicans*, and *The Prairie* followed over the next seven years, all receiving far greater attention than *Precaution* and winning Cooper a wide readership despite mixed reviews. As was typical of the time, the British periodical press took the critical lead, with most American journals content to wait upon a foreign opinion. One notable exception was the *Port Folio* that, in a February 1822 review (1243), praised *The Spy* for its characterizations, dialogue, high level of interest, and contribution to American literature.

Not all reviewers agreed, however, and two months later W. H. Gardiner, in *The North American Review* (1224), found only faint praise for the book, claiming it was not equal to the work of Sir Walter Scott. Gardiner, again writing for the *Review* (914), continued to express his reservations about Cooper in an article on *The Pioneers*, the first volume of the Leatherstocking Tales. While willing to acknowledge Cooper as America's foremost novelist, Gardiner believed this position would only last until someone better suited took the title from him. Typically, Gardiner found *The Last of the Mohicans* to have characters placed in impossible situations and to have too much action and a cluttered plot (982). William Cullen Bryant noted similar faults in a review of *The Prairie* (1060). Fortunately for Cooper, other reviewers

---

[*]Parenthetical figures refer to item numbers of reviews and criticism in the body of the book.

described these works as unequalled in description and narration, suspenseful, accurate in detail, and original in nature.

The Pilot, published in 1823, the same year as *The Pioneers*, was Cooper's first work to receive more positive than negative comment. British reviewers were especially eager to praise his first sea tale, comparing it favorably with the writings of Smollett and Scott (e.g., 1391, 1402, 1404). Leigh Hunt, in a well reasoned *Tatler* review (1390), proclaimed that Cooper had set the standard for American sea fiction with this book.

Lionel Lincoln, an 1825 Revolutionary War novel, appeared just prior to the *Mohicans* and *The Prairie*. Unlike its predecessors, it was a complete failure. With the exception of reasonably favorable reviews in the *U. S. Literary Gazette* (1299) and *Nepenthes* (1295), both American and British reviewers roundly criticized it. One reviewer went so far as to suggest that Cooper's earlier success was earned not through talent but by accident and that other writers would soon emerge to surpass him permanently (1293). An American, John Neal, writing for *Blackwood's Magazine* (1294) contributed to the attack, but did so with humor and a style untypical of most British publications of the time.

In 1828 Cooper tried his hand at nonfiction, but *Notions of the Americans* suffered much the same fate as *Lionel Lincoln* had three years previously. It was largely ignored by American reviewers and the British could find little positive to say about the work. A *Literary Gazette* (1867) review was so severe in its condemnation that other writers, while admitting to the book's flaws, also found it necessary to point out the unfairness of the *Gazette*'s evaluation (1860, 1869).

Despite the negative reception of *Notions*, Cooper refused throughout the 1830s to return to the romances of the sea and frontier that had brought him popularity. Instead, the decade saw his writings become increasingly more political in their pronouncements; consequently, the attacks upon him became more frequent and intense. *The Bravo*, published in 1831 as the first volume of his European trilogy, was an exception in that it was generally well received. Leigh Hunt, writing in the *Tatler* (1625), believed *The Bravo* to be Cooper's most exciting novel and compared him favorably with Scott. Unfortunately, *The Heidenmauer* and *The Headsman*, the last two works in the series, did not fare as well. Both were reviewed extensively in America and England and were largely condemned. The only favorable reviews of substance appeared in the New York *Evening Post* (1652, 1669).

Still, Cooper forged ahead, returning to nonfiction with the 1834 publication of *A Letter to His Countrymen*. While the British media paid little attention to the work, American critics were especially vicious in their attacks upon it. The *New-England Magazine* (1890), for example, considered it an absurd volume, full of hallucinations, written by a man who was losing his wits.

The Monikins, a bitter social satire, appeared the following year to scant notice from the media. The *Literary Gazette*'s statement (1739) that it was an able try, written with some ingenuity, proved to be the best that was said of the book. This faint praise, however, did not move other reviewers, some of whom claimed *The Monikins* was Cooper's worst attempt to date -- a vain, prejudiced, caricature, filled with rubbish that should never have been published.

Between 1836 and 1838 Cooper published a series of European travelogues. They received a somewhat better hearing than their immediate predecessors as reviewers seemed eager to point to anything that might revive their creator's literary fortunes. The *Knickerbocker Magazine* (1785), for instance, said that *Sketches of Switzerland* would go a long way toward restoration of a reputation that had been completely destroyed by *The Monikins*. While these volumes were praised by some reviewers for descriptions and reflections of interest to both Americans and Europeans, they were also considered to be ill-humored, ignorant, and prejudiced by others. A *Quarterly Review* essay (1832) on *Gleanings in England* went so far as to denounce Cooper as both writer and man. This review was widely distributed in the United States and, consequently, the travelogues did not become the positive influence that some believed they would.

Along with the final volume in the travelogue series, Cooper published three additional works in 1838. One book of nonfiction, *The American Democrat,* contained a comprehensive statement of his social and political philosophy and, for that reason alone, deserved to be extensively reviewed. It was not, but neither was it treated as harshly as some of its predecessors. Two novels that severely criticized American society, *Homeward Bound* and *Home as Found*, rounded out the year's work. While they were found to be exciting and lively by the *Athenaeum* (1694), they were most often compared to *The Monikins*. F. Bowen in the *North American Review* (1695) considered *Homeward Bound* to be tiresome, absurd, and stupid. A James Watson Webb review of *Home as Found* (1724) said that Cooper wrote the book only to make a profit in England and that Cooper was a traitor to his country and should leave it. Cooper promptly sued Webb for libel. *Home as Found* was also reviewed in the *Albany Evening Journal* (1725) where Thurlow Weed claimed that Cooper had only written the book as a means of attacking those who had offended him. It is important to note that Weed had earlier been sued by Cooper over comments in the same newspaper concerning Cooper's warning to trespassers on his land at Three Mile Point (see items 176-80). These novels, the legal action resulting from them, and the land controversy to which they became joined did little to improve the public's impression of Cooper as author or man. The 1830s drew to a close with the publication of *History of the Navy* in 1839. While it was generally praised in America, it was severely criticized in Great Britain. The *Edinburgh*

Review (1566) perhaps best expressed what British reviewers found to be the work's greatest fault--that Cooper did not consider British opinions or viewpoints in controversial areas. Thus, his historical accuracy was called into question. Some American critics, William A. Duer among them, gleefully pounced on this perceived defect as well. Cooper's response to Duer was to sue his editor as he had Webb and Weed earlier (see item 181).

Cooper's social and political views, his seemingly exaggerated sense of self-importance, and his tendency to expound upon subjects of which it appeared he had scant knowledge, had led his critics to implore him to return to the non-political sea and frontier romance lest his reputation be completely destroyed. This he did in the 1840s. The Littlepage trilogy (1845-46), born out of the anti-rent controversy, *The Crater* (1847) and *The Ways of the Hour* (1850) were exceptions to this trend. Consequently, these books were not well reviewed and, when they were noticed, reviewers not only found fault with Cooper's ideas, but with his exaggerations, repetitiveness, and the general uninteresting nature of his subject matter.

In juxtaposition to these volumes was Cooper's continuation of the Leatherstocking Tales during the early part of the decade. Both *The Pathfinder* in 1840 and *The Deerslayer* in 1841 were heralded for their lack of social and political commentary and were important vehicles in restoration of a reputation lost during the 1830s. Even *Wyandotte*, an 1843 novel described as dull, plotless, and devoid of action seemed to bring a sigh of relief from at least one reviewer who could find none of Cooper's usual social preachings in the text (1331). An Edgar Allen Poe review of the book in *Graham's Magazine* (1328) considered it unoriginal, obvious, and stylistically inferior, but nevertheless absorbing. In a like manner, *Oak Openings*, an 1848 frontier novel, was recognized for its return to the old themes necessary to bring back lost readers (1335). The 1840s was also the decade in which Cooper produced the majority of his sea fiction: seven tales if one considers *Afloat and Ashore* and *Miles Wallingford* as a single work. While these stories most often met with mixed reviews, critics seemed pleased that Cooper had forsaken his liberal use of political and social comment. Only in an 1848 *Brownson's Quarterly Review* of *The Sea Lions* (1544) was the subject discussed to any significant degree. In this case, however, rather than taking Cooper to task for his views, the author presented an explanation of America's failure to understand them.

Following his death in September 1851, Cooper quickly fell into disrepute and near oblivion with literary America. Thomas Lounsbury's assessment (114) of both Cooper's character and social and political views aided in this development. His critical demise was further assured by Mark Twain's attack in the July 1895, *North American Review* (653). While this was not the only time that Cooper had been satirized, having been parodied by William Makepeace Thackeray in *Punch* (286) nearly fifty years earlier and by

Bret Harte in *Muck-a-Muck: A Modern Indian Novel After Cooper* (798), the difference was the animosity that was evident in the Twain article.   Lance Schachterle and Kent Ljundquist have since taken Twain to task for an inaccurate appraisal of Cooper that was based upon scant evidence (1171). In a like manner, Tremaine McDowell, in a 1930 article (1266), claimed that Cooper was a conscientious critic of his own material and made more than nominal revisions of his work.

By the turn of the century a few writers, William Brownell (334-35), Brander Matthews (118, 506-8), and William Phelps (561) among them, sought to right some of the damage done by their nineteenth century colleagues. Because their work was highly biographical, however, little that was new or insightful about Cooper resulted.

It was not until after World War I that Cooper began to be studied as a serious American author.   Among the outstanding works of this period is Robert E. Spiller's *Fenimore Cooper: Critic of His Times* (619).   Spiller sought to illustrate that Cooper was indeed a profound social critic and not, as Twain suggested, a writer of boys' stories.   H. L. Mencken, in an intro-duction to a reprint of *The American Democrat* (1912), discussed Cooper's aristocratic notions, their impact on his ideas about social responsibility, and the number of Cooper's prophesies that had proven accurate.   In 1927, a Vernon Louis Parrington study (548) concluded that Cooper had been a Jeffersonian defender of the republic at odds with his aristocratic nature. Other important contributors also emerged, including John F. Ross (590), who considered Cooper a forerunner of modern day social critics; Dorothy Waples (668), who attributed Cooper's unpopularity to the Whig newspapers; and Ethel Outland (201), whose study of Cooper's libel suits resulted in conclusions opposing those of Waples.   James Grossman's 1954 article on Cooper's belief that the press had outlived its usefulness and that public opionion had become its prisoner is also significant to understanding the libel suits (1727).

To these and other early twentieth century critics must go the credit for what, by the mid-1900s, had resulted in a complete re-evaluation of Cooper and his works.   Forgotten were his lapses in style, his repetition and wordiness, his wooden characters, his historical inaccuracies, and his reputation as a juvenile author.   In their stead Cooper was praised as a pioneer in the development of the American social and political novel. Russell Kirk, writing in 1946, said that Cooper was the first to use social and political criticism in his writings (1615) and that his democratic principles called for political equality, progress, freedom, property rights, and gentility (472). Arthur M. Schlesinger (595) and John McClosky (1758) both found Cooper to be a conservative whose views changed as the country developed and expanded, while Marius Bewley (315), taking an opposing viewpoint, saw only continuity in Cooper's political opinions over his lifetime.   Others seeking to raise Cooper's stature included Thomas Philbrick (1376), who, in a full length study, concentrated on Cooper as the originator of the sea novel; Morton Frisch (1880), who claimed that Cooper's social and political theories showed a great understanding of his time; and James Folsom (705), who stressed the author's ability to see the social and moral implications of the westward movement. Both Folsom's volume and Donald Davie's *The Heyday of Sir Walter Scott* (943) stand in contrast to Henry Nash Smith's *Virgin Land* (874), a 1950 discussion of the Leatherstocking Tales. This is not to infer, however, that all recent writers have seen Cooper in a positive light. Roy Harvy Pearce, for example, in *"The Leatherstocking Tales Re-examined"* (850) states that they are complete failures as novels of ideas.

At the same time that scholars were concerning themselves with studies of Cooper's social and political thought and general importance to American literature, others were narrowing their focus to more one-dimensional themes. Thus, William Wasserstrom (1106), drawing on *The Prairie*, examined the similarities between Cooper and Freud in their concepts of the origin of society. Nearly twenty years later, both Stephen Railton (574) and Eric Sundquist (1733) explored influential events in Cooper's life and their Freudian impact on his works. Annette Kolodny made use of the psychological approach in two studies (475, 815) that investigated theme in the Leatherstocking Tales and Cooper's need to dominate nature. More recently, Mabel Dunham's introduction to marriage and the wilderness in *The Prairie* has been interpreted in psychological terms by Paul Rosenzweig (1137).

A second group of critics have chosen to explore the importance of religion in Cooper's life and its effect on his writings. Charles Brady's "James Fenimore Cooper" (328) provides an appraisal from a Catholic viewpoint, while Keith Burich (338) and J. Gary Williams (677, 1666) assess Cooper's attitudes toward Catholicism. Aspects of Trinitarianism have been found in Cooper's writings by Allan Axelrad (297) and Howard Mumford Jones (464). Henry S. Canby (350) and Howard Hintz (444) both concern themselves with Quaker influences on Cooper, while John Frederick's *Darkened Sky* (412) concludes that Cooper's early fiction shows aspects of Deism. Cooper has also been seen as an apologist for the Episcopal Church who took every opportunity to place Calvinism in a bad light (445, 823).

The search for sources used by Cooper has led critics in several directions. Warren S. Walker's folklore studies list over 200 proverbs found in Cooper's writings (665), investigate the use of folk elements in theme and narration (643), and discuss folk-types, the supernatural, and dialect (662). Several articles by Florence French examine the use of proverbs and folk-sayings (413, 1182-83). James Pickering (1200) and Joseph Slater (1202) comment on Cooper's knowledge of Anglo-Dutch customs; his understanding of sea lore, legend, and idiom are pointed out by John Clagett (1363); and William Bonner (1359) discusses his use of the Captain Kidd legend.

Cooper's contribution to the perpetuation of the folk-type (961, 1257) is illustrated by Harvey Birch (the Yankee peddler myth) and Billy Kirby (later development of the Paul Bunyan legend).

The real-life individuals Cooper used as sources for his characters have concerned several scholars. As early as 1823, it was claimed that David Gray, a Revolutionary War spy, was Cooper's model for Harvey Birch (1222). In 1831, H. L. Barnum named Enoch Crosby as the prototype (1221). This claim was disputed in two articles written in the 1890s by Guy Hatfield (1259-60). Hatfield was promptly challenged by James Deane (1254). More recently, Rufus Wilson (1285) and J. C. Pumpelly (1274) have supported the Crosby claim. Others continue to disagree, however, several of them putting forth their own candidates for the model (1247, 1255, 1283). Tremaine McDowell (1265) takes issue with all of the above writers, claiming Birch was a product of Cooper's imagination. Similarly, Edith Beaumont (760) has written of earlier attempts to identify Nathaniel and David Shipman as models for Natty Bumppo (761, 863, 888). Eleanor Franz (791) speculates that Nat Foster, an eighteenth century trapper, was Cooper's real-life hero. Marshall Fishwick (789) believes the character is based on Daniel Boone, while John Vlach (890) says Natty is a combination of Boone and Davey Crockett. There are similar studies of Hugh Willoughby in *Wyandotte* (1334), Paul Hoover in *The Prairie* (1100), Tom Hutter in *The Deerslayer* (1175), and Duncan Heyward in *The Last of the Mohicans* (1016).

Cooper's Indian characterizations were, from the beginning, criticized as being unreal and highly romanticized. In 1828 Lewis Cass (691) wrote that it was unfortunate that Cooper had relied upon John Heckewelder's *Account of the History, Manners, and Customs of the Indian Nations* as his source, a sentiment also expressed more recently by Paul Wallace (743, 896). Arthur Parker (847) finds that Cooper took his information from local legend, other writers, and personal acquaintances, but his real interest remained in creating works of fiction. In a like manner, Gregory Paine (846) writes that Cooper relied on sources he believed to be accurate, but his imagination often took over. The influence exerted by Heckewelder often led him to idealize his Indian portraits (1168). Elémire Zolla (907) states that Cooper's Indians were highly romanticized, but attributes this to his social, political, and religious beliefs. Opposing opinions have been expressed by Jason Russell (865) and Edwin Stockton (880), who emphasize that Cooper possessed reliable sources and stayed faithful to them. The examination of public records of Indian speech by John Frederick (708) tends to support this view, for they show that Cooper did not exaggerate his Indians' eloquence. In other studies, Richard Vanderbeets (1173) concludes that much of the Indian lore, characterization, and plot in *The Deerslayer* can be traced to an 1827 Indian captivity narrative; E. Muszynska-Wallace (1090) lists journals and histories of Lewis and Clarke, Charlevoix, Mackenzie, and Long among the sources used for *The Prairie*; and

Donald Ringe (1217) names Thacher's *Military Journal* as a source for *The Redskins*. Cooper's female characters have been examined as closely as his Indians. Kay Seymour House has written several sympahetic studies (447, 450 with Genevieve Belfiglio, 641) that conflict with the popular nineteenth century attitudes of Lowell (265), Howells (452) and others. The minor roles and poor delineation of Cooper's female characters were the result of the age in which he wrote, according to Nina Baym (759). Edna Steeves (877) says that Cooper's women were typically Victorian: they fainted, acted as sources for moral inspiration, stayed at home, and possessed great courage and resourcefulness when necessary. Mary Schriber (596-97) credits Cooper with being the first to create distinctly American women who are intelligent, spirited, experienced, and as important as their male counterparts. Among those who disagree are Sandra Zagarell (689), who illustrates how other writers quickly moved beyond Cooper in their treatment of women and their roles, and Joyce Warren (669), who sees Cooper's women as dependent upon males and lacking rights as individuals. Recent Ph.D. dissertations on the subject by Dodd (387), Elliott (782), Faver (947), and Fleischner (407) are also significant.

Cooper's contemporaries had little to say regarding his views on slavery, the South, or his characterization of blacks in general. Among twentieth century critics, Max Griffin (427) states that Cooper tried to be fair to the South as he considered constitutional law and the national interest. Russell Kirk (472) describes him as a man seeking a middle road between Northern capitalism and Southern separatism. Leona Davis (1905) writes of Cooper's pro-slavery views and Freimarck and Rosenthal (1908) find that he often reflected the opinions of slavery's adherents, whereas Robert Spiller (621) says that Cooper was not a pro-slavery apologist, but refused to speak out on the subject. Cooper is found to be in the tradition of the Southern novelist by John Seelye (601), partly as a result of his comic portrayal of blacks; Charles Nilon (533) blames him for much of the stereotypical black characterizations found in American literature until recent times; and Catherine Starke (1279) says his slave portrayals were meant to point out the virtues of the landed class.

Studies of Cooper's relationships with other literary figures, his knowledge of them, and their debt to him abound. Two articles by Edward Vandiver (655, 1103) address Cooper's knowledge of Shakespeare. Milton's influence has been noted by David Kesterton (721) and a Joann Krieg study (958) discusses Spenser's *The Faerie Queen* as a source for *The Pioneers*. That Cooper was familiar with Defoe's *Robinson Crusoe* is illustrated by incidents in *The Crater* according to W. B. Gates (1757). Articles by Thomas Palfrey (1686) and James Sheperd (1277) show that Cooper and Balzac borrowed from each other. Studies by Donald Goodfellow (1493) and David Seed (1046) demonstrate that Cooper also borrowed from Washington Irving.

The debt of Herman Melville to Cooper is explored by Nathalia Wright (1714), Morton Ross (1712), and Christine Bird (1358).   Studies of Cooper and Scott (944, 1089), Thackeray (1107), Poe (1025), Crane (1037), Algier (867), Karl May (1029), Conrad (1087, 1552), and Faulkner (379, 532, 717, 735, 899) also exist.

Lastly, *The Writings of James Fenimore Cooper Series* published by the State University Press of New York (307) should be noted.   Begun in 1980, as of 1990, seventeen individual works of fiction and nonfiction have been published, each with an historical introduction and textual notes by recognized Cooper scholars.   When completed, this series will form an important addition to the existing body of Cooper scholarship.

Cooper, the first American to earn his living from writing, was as widely read abroad as at home.   The translation of his works into every European language assured that his portrayal of America would be accepted by a large part of the world and that his works would play a significant role in the development of fiction in European countries (301, 534, 549, 568, 644, 646, 733, 839, 1029).   His desire to develop a truly American literature gave rise to the frontier and sea novel, the invention of America's first mythical hero (Natty Bumppo), and descriptions of nineteenth century life and society that are of value to social historians today.

JAMES FENIMORE COOPER

1

BIBLIOGRAPHY

1 Barnes, Warner. "American First Editions at TxU. XIII. James Fenimore Cooper (1789-1851)." LIBRARY CHRONICLE OF THE UNIVERSITY OF TEXAS 7 (Summer 1962):15-18.
    A description of those C. editions held by the University of Texas that are variants to the copies listed in Blanck's BIBLIOGRAPHY (item no. 3).

2 Beard, James F. "James Fenimore Cooper." FIFTEEN AMERICAN AUTHORS BEFORE 1900: BIBLIOGRAPHIC ESSAYS ON RESEARCH AND CRITICISM. Edited by Robert A. Rees and Earl N. Harbert. Madison: University of Wisconsin Press, 1971. Pp. 63-96. 1984 edition. Pp. 80-127.
    Covers bibliographies of C's. publications, his life, and critical material. Similar to Spiller's LITERARY HISTORY (item no. 20) in scope, but Beard provides more textual comments and criticism.

3 Blanck, Jacob. BIBLIOGRAPHY OF AMERICAN LITERATURE. Vol. 2. New Haven, Conn.: Yale University Press, 1957. Pp. 276-309.
    A worthy supplement to Spiller and Blackburn (item no. 19). Lists C. editions based upon trade periodical announcements. A descriptive bibliography.

4 Cairns, William B. BRITISH CRITICISMS OF AMERICAN WRITINGS, 1815-1833. University of Wisconsin Studies in Language and Literature, no. 14. Madison: University of Wisconsin Press, 1922. Pp. 112-57.
    Excerpts of reviews from 1822-33. C. was given little attention by some of the best British literary magazines, although he was reviewed widely. He probably received more negative criticism than he deserved for he gained

both political and personal enemies during his European stay.

5 Clavel, Marcel. FENIMORE COOPER AND HIS CRITICS: AMERICAN, BRITISH, AND FRENCH CRITICISM OF THE NOVELIST'S EARLY WORK. Aix-en-Provence, 1938.
      Largely a reprinting of criticism of PRECAUTION, THE SPY, THE PIONEERS, THE PILOT, LIONEL LINCOLN, and THE LAST OF THE MOHICANS.

6 Dekker, George and John P. McWilliams, eds. FENIMORE COOPER; THE CRITICAL HERITAGE. London & Boston: Routledge & Kegan Paul, 1973.
      A collection of early C. criticism from about fifty of his contemporaries.

7 Drescher, Rudolph. "My Cooper Collection." FREEMAN'S JOURNAL (Cooperstown), February 13, 1929.
      C. editions in German. See also the December 6, 1911 and November 14, 1918 issues for other articles relating to C. and Germany.

8 Hopkins, Frederick M. "The World of Rare Books." SATURDAY REVIEW OF LITERATURE 2 (November 14, 1925):307.
      A description of the material in the James Fenimore Cooper collection at the Sterling Memorial Library, Yale University. Includes several manuscripts of the L. S. TALES, three diaries, 300 letters to and from family members, and several hundred letters from other acquaintances of C's. (Irving, Scott, Samuel Morse, William Dunlap, Charles Wilkes, Lafayette, etc.).

9 Johnson, Merle. AMERICAN FIRST EDITIONS. New York: R. R. Bowker, 1932. Pp. 86-89.
      Primarily a list of first editions of C's. romances. Includes city of publication, date, number of volumes, and occasional notes.

10 Leary, Lewis. "Knickerbocker Literature at the Benjamin Collections." COLUMBIA LIBRARY COLUMNS 9 (February 1960):22-27.
      A collection of books, manuscripts, and periodicals covering New York from the mid-1830s to the mid-1860s. Includes C. material.

11 Libman, Valentina A. RUSSIAN STUDIES OF AMERICAN LITERATURE: A BIBLIOGRAPHY. Chapel Hill: University of North Carolina Press, 1969. Pp. 53-58.
      Comments on C. in Russian. Sixty-two items.

12 Mantz, Harold Elmer. FRENCH CRITICISM OF AMERICAN LITERATURE BEFORE 1850. New York: Columbia University Press, 1917. Pp. 39-44, 52-54, 65-69.

    Excerpts of reviews of C's. novels from French sources. Both he and Irving were favorably received.

13 THE NATIONAL UNION CATALOG; PRE-1956 IMPRINTS. VOL. 121. London: Mansell Information/Publishing Ltd., 1970. Pp. 591-673.

    List of C. novels reported as owned by the Library of Congress and other participating libraries. Information given is that available on the standard library catalog card.

14 New York State Historical Association. "James Fenimore Cooper Centennial Exhibition." NEW YORK HISTORY 32 (October 1951):474-87.

    A catalog of the C. exhibition held at the Fenimore House.

15 Nilon, Charles H. BIBLIOGRAPHY OF BIBLIOGRAPHIES IN AMERICAN LITERATURE. New York: R. R. Bowker Co., 1970. Pp. 68-70.

    Lists twenty-one bibliographies of C's. works, and criticism of them.

16 Pfennig, Hazel Tesh. "Periodical Literary Criticism (1800-65): A Study of the Book Reviews from 1800 to the Close of the Civil War Dealing With the Successive Works of Irving, Cooper, Poe, Hawthorne, Bryant, and Thoreau Which Appeared in American Publications Within the Lifetime of the Individual Authors." Ph.D. dissertation, New York University, 1932.

17 Sabin, Joseph. A DICTIONARY OF BOOKS RELATING TO AMERICA FROM ITS DISCOVERY TO THE PRESENT TIME. Vol. 4. New York: J. Sabin & Sons, 1871. Pp. 490-510.

    Records many foreign editions.

18 Spiller, Robert E. "Second Thoughts on Cooper as a Social Critic." NEW YORK HISTORY 35 (October 1954):540-57.

    A bibliographic essay on C. scholarship.

19 _____ and Philip C. Blackburn. A DESCRIPTIVE BIBLIOGRAPHY OF THE WRITINGS OF JAMES FENIMORE COOPER. New York: R. R. Bowker Co., 1934. Reprint edition, N. Y. Burt Franklin, 1968.

    Includes the first and early editions (both in English and foreign languages) for each novel, with complete bibliographical information; American, French, and German editions of his collected works; contributions to periodicals, etc.; material attributed to him; and adaptations of his work.

20 _____ et al. LITERARY HISTORY OF THE UNITED STATES: BIBLIOGRAPHY. 3d ed. rev. New York: Macmillan Co., 1963. Pp. 97-98, 452-54.

> Two bibliographic essays, one updating the other. Far from complete, but they give mention to much of the best C. criticism.

21 Trent, William Peterfield et al., eds. THE CAMBRIDGE HISTORY OF AMERICAN LITERATURE. Vol. 1. New York: G. P. Putnam's Sons, 1921. Pp. 530-34.

> A list of C's collected and single works in English, his contributions to periodicals, and about 50 references to C. criticism and biography.

22 Tucker, Martin, ed. THE CRITICAL TEMPER: A SURVEY OF MODERN CRITICISM ON ENGLISH AND AMERICAN LITERATURE FROM THE BEGINNINGS TO THE TWENTIETH CENTURY. Vol. 3. New York: Frederick Ungar Publishing Co., 1969. Pp. 253-61.

> Selections from fourteen twentieth century critics.

23 _____, ed. MOULTON'S LIBRARY OF LITERARY CRITICISM OF ENGLISH AND AMERICAN AUTHORS THROUGH THE BEGINNING OF THE TWENTIETH CENTURY. Vol. 3. New York: Frederick Ungar Publishing Co., 1966. Pp. 219-31.

> Selections from twenty-eight nineteenth century critics.

24 Virginia. University of. Library. Clifton Waller Barrett Library. THE FICTION OF JAMES FENIMORE COOPER. AN EXHIBITION OF AMERICAN, ENGLISH AND CONTINENTAL EDITIONS AND MANUSCRIPTS FROM THE CLIFTON WALLER BARRETT LIBRARY, UNIVERSITY OF VIRGINIA. APRIL-JUNE 1974. Charlottesville: Department of Rare Books, University of Virginia Library, 1974.

25 Ward, William S. "American Authors and British Reviewers, 1798-1826: A Bibliography." AMERICAN LITERATURE 49 (March 1977):1-21.

> Includes fifty-three reviews of C's. first six novels. No annotations.

26 Wegelin, Oscar. EARLY AMERICAN FICTION, 1774-1830. Stamford, Conn.: Published by the Compiler, 1902. Pp. 11-12.

> Titles published before 1831.

27 Woodress, James. "The Fortunes of Cooper in Italy." STUDI

AMERICANI 11 (1965):53-76.
Bibliography of Italian editions of C. and of C. criticism in Italian.

28 Wright, Lyle H. AMERICAN FICTION, 1774-1850: A CONTRIBUTION TOWARD A BIBLIOGRAPHY. 2d rev. ed. San Marino Cal.: Huntington Library, 1969. Pp. 82-100.
American editions of C's. novels only. Little description, no variation between copies noted.

2

BIOGRAPHY

29 Adams, James Truslow. HISTORY OF THE TOWN OF SOUTHHAMP-
TON. Bridgehampton, L. I.: Hampton Press, 1918. Pp. 160, 237.
   On C's. whaling activities and Fordham's Inn where he may have
written PRECAUTION.

30 Adkins, Nelson Frederick. FITZ-GREENE HALLECK; AN EARLY
KNICKERBOCKER WIT AND POET. New Haven, Conn.: Yale University
Press, 1930. Pp. 151-57.
   Halleck's relations with C. and the Bread and Cheese Club.

31 _____. "Glimpse of Fenimore Cooper in His Last Years." NOTES AND
QUERIES (London) 167 (August 11, 1934):96-97. A reprint of the "Preface"
from Ben Shadow. ECHOES OF A BELLE; OR, A VOICE FROM THE
PAST. New York: George P. Putnam, 1853.
   An 1849 statement that shows that C. did not spend his last years as
a bitter and disillusioned man.

32 _____. "James Fenimore Cooper and the Bread and Cheese Club."
MODERN LANGUAGE NOTES 47 (February 1932):71-79.

33 _____. "James Fenimore Cooper in France, 1830-1832." NOTES AND
QUERIES (London) 173 (September 25, 1937):222-24.
   Information gleaned from Emma Willard's JOURNAL (item no.
288) AND N. P. Willis' HURRYGRAPHS (item no. 168). Includes comments on C's. relations with Lafayette, French opinions of him as an author,
and his work with the polish refugees.

34 Avanzi, William A. "The Bread and Cheese Club." Master of Arts degree, Columbia University, 1936.

35 Baldensperger, Fernand. "James Cooper [1789-1851] in France." LEGION OF HONOR MAGAZINE 11 (1940):163-69.

36 _____. JAMES FENIMORE COOPER IN FRANCE. Franco American Pamphlets, 2. New York, 1940.

37 Bandy, W. T. "Two Uncollected Letters of James Fenimore Cooper." AMERICAN LITERATURE 20 (January 1949):441-42.
          The first, undated, is the only known letter by C. to have been written in French. It first appeared in L'AUTOGRAPHE August 1, 1864, in facsimile. It concerns an estimate of the author J. G. Lockhart. The second, dated May 27, 1848, is written to C's. English publisher of OAK OPENINGS. It was reprinted earlier in THE AUTOGRAPHIC MIRROR 1 (1864):27.

38 Beard, James F. "Cooper, Lafayette, and the French National Budget: A Postscript." American Antiquarian Society, PROCEEDINGS 95 (1985):81-99.
          C's. friendship with Lafayette, letters between the two men, and C's. part in the "Finance Controversy."

39 Beard, James F. "James Fenimore Cooper Aids the Collectors." MANUSCRIPTS 6 (Fall 1953):22-26.
          On letters written by C. in response to autograph collectors.

40 Birdsall, Ralph. "Fenimore Cooper in Cooperstown." New York State Historical Association, PROCEEDINGS 16 (1917):137-49.
          Concerning C's. daily routine, his appearance, his relationship with the townspeople,and the Three Mile Point controversy.

41 _____. FENIMORE COOPER'S GRAVE AND CHRIST CHURCH-YARD. New York: F. H. Hitchcock, 1911.

42 _____. THE STORY OF COOPERSTOWN. Cooperstown, N. Y., 1917.
          Includes facts and incidents relating to C's. life.

43 Bolander, Louis. "The Naval Career of James Fenimore Cooper." U. S. Naval Institute, PROCEEDINGS 66 (1940):541-50.

44 Boyd, William. "An Unpublished Letter of J. Fenimore Cooper." Trinity

College Historical Society, HISTORICAL PAPERS, ser. 8 (1908-09):1-2.
    Letter from C. to Bedford Brown.

45 Boynton, Henry Walcott. JAMES FENIMORE COOPER. New York:
Century Co., 1931.
    Biography of C. from boyhood to death with little literary criticism.
More favorable to C. as a person then Lounsbury (item no. 114). Dislikes his
social satire and emphasizes his ill health.

46 Bronson, Walter C. A SHORT HISTORY OF AMERICAN LITERA-
TURE. Boston: D. C. Heath, 1900. Pp. 126-36.
    Biographical sketch with short descriptive/critical comments on sev-
eral C. novels. Written for use in high school and college English courses.

47 Browning, Charlotte Prentiss. FULL HARVEST. Philadelphia: Dorrance
& Co., 1932. Pp. 91-118. Partially reprinted in "She Remembers Fenimore
Cooper." LITERARY DIGEST 114 (November 12, 1932):14-15.
    As a friend of C's. daughters, Charlotte Browning's reminiscences
include a portrait of the author.

48 Bruccoli, Matthew J. and Richard Layman, eds. CONCISE DICTION-
ARY OF AMERICAN LITERARY BIOGRAPHY; COLONIZATION TO
THE AMERICAN RENAISSANCE, 1640-1865. Detroit: Gale Research Co.,
1988. Pp. 38-61.

49 Cameron, Kenneth Walter, ed. "Melville, Cooper, Irving, and Bryant on
International Matters." EMERSON SOCIETY QUARTERLY no. 51 (2d
quarter 1968):108-36.
    Fascimiles of documents on free trade and copyright.

50 Campbell, Killis. "The Kennedy Papers." SEWANEE REVIEW 25 (April
1917):193-208.
    Letter from C. to John Pendleton Kennedy, dated April 22, 1846,
concerning an inquiry about Mrs. Oldfield (p. 200).

51 Charvat, William. THE PROFESSION OF AUTHORSHIP IN AMERI-
CA, 1800-1870: THE PAPERS OF WILLIAM CHARVAT. Edited by Matthew J. Bruccoli. Columbus: Ohio State University Press, 1968. Scattered references.
    On C's. relationship with his publishers, his popularity, his success,
and etc.

52 Chubb, E. W. STORIES OF AUTHORS, BRITISH AND AMERICAN.

New York: Sturgis & Walton, 1910. Pp. 242-48.
　　　　Anecdotal sketch.

53 Clark, Lewis Gaylord. "Cooper, Scott and Lockhart." LIPPINCOTT'S MAGAZINE OF POPULAR LITERATURE AND SCIENCE 8 (December 1871):625-29.
　　　　Clark asserts that C's. attack on Lockhart's LIFE OF SCOTT was the result of unfair treatment given him in the QUARTERLY REVIEW at the hands of Lockhart. C's. review is found in the KNICKERBOCKER MAGAZINE 12 (October 1838):349-66. It has been partially reprinted in Banks, Stanley, ed. AMERICAN ROMANTICISM; A SHAPE FOR FICTION. New York: G. P. Putnam's Sons, 1969. Pp. 125-27. C. concluded that Lockhart's LIFE OF SCOTT "is false in principles, dangerous to the young, and far from being free from the imputation of mystification and insincerity." This review drew an immediate response from several critics. See "Epaminodas Grubb, or Fenimore Cooper *Versus* the Memory of Sir Walter Scott." FRASER'S MAGAZINE FOR TOWN AND COUNTRY 19 (March 1839):371-77; reprinted in MUSEUM OF FOREIGN LITERATURE, SCIENCE AND ART 35 (April 1839): 529-32; NEW YORK LITERARY GAZETTE 1 (April 6, 1839):79; "J. Fenimore Cooper *vs.* Sir Walter Scott." NEW-YORK MIRROR 16 (November 17, 1838):165-66; "The Knickerbocker for October." NEW-YORKER 6 (October 13, 1838):61; "Reply to Cooper's Attack Upon Sir Walter Scott." NEW-YORKER 6 (December 29, 1838):228; and "A Reply to the Attack on Sir Walter Scott, in 'The Knickerbocker' for October." KNICKERBOCKER MAGAZINE 12 (December 1838):508-20.

54 Clymer, William Branford Shubrick. JAMES FENIMORE COOPER. Boston: Small, Maynard & Co., 1900.
　　　　Short laudatory biography of C. as a man and writer. As the former he possessed great political and social significance. As the latter he expressed a high degree of originality that more than compensated for his lack of technical ability.

55 Coffin, R. B. [Barry Gray]. THE HOME OF COOPER AND THE HAUNTS OF LEATHERSTOCKING. New York: Russell Bros., 1872.
　　　　Pamphlet. A history of Cooperstown, specifically as it refers to C. Includes references to other authors who have alluded to Cooperstown in their writings.

56 Cooper, James Fenimore. CORRESPONDENCE OF JAMES FENIMORE COOPER. 2 vols. Edited by James Fenimore Cooper, III. New Haven, Conn.: Yale University Press, 1922.
　　　　Letters (1800-1851) by and to C. in possession of the family, plus

the 1848 JOURNAL.   Includes SMALL FAMILY MEMOIRS by Susan Cooper.

57 _____. THE LETTERS AND JOURNALS OF JAMES FENIMORE COOPER. 6 vols.   Edited by James F.   Beard. Cambridge, Mass.: Belknap Press of Harvard Universi- ty Press, 1960-68.
　　　　　Includes a short biographical sketch by the editor, an introduction to each of the twenty-eight sections, letters for 1800-51, and entries from C's. European JOURNALS. Notes, index, chronological arrangement.

58 Cooper, James Fenimore, III.   "Cooperstown, N. Y." COUNTRY LIFE 27 (December 1914):48-49.

59 _____. THE LEGENDS AND TRADITIONS OF A NORTHERN COUNTRY. New York & London: G. P. Putnam's Sons, 1921.
　　　　　Documents and other material important to the C. family: pp. 156-57, the earliest known C. letter; pp. 174-75, 190-91, two additional C. letters; and pp. 201-22, a portion of Susan Cooper's 1883 essay on her father's life and character.   Includes the conditions under which PRECAUTION was written, its early acceptance, the writing of THE SPY, and the claim that Harvey Birch was not based upon a real person.

60 _____.   "Unpublished Letters of James Fenimore Cooper." YALE REVIEW 5 (July 1916):810-31.
　　　　　A selection of letters from 1800-51 that remained in the possession of the C. family at this time.

61 _____.   "Unpublished Letters of James Fenimore Cooper.: YALE REVIEW 11 (January 1922):242-68.
　　　　　Letters written by C. from 1826-32 during his travels in Europe. Two or three of these selections were reprinted in the NEW YORK TIMES, December 18, 1921, Sect. II, p. 8.

62 Cooper, W. W. "Cooper Genealogy." New York Historical Association, PROCEEDINGS 16 (1917):193-211.
　　　　　C. genealogy from 1661 to the mid-1880s.

63 [Cushing, Caleb.] A REPLY TO THE LETTER OF J. FENIMORE COOPER, BY ONE OF HIS COUNTRYMEN. Boston: J. T. Buckingham, 1834.
　　　　　A defense of the right of the legislature to criticize President Jackson.

64 Davidson, Levette Jay, ed. "Letters from Authors." COLORADO MAGAZINE 19 (July 1942):122-26.
        Includes a letter dated January 3, 1849, from C. to Major General Winfield Scott recommending E. L. Berthoud for a surveyor's position. Other C. letters are also found in the Colorado State Historical Society.

65 Davis, Elizabeth E. "James Fenimore Cooper Lived Here." LONG ISLAND FORUM 3 (1940):253-54.

66 DETROIT DAILY ADVERTISER, June 23, 1847.
        On C's. arrival in Detroit from Buffalo.

67 _____, June 21, 1849.
        A reference to C. _vs._ Gibbs and Gordon concerning land litigation.

68 Dewey, Franklin S. "The Story of a Famous Lenawee County Landmark." ONSTED NEWS, September 24, 1914.
        On C's. visit to Cambridge Junction, Michigan.

69 Dunlap, William. "Diary of William Dunlap, March 16, 1832-June 25, 1833, Vol. III." New York Historical Society, COLLECTIONS 64 (1930). Scattered references.
        Numerous mentions of C. and his relationship to painting, the theater, and literary criticism. Includes the text of several C. letters.

70 _____. HISTORY OF THE RISE AND PROGRESS OF THE ARTS AND DESIGN IN THE UNITED STATES. Vol. 3. New ed., rev. & enl. Edited by Alexander Wyckoff. New York: Benjamin Blom, 1965. Scattered references.
        C. and his relations with the National Academy of Design, Horatio Greenough, Lafayette, and Samuel Morse.

71 Dunn, James Taylor. "Troskolaski and Cooper." NEW YORK HISTORY 30 (April 8 1949):253-56.
        On C's. relationship with Joseph Troskolaski, a Polish refugee, who appealed to the writer to aid him in his establishment in the United States.

72 Durand, John. THE LIFE AND TIMES OF A. B. DURAND. New York: Charles Scribner's Sons, 1894. Pp. 64-65.
        Letter from C. to William Dunlap dated July 29, 1830, on the commission given by C. to the sculptor Horatio Greenough.

73 "Editor's Study." NEW YORK MIRROR 9 (March 4, 1832):278-79.

Extract of a letter from Horatio Greenough to Rembrandt Peale dated November 8, 1831, concerning his bust of C. and the acceptance of THE BRAVO in France.

74 Edmiston, Susan and Linda D. Cirino. LITERARY NEW YORK: A HISTORY AND GUIDE. Boston: Houghton Mifflin Co., 1976. Pp. in New York City.

A description of C's. residences and his relationships in New York City.

75 Evans, Constantine. "An Unpublished Reminiscence of James Fenimore Cooper." Syracuse University Library Associates, COURIER 24 (Fall 1989):45-53.

An 1840s portrait of C. William Mather written in 1889. Contains information on the Three Mile Point controversy.

76 Farmer, Silas. HISTORY OF DETROIT AND WAYNE COUNTY AND EARLY MICHIGAN. Vol. 1. Detroit, 1890. P. 708.

On C's. visit to Michigan in June 1848.

77 Fenimore, Constance [Constance Fenimore Woolson]. "The Haunted Lake." HARPER'S NEW MONTHLY MAGAZINE 44 (December 1871):20-30.

Largely biographical, but also deals with Cooperstown and its surrounding area.

78 Field, Maunsell B. MEMORIES OF MANY MEN AND SOME WOMEN. New York: Harper & Bros., 1875. Pp. 178-79.

79 Fisher, George P. LIFE OF BENJAMIN SILLIMAN, M.D., LL.D. Vol. 1. New York: Charles Scribner, 1866. Pp. 334-38.

Letter from C. to Silliman dated June 10, 1831, on politics and the press.

80 Fox, Dixon Ryan. "Fenimore Cooper in Scarsdale." Westchester County Historical Society, BULLETIN 6 (July 1930?):59-60

Not seen. Citation from WRITINGS IN AMERICAN HISTORY, 1930, p. 256.

81 Francis, John W. OLD NEW YORK: OR, REMINISCENCES OF THE PAST SIXTY YEARS, 1865. Reprinted, New York: Benjamin Blom, 1971. P. 291.

The Bread and Cheese Club.

82 Fynmore, R. J. "Fenimore Cooper: A Coincidence." NOTES AND QUERIES 10, 11th series (July 11, 1914):26.

      The name Fenimore was derived from C's. mother who was a daughter of Richard Fenimore of Burlington County, New Jersey.

83 Glicksberg, Charles I. "Cooper & Bryant: A Literary Friendship." COLOPHON part 20 (1935):unpaged.

      Includes the Bryant-C. friendship, Bryant's reviews and comments on C's. novels (mostly favorable), and reprints from the EVENING POST (New York) dealing with politics and copyright.

84 Godwin, Parke. A BIOGRAPHY OF WILLIAM CULLEN BRYANT, WITH EXTRACTS FROM HIS PRIVATE CORRESPONDENCE. 2 vols. New York: D. Appleton, 1883. Scattered references.

      The Bryant-C. relationship.

85 Goggio, Emilio. "The Italy of James Fenimore Cooper." MODERN LANGUAGE JOURNAL 29 (January 1945):66-71.

      On C's. social life in, and impressions of, Italy.

86 Goodrich, Samuel Griswold. RECOLLECTIONS OF A LIFETIME, OR MEN AND THINGS I HAVE SEEN. Vol. 3. New York: Miller, Orton, and Mulligan, 1857. Pp. 134-35, 201-03.

      Includes a physical description of C., his meeting with James Gates Percival, J. G. Lockhart on THE PIONEERS, and Scott on THE PILOT.

87 Green, George Washington. "James Fenimore Cooper." NEW YORK QUARTERLY 1 (June 1852):215-28.

88 Greenough, Horatio. "The Cooper Monument." A MEMORIAL OF HORATIO GREENOUGH. Edited by Henry T. Tuckerman. New York: G. P. Putnam, 1853. Pp. 184-87.

      Mainly concerned with the monument, little information on C.

89 _____. LETTERS OF HORATIO GREENOUGH: AMERICAN SCULPTOR. Edited by Nathalia Wright. Madison: University of Wisconsin Press, 1972. Scattered references.

      Includes thirty-one letters from Greenough to C.

90 _____. LETTERS OF HORATIO GREENOUGH TO HIS BROTHER, HENRY GREENOUGH. Edited by Francis Greenough. Boston: Ticknor, 1887. Pp. 47, 83, 87-89, 152, 237, 238.

      Letters not found in the above collection.

91 Griggs, Earl Leslie. "James Fenimore Cooper on Coleridge." AMERICAN LITERATURE 4 (January 1933):389-91.

Concerns C's. first meeting with Coleridge in 1828 in London, his favorable impression of the poet, and his desire to renew the acquaintanceship.

92 Griswold, Rufus W. PASSAGES FROM THE CORRESPONDENCE AND OTHER PAPERS OF RUFUS W. GRISWOLD. Cambridge, Mass.: M. Griswold, 1898. Pp. 114-15, 154, 269-70, 277-78.

Two letters from C. to Griswold (one on Irving dated August 7, 1842, and one on Mrs. Ralph Izard dated April 27, 1851), one letter from C. F. Hoffman containing contemporary comments on C. as a writer (June 12, 1844?), and one from Susan Cooper expressing her gratitude to Griswold following her father's death (October 2, 1851).

93 Hemstreet, Charles. "Literary Landmarks of New York." THE CRITIC 42 (February 1903):143-48.

Includes comments on C's. house and the Bread and Cheese Club.

94 _____. LITERARY NEW YORK: ITS LANDMARKS AND ASSOCIA-TIONS. New York: G. P. Putnam's Sons, 1903. Pp. 125-44.

On C's. life in New York City, his friends, and the places he frequented.

95 ["Homes"]. BOOKMAN (New York) 10 (October 1899):102-05.

C's. Burlington and Cooperstown homes.

96 Howe, Mark A. De Wolfe. AMERICAN BOOKMEN: SKETCHES, CHIEFLY BIOGRAPHICAL OF CERTAIN WRITERS OF THE NINE-TEENTH CENTURY. New York: Dodd, Mead, 1898. Pp. 29-51.

Mostly a favorable sketch of C's. life, including the lawsuits. Little literary comment.

97 Ingraham, Charles Anson. "James Fenimore Cooper: An Intimate Account of the Life, Work, Character, and Personal Peculiarities of America's Famous Novelist." JOURNAL OF AMERICAN HISTORY 11 (2d quarter 1917):223-43.

98 Irving, Washington. LIFE AND LETTERS OF WASHINGTON IRVING. Vol. 4. Edited by Pierre Monroe Irving. New York: G. P. Putnam, 1864. Pp. 103-04, 313.

Short notes on C.: one by the editor concerning the C./Irving relationship and the other by Irving alluding to C's. immortality as a novelist.

99 Jackson, Stuart W. "Lafayette Letters and Documents in the Yale Cooper Collection." Yale University Library GAZETTE 8 (April 1934):112-46.

Approximately fifty letters written by Lafayette, most between 1826-38. Not all relate to C.

100 "James Fenimore Cooper." APPLETON'S CYCLOPAEDIA OF AMERICAN BIOGRAPHY. Vol. 1. Edited by James Grant Wilson and John Fiske. New York: D. Appleton, 1888. Pp. 725-30.

101 "James Fenimore Cooper." THE NATIONAL CYCLOPEDIA OF AMERICAN BIOGRAPHY. Vol. 1. New York: James T. White, 1891. Pp. 398-401.

Some critical comment. Bemoans the fact that C. allowed his social ideas to over shadow his artistic abilities in later life.

102 "James Fennimore [sic] Cooper." PORTLAND MAGAZINE 1 (December 1, 1834):90-91.

Brief, uncritical biography.

103 Johnson, Clifton. NEW ENGLAND AND ITS NEIGHBORS. New York: Macmillan Co., 1902. Pp. 106-23.

Biographical sketch that includes material on Cooperstown and the C. lawsuits.

104 Keese, G. Pomeroy. "Memories of Distinguished Authors. James Fenimore Cooper." HARPER'S WEEKLY, July 29, 1871, supp., pp. 707-11.

Reminiscences by C's. grandnephew.

105 Kouwenhoven, John A. "Cooper and the American Copyright Club: An Unpublished Letter." AMERICAN LITERATURE 13 (November 1941):265.

Reprint of a September 25, 1843, C. letter refusing membership in the American Copyright Club.

106 Kunitz, Stanley J. and Howard Haycroft. AMERICAN AUTHORS: 1600-1900: A BIOGRAPHICAL DICTIONARY OF AMERICAN LITERATURE. New York: H. W. Wilson, 1938. Pp. 177-79.

Biographical sketch with little assessment of C. as a writer beyond ascribing vitality to his novels and suggesting that he was the first to make sea fiction of interest to the reader.

107 "Letter of James Fenimore Cooper." AUTOGRAPH 1 (December 1911):22-24.

An 1848 letter concerned with the presidential veto. Includes remarks on Zachary Taylor.

108 "Letter of James Fenimore Cooper." MAGAZINE OF HISTORY 19 (October-November 1914):225-27.
Letter dated November 15, 1831, on Dr. Chester, reminiscences of Albany, N. Y., and European politics.

109 "Letter of Mr. Cooper." HISTORICAL MAGAZINE AND NOTES AND QUERIES 5 (May, August 1861):140-42, 229-36.
Correspondence in 1848 between C., H. C. Van Schaak, Henry Onderdonk, Jr., and others on the death of General Nathaniel Woodhull.

110 "Letters of Cooper." BOOKMAN (New York) 43 (August 1916):570-75.
Makes use of letters reprinted by J. F. Cooper, III, in the July issue of the YALE REVIEW (item no. 60) to throw light on C's. character.

111 "Literary Characters: James Fenimore Cooper." ARIEL 5 (June 25, 1831):66-67.

112 Littel, W. R., ed. A HISTORY OF COOPERSTOWN. Cooperstown, N. Y., 1929.

113 Livermore, Samuel T. A CONDENSED HISTORY OF COOPERSTOWN, WITH A BIOGRAPHICAL SKETCH OF J. FENIMORE COOPER. Albany: J. Munsell, 1862.
A republication of C's. CHRONICLES OF COOPERSTOWN with notes and additions.

114 Lounsbury, Thomas R. JAMES FENIMORE COOPER. Boston: Houghton Mifflin, 1883. Excerpted in Stedman, Edmund Clarence and Ellen MacKay Hutchinson, eds. A LIBRARY OF AMERICAN LITERATURE FROM THE EARLIEST TO THE PRESENT TIME. Vol. 9. Charles L. Webster, 1889. Pp. 578-87.
A negative assessment. C. is described as cold, gloomy, cynical, and wrong in concerning himself with social and political criticism.

115 Lutes, Della Thompson. "In the Land of the Deerslayer." AMERICAN HISTORICAL MAGAZINE 4 (May 1909):312-15.
Description of the area surrounding Cooperstown that gave rise to many of C's. scenes.

116 Madison, R. D. "Fenimore Cooper to Rufus Griswold: A Puff." STUDIES IN AMERICAN RENAISSANCE (1980):119-22.

117 Marckwardt, Albert H. "The Chronology and Personnel of the Bread and Cheese Club." AMERICAN LITERATURE 6 (January 1935):389-99.

118 Matthews, Brander. GATEWAYS TO LITERATURE AND OTHER ESSAYS. New York: Charles Scribner's Sons, 1912. Pp. 243-76. Originally ATLANTIC 100 (September 1902):329-41. Reprinted in part in REVIEW OF REVIEWS 36 (October 1907):503-04.
	A speech that was delivered at the centenary incorporation of Cooperstown. It is basically a biographical sketch, but describes C's. genius as a story teller, recognizes his deficiencies in style, and praises him for his characterizations.

119 _____. AN INTRODUCTION TO THE STUDY OF AMERICAN LITERATURE. New York: American Book Co., 1896. Pp. 56-68.
	Biographical sketch with illustrations. A positive and negative assessment of C. as a writer included.

120 "Medal Presented to Lafayette." NEW YORK MIRROR 10 (April 27, 1833):337. An article describing the medal cast for Lafayette in appreciation for his efforts in the Revolutionary War, and C's. presentation of it to him in Paris.

121 "Mr. Cooper's Will." NATIONAL ERA 6 (January 1, 1852):2.

122 Morse, Samuel F. B. SAMUEL F. B. MORSE: HIS LETTERS AND JOURNALS. 2 vols. Edited by Edward Lind Morse. Boston & New York: Houghton Mifflin, 1914. Scattered references.
	On C's. character, novels, political beliefs, and relations with Morse. See also EVENING POST (New York), June 28, 1833, for further comments by Morse.

123 Mulford, Anna. A SKETCH OF DR. JOHN SMITH SAGE. Sag Harbor, N. Y., 1897. Pp. 28-36.
	C's. experiences as part owner of a whaling ship.

124 Mulford, William Remsen. "James Fenimore Cooper, His Ancestory and Writings." NEW YORK GENEALOGICAL AND BIOGRAPHICAL REC-ORD 15 (January 1884):9-15.
	Contrary to the article's title, it contains almost nothing on C's. writings.

125 Myers, Andrew B. "Europe as Found: Cooper Writes Home." COLUMBIA LIBRARY COLUMNS 31 (February 1982):28-36.

To Mary Rutherford Clarkson Jay on Greenough and ITALY.

126 NATIONAL PORTRAIT GALLERY OF DISTINGUISHED AMERI-
CANS; WITH BIOGRAPHICAL SKETCHES BY CELEBRATED AUTH-
ORS. Vol. 1. Philadelphia: Rice, Rutter & Co., 1865. Unpaged.

127 Neuhauser, Rudolf. "Notes on Early Russian-American Cultural
Relations. (James Fenimore Cooper and Russia)." CANADIAN SLAVIC
STUDIES 1 (Fall 1967):461-73.
        C. was an extremely popular writer in Russia and left a definite
imprint on novelists of the 1830s and 1840s.   While in Paris he became
acquainted with several prominent Russians and soon developed a high opinion
of the people that even his work for the Polish refugees could not dampen.

128 NEW YORK TIMES, September 22, 1889, p. 4.
        Reprint of a letter from C. to S. C. Hall, undated, concerning his
ancestors, marriage, Europe, and THE PIONEERS.

129 _____, June 20, 1897, p. 14.
        Cooperstown Park created, Leatherstocking's cave found.

130 _____, "Book Review Section," January 8, 1899, pp. 10-11.
        On the Cooperstown home that burned in 1853 and the
surrounding grounds. By G. Pomeroy Keese.

131 _____, "Book Review Section," October 20, 1900, p. 720.
        C's. failure to be included in the Hall of Fame.

132 _____, "Book Review Section," November 3, 1900, p. 756.
        Comments by Clarence Adams, Joseph B. Gilder, Carl Damm,
and Charles H. Ward on the above oversight.

133 _____, September 9, 1923, Sect. II, P. 1; November 24, 1923, p. 8.
        On C's. Burlington house.

134 _____, May 4, 1930, Sect II, p. 3.
        C. inducted into the Hall of Fame along with eight others.

135 Oakley, Kate Russell. "James Fenimore Cooper and 'Oak Openings.'"
MICHIGAN HISTORY MAGAZINE 16 (Spring 1932):309-20.
        Description of C's. visit to Michigan and a plot outline of OAK
OPENINGS with little critical material.

136 "The 'Palpable Sin of Omission' of the Hall of Fame." CURRENT LITERATURE 43 (October 1907):399-400.
    ON C's. failure to be included in New York's Hall of Fame.

137 Phillips, Mary E. JAMES FENIMORE COOPER. New York: John Lane Co., 1913.
    An anecdotal biography of C's. personal life. Many illustrations, little literary criticism.

138 Phinney, Elihu. REMINISCENCES OF THE VILLAGE OF COOPERS-TOWN. Cooperstown, N. Y., 1891.

139 Poe, Edgar Allan. "A Chapter on Autobiography." THE WORKS OF EDGAR ALLAN POE. Vol. 9. Edited by Edmund Clarence Stedman and George Edward Woodberry. New York: The Colonial Co., 1903. P. 212.
    On C's. penmanship.

140 "The Poles." NILES' WEEKLY REGISTER 41 (September 10, 1831):-20.
    C's. Paris efforts to raise money for Polish refugees. Includes a letter from C. to Lafayette (July 10) and Lafayette's response (July 14).

141 Prime, Samuel Irenaeus. THE LIFE OF SAMUEL F. B. MORSE, LL.D., INVENTOR OF THE ELECTRO-MAGNETIC RECORDING TELEGRAPH. New York: Appleton, 1875. Scattered references.

142 Proctor, Bryan Waller [Barry Cornwall]. AN AUTOBIOGRAPHICAL FRAGMENT AND BIOGRAPHICAL NOTES. Boston: Roberts Bros., 1877. Pp. 74-77.
    On C's. rude behavior in Europe.

143 Putnam, George Haven. GEORGE PALMER PUTNAM: A MEMOIR. New York: G. P. Putnam's Sons, 1912. Pp. 28, 33, 143, 155.

144 Russell, Frank Alden. AMERICAN PILGRIMAGE. New York: Dodd, Mead & Co., 1942. Pp. 33-50.
    A sketch of C's. life with little criticism of his work.

145 Scharf, John Thomas. HISTORY OF WESTCHESTER COUNTY. Vol. 1. New York & Philadelphia: L. E. Preston & Co., 1886. Pp. 608-10.

146 Scott, Walter. THE LETTERS OF SIR WALTER SCOTT. Vol. 10. Edited by H. J. C. Grierson. London: Constable & Co., 1936. Pp. 122-24,

437-39.
> Eighteen twenty-six and 1828 letters from Scott to C.

147 _____. MEMOIRS OF SIR WALTER SCOTT. Vol. 5. Edited by J. G. Lockhart. London: Macmillan, 1900. Pp. 62, 64-65.
> On the meeting of C. and Scott in Paris.

148 Sedgwick, Catharine M. LIFE AND LETTERS OF CATHARINE M. SEDGWICK. Edited by Mary E. Dewey. New York: Harper & Bros., 1872. Pp. 285-86.
> Letter, Sedgwick to K. S. Minot, June 6, 1843, on her meeting with C.

149 Shaw, S. M., ed. A CENTENNIAL OFFERING. BEING A BRIEF HISTORY OF COOPERSTOWN. Cooperstown: Printed at The Freeman's Journal Office, 1886.
> Includes a chapter on Lake Otsego, the role it played in THE DEERSLAYER (pp. 130-40), and a tribute to C. by Isaac N. Arnold (pp. 192-211).

150 Simison, Barbara Damon, ed. "A New Cooper Letter." Yale University Library GAZETTE 25 (July 1950):29-32.
> Letter dated January 22, 1834, to John Whipple of Providence, R. I. Includes insights into C's concern for the nation, the acceptance of his books, and his countrymen's attitudes toward him as a person.

151 Spiller, Robert E. "Fenimore Cooper and Lafayette: Friends of Polish Freedom." AMERICAN LITERATURE 7 (March 1935): 56-75.
> Lafayette, who looked to C. for American aid in the Polish struggle against Russia in the 1830s, was not disappointed. C. organized a committee of Americans in Paris who raised money and expressed their sympathy for the Polish cause.

152 _____. "Fenimore Cooper and Lafayette: The Finance Controversy of 1831-1832." AMERICAN LITERATURE 3 (March 1931):28-44.
> On C's. support of Lafayette in the latter's defense of the economic advantages enjoyed by a republican form of government over a limited monarchy.

153 _____, ed. LETTER TO GEN. LAFAYETTE BY JAMES FENIMORE COOPER AND RELATED CORRESPONDENCE ON THE FINANCE CONTROVERSY. Language and Literature Series I, Vol. 6. New York: Columbia University Press for The Facsimile Text Society, 1931.

A reproduction of the Paris editions of 1831 and 1832. C's. letter is in Eng-lish. Those of Lafayette and others are in French. Includes a bibliographical note on the subject.

154 Stanton, Theodore, ed. A MANUAL OF AMERICAN LITERATURE. New York: G. P. Putnam's Sons, 1909. Pp. 25-32.
      Stanton describess C. as one of the most powerful novelists of his time, but also as one of the most hated men.

155 Stedman, Edmund Clarence. "Poe, Cooper and the Hall of Fame." NORTH AMERICAN REVIEW 185 (August 16, 1907):801-12.
      On the failure of C. and Poe to be voted into the newly created Hall of Fame.

156 Stokes, Anson Phelps. "James Fenimore Cooper: A Memorial Sermon." NEW YORK HISTORY 22 (January 1941):36-45.
      An analysis of C's. character in Christian terms, taking into account his family background. Independence, loyalty to country, devoutness, and morality are all ascribed to him.

157 Strout, Alan Lang. "Some Unpublished Letters of John Gibson Lockhart to John Wilson Croker." NOTES AND QUERIES (London) 185 (October 9, 1943):217-23.
      Reprint of a letter dated June 8, 1837 (p. 219) that describes C. "as being either a very surly fellow, or suffering under extreme uneasiness."

158 Sumner, Charles. MEMOIR AND LETTERS OF CHARLES SUMNER. Edited by Edward L. Pierce. Boston: Roberts Bros., 1877. Pp. 23, 38, 105.

159 Tappan, Lucy. TOPICAL NOTES ON AMERICAN AUTHORS. New York: Silver, Burdett, 1896. Pp. 39-56.
      Includes extracts from several of C's. works, a bibliography, an outline of his life, "Appellations," and notes on his writings of a miscellaneous nature.

160 Triesch, Manfred O. "James Fenimore Cooper and His Russian Friends." AMERICAN BOOK COLLECTOR 16 (1966):17.
      A letter to Prince Dolgoroucki.

161 [Tuckerman, Henry Theodore.] "Cooper." HOMES OF AMERICAN AUTHORS; COMPRISING ANECDOTAL, PERSONAL AND DESCRIP-TIVE SKETCHES, BY VARIOUS WRITERS. New York: G. P. Putnam, 1852. Pp. 179-215.

A highly laudatory biographical sketch with little critical material.

162 Underwood, Francis H. THE BUILDERS OF AMERICAN LITER-
ATURE. First Series. Boston: Lee & Shepard. 1893. Pp. 82-85.

163 Van Doren, Carl. "James Fenmimore Cooper. DICTIONARY OF
AMERICAN BIOGRAPHY." Vol. 4. Edited by Allen Johnson and Dumas
Malone. New York: Scribner's Sons, 1930. Pp. 400-06.

164 Waples, Dorothy, ed. "A Letter from James Fenimore Cooper." NEW
ENGLAND QUARTERLY 3 (January 1930):123-32.
        Reprint of an 1846 invitation to lecture at the Mercantile Library
Association of Boston and C's. reply. A portion of the letter discusses
Boston's unfavorable acceptance of C's. HISTORY OF THE NAVY. Waples'
introduction explores additional reasons for C's. dislike of New England.

165 Ward, Julius H. THE LIFE AND LETTERS OF JAMES GATES
PERCIVAL. Boston: Ticknor and Fields, 1866. Scattered references.
        Percival's recollections of C., a man he considered a literary
parasite.

166 Whitfield, Francis J. "Mickiewicz and American Literature." ADAM
MICKIEWICZ IN WORLD LITERATURE. Edited by Waclaw Lednicki.
Berkeley & Los Angeles: University of California Press, 1956. Pp. 339-52.
        Maintains that while C. and Mickiewicz had little influence on
each other's writing, it was the latter who was partially responsible for C's.
prolonged and active interest in the Poles.

167 Whiting, Frank P. "Fynmere; the House of Cooper." ARCH-
ITECTURAL RECORD 30 (October 1941):360-67.
        Floor plan and photographs.

168 Willis, N. Parker. HURRY-GRAPHS; OR, SKETCHES OF SCENERY,
CELEBRITIES AND SOCIETY, TAKEN FROM LIFE. Detroit: Keer,
Doughty & Lapham, 1853. Pp. 210-12.
        On C's. hospitality and his relationship with Lafayette.

169 _____. OUTDOORS AT IDLEWILD; OR, THE SHAPING OF A
HOME ON THE BANKS OF THE HUDSON. New York: Charles Scribner,
1855. Pp. 126-32.
        A description of C's Cooperstown home that had been made into a
hotel shortly after its owner's death. Includes information on Natty Bumppo's
cave and the surrounding area.

170 _____. PENCILLINGS BY THE WAY: WRITTEN DURING SOME YEARS OF RESIDENCE AND TRAVEL IN EUROPE. Auburn, N. Y.: Alden, Beardsley & Co.; Rochester, N. Y.: Wanzer, Beardsley & Co., 1853. Scattered references.

Comments on C's. art patronage (Greenough), his physical characteristics, his work with the Polish refugees, his acceptance in France and England, and his patriotism.

171 _____. RURAL LETTERS AND OTHER RECORDS OF THOUGHT AT LEISURE. New York: Baker & Scribner, 1849. Pp. 314-23.

The author's visit to Cooperstown.

172 Wilson, James Grant. BRYANT AND HIS FRIENDS: SOME REMINISCENCES OF THE KNICKERBOCKER WRITERS. New York: Fords, Howard & Hulbert, 1886. Pp. 230-44.

A short, laudable biographical sketch making use of opinions and statements by people known to C. Includes a letter by Susan Cooper on Lounsbury's biography.

173 _____. "Recollections of American Authors, No. 4. James Fenimore Cooper." BOOK NEWS MONTHLY 30 (October 1911):117-22.

Largely biographical, but with some general criticism.

174 Wright, Nathalia. "The Chanting Cherubs: Horatio Greenough's Marble Group for James Fenimore Cooper." NEW YORK HISTORY 38 (April 1957):177-97.

Description of C's. encounter with Greenough in Italy in 1828 and the commissions that resulted.

175 _____, ed. "Letters by Horatio Greenough in the Library." Boston Public Library, QUARTERLY 11 (April 1959):75-93.

A series of nine letters, the last one being a proposal for erecting a monument to C.

LIBEL SUITS

Cooper was involved in several libel suits beginning in July 1837. Although long and drawn out, they can be summarized as follows:

176 FREEMAN'S JOURNAL (Cooperstown), July 31, 1837.

C. warns residents of Cooperstown against trespassing on his land known as Three Mile Point.

177 ALBANY EVENING JOURNAL, August 12, 1837.
>Thurlow Weed reprints an Elius P. Pellet editorial from the CHENANGO TELEGRAPH giving the town's view of the controversy. C. sues for libel.

178 OTSEGO REPUBLICAN (Cooperstown), August 14, 1837.
>Andrew M. Barber reprints the CHENANGO TELEGRAPH editorial, adding comments of his own. He is sued by C. also.

179 ALBANY EVENING JOURNAL, August 18, 1837.
>Weed reprints the OTSEGO REPUBLICAN article, adding his own comments.

180 _____, November 2, 1838.
>Weed reviews HOME AS FOUND, relating it to the Three Mile Point controversy (item no. 1725).

181 COMMERCIAL ADVERTISER (New York), June 8, 19, 1839.
>A derogatory review of C's. HISTORY OF THE NAVY, written by William A. Duer (item no. 1565) results in a suit against William Leete Stone, the newspaper's editor.

182 _____, July 6, 1842.
>Further comments lead to a second suit.

183 MORNING COURIER AND NEW YORK ENQUIRER, November 22, 1838.
>James Watson Webb reviews HOME AS FOUND (item no. 1724). C. sues him for libel.

184 _____, May 24, 1839.
>Comments on the above indictment result in a second suit against Webb.

185 _____, September 13, 1839.
>On postponement of the trial. C. tries five times to indict Webb for this letter.

186 NEW WORLD, May-September 1840.
>Park Benjamin is sued for material copied from Webb's newspaper and placed in the NEW WORLD in May 1840. Benjamin's reviews of HOMEWARD BOUND and HOME AS FOUND followed in the NEW WORLD under the title of "Fenimore Cooper's Libels on America and

Americans," August 29, 1840, pp. 193-95 and September 5, 1840, pp. 210-15 (item no. 1671).

187 NEW-YORK TRIBUNE, November 20, 1841.
        Horace Greeley comments upon Webb's trial. He is sued by C.

188 _____, December 12, 1842.
        Greeley publishes a report of his trial. This creates a second suit.

During this period, the press and other sources are full of material bearing on the subject. The following represent only a few of the possible records:

189 BRIEF STATEMENT OF THE PLEADINGS AND ARGUMENT IN THE CASE OF J. FENIMORE COOPER, VERSUS HORACE GREELEY AND THOMAS MCELRATH, IN AN ACTION FOR LIBEL . . . DECEMBER 9, 1842 . . . New York: Greeley & McElrath, 1843.

190 "Look Out." POUGHKEEPSIE CASKET 4 (May 30, 1840):31.
        A satirical jab at C. warning newspaper publishers to take care of what they print for fear of being sued.

191 "M'Henry and Cooper, the Novelists." NEW-YORK MIRROR 12 (July 19, 1834):17-19.
        Further attacks on C.

192 "Mr. Cooper and the Press." BROTHER JONATHAN 1 (January 1, 1842):15-22.
        Letter from C. justifying the libel suits. Includes extracts from the NEW YORK COURIER AND ENQUIRER and HOME AS FOUND that are relevant.

193 NEW WORLD 1 (October 3, 1840, December 5, 1840):284, 429; 2 (April 17, 1841):256; and 3 (November 27, 1841):348-49.
        Highly derogatory toward C.

194 NEW-YORK TRIBUNE, February 27, 1842.
        An editorial discussion.

195 NILES WEEKLY REGISTER 58 (May 23, 1840):192.
        Mention of the lawsuit against Benjamin amounting to $5,000 in damages.

196 "The Quarrels of Authors." NEW-YORKER 9 (May 16, 1840):142.
    The Colonel Stone lawsuit.

A considerable amount of information, written at a later time exists as well.
For example:

197 Greeley, Horace. THE AUTOBIOGRAPHY OF HORACE GREELEY,
OR RECOLLECTIONS OF A BUSY LIFE. New York: E. B. Treat, 1872.
Pp. 261-64.

198 Hudson, Frederic. JOURNALISM IN THE UNITED STATES FROM
1690 TO 1872. New York, 1873. Pp. 744-48.
    An article from the NEW YORK HERALD of 1869 is reprinted
here that gives a brief historical sketch of United States libel laws and
important cases, including C's, that influenced them. Also included (p. 248)
is a reprint of a letter from C. to the editors of the ALBANY EVENING
JOURNAL (May 21, 1845) concerning that newspaper's alleged libel against
him.

199 Ingersoll, L. D. THE LIFE OF HORACE GREELEY, FOUNDER OF
THE "NEW YORK TRIBUNE." Union Publishing Co., 1873. Pp. 132-44.
    Concerned mostly with reprints of material from the TRIBUNE
about libel.   Included is a Thurlow Weed telegram published there on
November 17, 1841, and Greeley's account of the trial as it was reported in
the TRIBUNE.

200 NEW YORK TIMES, "Book Review Section".
        Stone, William L. "Fenimore Cooper Conflicts with His
        Neighbors--Col. William Stone." September 15, 1900, p. 620.
            Written by Col. Stone's son, this article describes C. as an
            "aristocratic . . . detestable . . . and obnoxious" person.
        Keese, G. Pomeroy. "Fenimore Cooper and His Neighbors."
        September 22, 1900, p. 628.
            A reply to Stone's article.
        Stone, William L. "Mr. Cooper and His Neighbors Again."
        September 29, 1900, p. 642.
            A Reply to Keese.
        "Cooper--A Contemporary's Opinion." October 27, 1900, p. 738.
            An evaluation of C. taken from Bryan Waller Proctor's (Barry
            Cornwall) REMINISCENCES, entry of May 27, 1828.
        Keese, G. Pomeroy, "Barry Cornwall's Criticism Refuted by
        Observers." November 3, 1900, p. 756.

201 Outland, Ethel R. THE "EFFINGHAM LIBELS" OF COOPER; A DOCUMENTARY HISTORY OF THE LIBEL SUITS OF JAMES FENIMORE COOPER CENTERING AROUND THE THREE MILE CONTROVERSY AND THE NOVEL "HOME AS FOUND", 1837-1845. Studies in Language and Literature, no. 28. Madison: University of Wisconsin, 1929.

Through an examination of C's. libel suits, Outland attempts to show that his legal disputes were instrumental in the creation of New York libel laws.

202 Parton, James L. LIFE OF HORACE GREELEY, New York: Mason Bros., 1855. Pp. 224-39.

Newspaper accounts and other material from the TRIBUNE.

203 Weed, Thurlow. AUTOBIOGRAPHY OF THURLOW WEED. Vol. 1. Edited by Harriet A. Weed. Boston: Houghton, Mifflin, 1884. Pp. 520-27.

204 Zabriske, Francis Nicoll. HORACE GREELEY THE EDITOR. New York: Funk & Wagnalls, 1890. Pp. 88-92.

OBITUARIES

205 "Death of James Fenimore Cooper." ILLUSTRATED LONDON NEWS 19 (October 4, 1851):408.

Admires the morality displayed by C's. writings, but regrets that he allowed politics to enter his fiction.

206 "Death of James Fenimore Cooper." LITTEL'S LIVING AGE 31 (October 11, 1851):87-89.

Reprints from the EVENING POST (New York) and the NEW-YORK TRIBUNE.

207 "Death of Mr. Cooper." LITERARY WORLD 9 (September 20, 1851):229.

208 Francis, John W. "Reminiscences of the Late Mr. Cooper--His Last Days." INTERNATIONAL MAGAZINE OF LITERATURE, ART, AND SCIENCE 4 (November 1, 1851):453-56.

Laudatory sketch.

209 "James Fenimore Cooper." ATHENAEUM [24] (October 4, 1851):1047-48.

The most original of American writers whose good qualities exceed his faults.

210 "James Fenimore Cooper." LITERARY GAZETTE 35 (October 18, 1851):709-10.
From the LITERARY WORLD and the NEW YORK HERALD.

211 "James Fenimore Cooper." LITERARY WORLD 9 (September 27, 1851):247-48.
C. was the first writer to attempt to delineate the American character. While his works were without humor or grace, they possessed substance and adventure.

212 "James Fenimore Cooper, Esq." GENTLEMAN'S MAGAZINE 191 (November 1851):546-48. Reprinted from the LITERARY WORLD.

213 "The Late James Fenimore Cooper." NATIONAL ERA 5 (September 25, 1851):155.

214 NEW YORK TIMES, September 18, 1851, p. 2.
Other material relating to C's. death includes: September 23, 1851, p. 4 (funeral); September 25, p. 2 (commemorative meeting); November 25, 1851, p. 1 (proposal for a statue in C's. honor); November 25, 1851, p. 3 (will); February 26, 1852, p. 1 (testimonial held); December 26, 1859, p. 4 (statute erected in Cooperstown).

215 "Public Honors to the Memory of Mr. Cooper." INTERNATIONAL MAGAZINE OF LITERATURE, ART, AND SCIENCE 4 (November 1, 1851):456-60.
Reprint of letters from the EVENING POST (New York) written by Irving, Bryant, G. W. Doane, Bancroft, John P. Kennedy, C. J. Ingersoll, and Edward Everett.

CENTENNIAL OF DEATH

216 NEW YORK TIMES, February 21, 1951, p. 29; September 6, 9, 1951, pp. 30, 59.

SESQUICENTENNIAL OF BIRTH

217 "Memorabilia." NOTES AND QUERIES (London) 180 (March 1,

1941):145.

Favorable comments on C. as a writer and as a person from speakers at the sesquicentennial celebration in Cooperstown.

218 NEW YORK TIMES, July 28, 1940, Sect. II, p. 2; August 30, 31, 1940, pp. 16, 12; September 1, 1940, Sect. I, p. 23; September 2, 1940, p. 18.

3

GENERAL STUDIES

ARTICLES AND REVIEWS CONTEMPORARY WITH COOPER

219 "America and American Writers." ATHENAEUM [2] (October 14, 1829):637-39.
On the failure of America to create a native literature and C's. imitation of Scott.

220 "American Authors, No. II: James Fenimore Cooper." AMERICAN MUSEUM OF LITERATURE AND THE ARTS 2 (January 1839):1-8.
C. is a genius as a writer of romance, but it is unfortunate that he has turned to the political sphere. These latter works, along with his review of Lockhart's LIFE OF SCOTT, have done much to destroy his reputation.

221 "American Drama." AMERICAN QUARTERLY REVIEW 1 (June 1827):331-57.
C's. success is proof that the American public is ready to accept American literature with a native theme. (p. 341)

222 "American Literary Biography. No. II: James Fenimore Cooper, Esq." NEW-YORKER 5 (June 23, 1838):211-12.
Brief reviews of each of C's. novels up to 1838. Largely favorable.

223 "American Novels." BRITISH CRITIC 2, 3d series (July 1826):406-39.
INcludes reviews of five C. novels--LIONEL LINCOLN, THE SPY, THE PILOT, THE LAST OF THE MOHICANS, and THE PIONEERS.

224 THE ARIEL 3 (March 6, 1830):183.
        Negative assessment. THE PILOT is his best work, especially the descriptions, but the remainder is ordinary.

225 _____ 4 (February 19, 1831):171.
        C's. latest novels have earned him $18,000 each.

226 "Biographical Sketches of Living American Poets and Novelists. No. II. James Fenimore Cooper, Esq." SOUTHERN LITERARY MESSENGER 4 (June 1838):373-78.
        Brief notices of each of C's. books.

227 "Cooper: His Genius and Writings." MAGNOLIA 1 n.s. (September 1842):129-239.
        An essay criticizing several novels concluding that C's. recent satires have been written at the wrong time and in the wrong spirit. He is, however, a patriot who has written both good and bad romances.

228 "Cooper's Novels." NEW-YORK MIRROR 5 (August 4, 11, 1827):31, 39.
        C's. works, in general, have deteriorated with time. THE SPY and THE PIONEERS were both highly successful, Leatherstocking was drawn with consummate skill, and THE PILOT added to his reputation, especially the portrayal of Tom Coffin. THE LAST OF THE MOHICANS and THE PRAIRIE, however, in spite of occasional brilliance, do not equal those novels that preceded them.

229 "Cooper's Works." UNITED STATES MAGAZINE AND DEMO-CRATIC REVIEW 25 (July 1849):51-55.
        On native literature, the problems of being an American author, a publishing history of THE SPY , and comments on C. as a novelist.

230 "Cooper the Novelist." NEW MONTHLY MAGAZINE 22 (April 1828):387. Reprinted in MUSEUM OF FOREIGN LITERATURE, SCIENCE, AND ART 13 (June 1828):187-88.
        Original, fresh, thrilling--a genius.

231 CRITIC 15 (September 14, 1889):126-27.
        Letters to the editor in praise of THE CRATER, THE SEA LIONS, and the L. S. TALES.

232 EDINBURGH LITERARY JOURNAL no. 42 (August 29, 1829):171-73.

A retrospective review of C's. works that finds his language "copious," his sentence structure "careless," his plots poorly conceived, but his characters strongly drawn. THE RED ROVER is his best book, accomplishing what THE PILOT failed to do.

233 EDINBURGH REVIEW 61 (April 1835):21-40.
From a review of SELECTIONS FROM THE AMERICAN POETS. C. is the undeniable master of the sea and frontier, but sinks to little more than a second-rate novelist when his subject becomes polite society. (pp. 23-24)

234 _____ 89 (January 1849):83-114.
From a review of CHARLES VERNON by Lieutenant-Colonel Senior. Childish plots, unreal characters, but the master as a creator of scenery. (p. 91)

235 Emerson, Ralph Waldo. THE LETTERS OF RALPH WALDO EMERSON. 6 vol. Edited by Ralph L. Rusk. New York: Columbia University Press, 1939. Scattered references.
Includes comments on THE CHAINBEARER, THE PIONEERS, THE REDSKINS, SATANSTOE, and THE SPY.

236 [Everett, A. H.] "American Literature." NORTH AMERICAN REVIEW 31 (July 1830):26-66.
C., along with Irving, stands at the forefront of American literature. Their reputations are international in scope and few writers in the world can compete with them. (pp. 33, 37, 38-39)

237 Finkelstein, Sidney, ed. "Introduction." JAMES FENIMORE COOPER: SHORT STORIES FROM HIS WORKS. New York: International Publishers, 1970.

238 Ford, Paul Leicester, Edward Everett Hale, and Alfred T. Mahan, eds. "Introduction." THE WORKS OF J. FENIMORE COOPER. Ideal Edition. New York: Appleton, 1901.

239 FOREIGN AND COLONIAL QUARTERLY REVIEW (October 1843):474.
Not seen. Citation from Clavel, p. 240 (item no. 5).

240 Fuller, Margaret. THE WRITING OF MARGARET FULLER. Edited by Mason Wade. New York: Viking Press, 1941. Pp. 25, 363.
C. possessed greater faults than merits, not only as a man , but as

a writer. He is saved from oblivion by his sea and forest sketches.

241 Gould, Edward S. "American Criticism on American Authors." NEW-YORKER 1 (April 23, 1836):66.

      C., while not a favorite of Gould's, is considered by him to be superior to George Payne Rainsford James, a novelist who gained repute far beyond his talent.

242 Griswold, Rufus W. "James Fenimore Cooper." GRAHAM'S MAGAZINE 26 (August 1844):90-93.

      A short critical assessment of each of C's. books.

243 _____. "Memoir of James Fenimore Cooper, the Author of 'The Pilot,' 'The Spy,' etc." BENTLEY'S MISCELLANY 21 (1847):533-40. Also in ECLECTIC MAGAZINE 11 (July 1847):430-36.

      A biographical sketch with appraisals of nearly all of C's. novels. A highly positive evaluation that credits the Littlepage Trilogy with expressing important truths and describes THE BRAVO as one of C's. best novels. The press is attacked for not defending him against his foreign detractors.

244 _____. THE PROSE WRITERS OF AMERICA. 3d ed., rev. Philadelphia: Carey & Hart, 1849. Pp. 263-83. Reprinted in SOUTHERN LITERARY MESSENGER 16 (April 1850):230-40.

      Short comments, both negative and positive, on each of C's. books.

245 ["Harvey Birch and the Skinner Engraving".] COLUMBIAN LADIE'S AND GENTLEMAN'S MAGAZINE 7 (January 1847):40.

      At the time that he wrote THE SPY, C. was neither a moralist, nor had he attempted to educate Americans in the areas of manners, democracy, or libel law.

246 Hazlitt, William. THE COLLECTED WORKS OF WILLIAM HAZLITT. Vol. 20. Edited by A. R. Waller & Arnold Glover. London: J. M. Dent, 1904. Pp. 312-14. Reprinted from a review of W. E. Channing's SERMONS AND TRACTS in the EDINBURGH REVIEW 50 (October 1829):128-29.

      C. provides much detail in his fiction, but his stories stand still and become drudgery for the reader.

247 "The Historical Romance." BLACKWOOD'S MAGAZINE 58 (September 1845):341-56.

      C's. portrayal of the national character, the Indian, and nature has given him his well deserved reputation. He is a failure, however, when he moves to Europe or attempts to comment upon society.

248 Hone, Philip. THE DIARY OF PHILIP HONE, 1828-1851. 2 vols. Edited by Allan Nevins. New York: Dodd, Mead & Co., 1927. 1:103, 346, 360-62; 2:604.
        Comments on C. as a novelist, his critique of Lockhart's LIFE OF SCOTT, his social criticism, and his libel suit against the COMMERCIAL ADVERTISER.

249 ILLUSTRATIONS FROM "THE SPY," "THE PIONEERS" AND THE WAVERLY NOVELS, WITH EXPLANATORY AND CRITICAL REMARKS. Philadelphia: Published at the Port Folio Office, 1826.

250 Irving, Washington. JOURNALS & NOTEBOOKS. Edited by Walter A. Reichart. Madison: University of Wisconsin Press, 1969.   Scattered references.

251 _____. THE LIFE & LETTERS OF WASHINGTON IRVING. 4 vols. Edited by Pierre Monroe Irving. New York: G. P. Putnam, 1864. Scattered references.

252 "J. Fenimore Cooper." AURORA 1 (November 22, 1834):249.
        Criticism of attempts to denounce C's. political views and literary character.

253 "James F. Cooper." AMERICAN MAGAZINE 2 (February 1836): 231.
        C's. early novels are fresh and original with graphic descriptions and real characters. His later books, however, are far too verbose and mean.

254 "James Fenimore Cooper." HARTFORD PEARL AND LITERARY GAZETTE 4 (August 20, 1834):5-6.
        C's. European novels, his failure in portraying gentility, and his inability to develop or provide proper dialogue for his female characters, are his greatest shortcomings.

255 "James Fenimore Cooper." INTERNATIONAL MAGAZINE OF LITERATURE, ART AND SCIENCE 3 (April 1851):1-7.
        C. has managed to retain a rational style while displaying great imagination and originality in his works.

256 "James Fenimore Cooper." RURAL REPOSITORY 14 (November 25, 1837):93-94.

C's. characterizations are superior to Smollett's. The forest scenes are successfully done. Those who criticize him for integrating politics with romance have done so through "ill-grace."

257 "James Fenimore Cooper." YALE LITERARY MAGAZINE 5 (March 1840):249-59.

C. was the first to design a truly American novel. As such he has had unequalled success as a portrayer of the American scene, while keeping a high moral tone in his stories. Unfortunately, except for his Indians, his characterizations are poorly drawn and his plots are not well thought out.

258 KNICKERBOCKER MAGAZINE 11 (April 1838):380-86.

Letters from C. plus material on relations between he and Scott.

259 _____ 13 (February 1839):172-73.

A criticism of an article in the NEW-YORK REVIEW of January 1839 that had attacked C. for inaccuracies in language usage.

260 "Letters on the United States of America." SOUTHERN LITERARY MESSENGER 1 (May 1835):482-83.

The romances of C. and Scott are preferred to all others, including those of Charles B. Brown. Although Scott possesses great knowledge of history, manners, and customs, C. is superior to him when dealing with the sea.

261 "Literature of the Nineteenth Century. America." ATHENAEUM [8] (January 3, 1835):9-13.

C. has never been treated in America with the respect he deserves, although foreigners have recognized and praised his genius.

262 "Living Literary Characters, No. IV. James Fenimore Cooper." NEW MONTHLY MAGAZINE 31 (May 1831):356-62. Reprinted in "James Fenimore Cooper." MUSEUM OF FOREIGN LITERATURE, SCIENCE AND ART 18 (June 1831):561-65.

Highly complimentary biographical sketch that credits C. with being an acute observer of life. His characterizations, his fiction as national literature, THE LAST OF THE MOHICANS, THE SPY, THE PRAIRIE, THE RED ROVER, and THE PILOT are discussed.

263 "Living Novelists, No. III." SOUTHERN LITERARY MESSENGER 13 (December 1847):745-52.

The most creative and dramatic American novelist. A poetic genius whose characterizations are surpassed only by those of Scott.

264 "Living Pictures of American Notabilities, Literary and Scientific, No. VIII. Sketched by Motley Manners, ESQ. James Fenimore Cooper." HOLDEN'S DOLLAR MAGAZINE 3 (February 1849): 89-91.

        C. wrote some good books, was a pioneer in American literature, but not a great novelist. He ranks below Scott.

265 Lowell, James Russell. A FABLE FOR CRITICS. New York: G. P. Putnam, 1848. Pp. 48-50.

        A lengthy poem on Lowell's contemporaries. Claims that C. created only one character, Natty Bumppo. All others were models of him. His women are described as "sappy . . . and flat."

266 "Mr. Cooper and the Reviewers." BALTIMORE LITERARY MONU-MENT 1 (November 1838):82.

        Comments on C. as writer and criticizes those who have reviewed him.

267 [Neal, John.] "American Writers. No. II." BLACKWOOD'S MAGA-ZINE 16 (October 1824):415-28.

        PRECAUTION--very poor; THE SPY--C's. best, but "too full of stage-tricks"; THE PIONEERS--often repetitious; THE PILOT--style greatly improved. C. is talented, but not a genius, nor even a great writer. (pp. 427-28)

268 NEW WORLD 3 (September 4, 1841):160.

        C. should cease writing or create new scenes and characters. There is no freshness or life in his latest works.

269 _____ 3 (November 6, 1841):293.

        Using C's. signature, this article purports to analyze his handwriting. As usual in this publication, C. is seen in very negative terms.

270 NEW-YORKER 6 (December 15, 1838):205.

        An assertion that C. is having a difficult time selling his books at his inflated estimate of their value.

271 Paulding, James Kirke. THE LETTERS OF JAMES KIRKE PAUL-DING. Edited by Ralph M. Aderman. Madison: University of Wisconsin Press, 1962. Scattered references.

        Letters to C. and comments on C. in letters to other friends.

272 Peck, G. W. "The Works of J. Fenimore Cooper." AMERICAN WHIG REVIEW 11 (April 1850):406-17.

C's. 'forte' is his imagination (scenes and objects). He, however, distorts everyday life, being uneasy in the parlor or on the street.

273 PHILADELPHIA MONTHLY MAGAZINE 1 (March 15, 1828):294.

C's. faults result from his following the Scottish model. His positive qualities include characterizations, accurate observations of places, and the reader interest he arouses. Unnecessary characters are often included.

274 Powell, Thomas. THE LIVING AUTHORS OF AMERICA. New York: Stringer & Townsend, 1850. Pp. 9-48.

While Irving was more of an English author, C. is the first truly American one. Even so, his novels lack imagination, are full of lectures, and become monotonous due to observations that possess no universal appeal.

275 [Prescott, W. H.] "English Literature of the Nineteenth Century." NORTH AMERICAN REVIEW 35 (July 1832):165-95.

C's. greatest defect is his failure to write well of genteel society. He has, however, far outdistanced any of his rivals who write in the imitation of Scott. (pp. 190-91)

276 "Present State of Literature." GENTLEMAN'S MAGAZINE 95 (September 1825):193-99.

An imitator of Scott, but superior to any of his (C's.) American imitators. (pp. 97-98)

277 RETROSPECTIVE REVIEW 9, part 2 (1824):323-26.

A talented author, more dramatic than Brown, but lacking emotion and narrative strength.

278 Scott, Walter. THE JOURNAL OF SIR WALTER SCOTT. Edited by W. E. K. Anderson. Oxford: At the Clarendon Press, 1972. Scattered references.

Comments on THE PILOT, THE RED ROVER, and THE PRAIRIE.

279 "Scott and Cooper." THE ARIEL 1 (November 17, 1827):120.

C. cannot be compared favorably to Scott. He has power, but not genius, fails to vary characters, and draws landscapes, whereas Scott creates them from the heart.

280 S[ealsfield, Charles.] "The Works of the Author of 'The Spy.'" NEW-YORK MIRROR 8 (February 12, 1831):252-54.

Sealsfield discusses C's. Indians ("sophisticated"), action scenes, excessive narrative, descriptive powers, and characterizations in general.

281 Simms, William Gilmore. "Cooper, His Genius and Writings." MAGNOLIA 1 n.s. (September 1842):129-39. Reprinted in VIEWS AND REVIEWS IN AMERICAN LITERATURE, HISTORY AND FICTION. 1st series. New York: Wiley and Putnam, 1845. Pp. 210-38; VIEWS AND REVIEWS IN AMERICAN LITERATURE, HISTORY AND FICTION. Edited by C. Hugh Holman. Cambridge: Belknap Press of Harvard University Press, 1962. Pp. 258-92; and Perkins, George, ed. THE THEORY OF THE AMERICAN MIND. New York: Holt, Rinehart & Winston, 1970. Pp. 35-37 (excerpted).
    C. was a persecuted man who wrote his social commentaries at the wrong time and in the wrong spirit.

282 "Sir W. Scott--'Lives of the Novelists'". QUARTERLY REVIEW 34 (September 1826):349-78.
    With only one or two exceptions, C. will not be remembered for long. His success is due to his superior materials. An inferior imitator of Scott.

283 SOUTHERN LITERARY MESSENGER 1 (February 1835):315.
    Bird, the author of CALAVAR; OR THE KNIGHT OF THE CONQUEST is superior to C. in his dialogue, buy fails to depict his female characters as expertly.

284 SOUTHERN QUARTERLY REVIEW 16 (October 1849):269-70.
    On the Putnam 1849 reprint of C's. works. A favorite author who has revised his novels, provided new introductions, as well as explanatory and illustrative notes.

285 SPIRIT OF LITERATURE 1 (October 30, 1830):425-28.
    Critical evaluations of THE WATER WITCH, PRECAUTION, THE SPY, THE PIONEERS, THE PILOT, LIONEL LINCOLN, and THE LAST OF THE MOHICANS.

286 Thackeray, William Makepeace. "The Stars and Stripes." THE WORKS OF WILLIAM MAKEPEACE THACKERAY. Vol. 6. London: Smith, Elder & Co., 1902. Originally in PUNCH, October 9, 1847, pp. 528-34.
    A parody of C's. romances.

287 UNITED STATES LITERARY GAZETTE 1 (December 1, 1824):254.
    C's. reputation in England as a major author is one that is well deserved.

288 Willard, Emma. JOURNAL AND LETTERS FROM FRANCE AND GREAT BRITAIN. Troy, N. Y.: Tuttle, 1833. P. 90.

      Letter to Mrs. A. H. Lincoln, December 7, 1830, on C's. ability to describe scenery and the charge that he borrowed the plot for THE WEPT OF WISH-TON-WISH from Sedgwick's HOPE LESLIE.

289 [Willis, N. Parker]. "First Impressions of Europe." NEW-YORK MIRROR 10 (July 7, 1832):4.

      C. is a true patriot and a gifted writer.

290 "Works of Fenimore Cooper." AMERICAN QUARTERLY REVIEW 17 (June 1835):407-30.

      C. has used his books as vehicles for expressing the noble ideas of love of country and freedom. Includes comments on C's. humor, characterizations (male and female), style, and social and political views.

291 "The Writings of Charles Sealsfield." FOREIGN QUARTERLY REVIEW 37 (July 1846):222-38.

      C. is unequalled as a writer of nautical romance, although not an accurate descriptor of sea life. Neither are his Indians or frontiersmen faithfully portrayed. One might read him for amusement, but he must be viewed with caution and little faith.

ARTICLES FROM COOPER'S DEATH TO THE PRESENT

292 Abcarian, Richard. "Cooper's Critics and the Realistic Novel." TEXAS STUDIES IN LITERATURE AND LANGUAGE 8 (Spring 1966):33-41.

      Few critics were fully satisfied with C's. early romances as realistic novels, but it was not until he introduced political and social themes that they fully condemned him. Indignant that he could find little to recommend the American dream, they urged him to return to the historical romance of the 1820s.

293 _____. "The Literary Reputation of James Fenimore Cooper in America, 1820-1955." Ph.D. dissertation, University of California at Berkeley, 1961.

294 Adams, Charles H. "'The Guardian of the Law': Authority and Identity in James Fenimore Cooper." Ph.D. dissertation, University of Virginia, 1985.

      Law and legal issues are central to C's. novels and their use often goes far toward determining dialogue, form and characterization.

295 Alden, William L. "J. Fenimore Cooper's Rank as Novelist." LITER-
ARY DIGEST 18 (March 25, 1899):339.

> C's. heroines, Indians, and sailors may not be lifelike, but he is
the best storyteller America has produced.

296 Arndt, Karl J. "New Letters from James Fenimore Cooper." MODERN
LANGUAGE NOTES 52 (February 1937):117-20.

> A letter from Cooper dated November 6, 1831, to his publisher
Carey and Lea in Philadelphia on THE HEIDENMAUER, and one dated
March 31, 1849, on his HISTORY OF NEW YORK.

297 Axelrad, Allan M. "History and Utopia: A Study of the World View of
James Fenimore Cooper." Ph.D. dissertation, University of Pennsylvania,
1974. Also in book form: Norwood, Pa., Norwood Press, 1978.

> C's. view of history was composed of both classical ideas (repeat-
ing cycles) and Christian ideas (a single cycle culminating in heaven on earth).
Formed early in life, a study of C's. world view shows that he did not change
from a liberal democrat to a conservative upon his return from Europe. Sees
C. as a Trinitarian.

298 Baldwin, Roger S. "Literary Pioneer." YALE LITERARY MAGAZINE
57 (March 1892):229-31.

> The period in American history in which C. wrote was important
to the influence he wielded. The practical nature of the country created a de-
mand for entertaining, rather than more scholarly, literature.

299 Ball, Roland C. "American Reinterpretations of European Romantic
Themes: The Rebel-Hero in Cooper and Melville." International Comparative
Literature Association, IVth Congress of, PROCEEDINGS. Edited by Francis
Jost. The Hague & Paris: Mouton & Co., 1966. Pp. 1113-21.

> As a romantic, C's. rebellion against American society failed to
reach the point of total rejection that was characteristic of many of his European counterparts. His conservatism called for a ruling aristocratic class based
upon landed wealth, while his orthodox religious convictions and a strict moral
code removed him even further from his contemporary romantics.

300 Banks, Stanley M., ed. AMERICAN ROMANTICISM: A SHAPE FOR
FICTION. New York: G. P. Putnam's Sons, 1969. Pp. 110-52.

> Sees C. as both a romantic writer and an historian. Reprints the
Prefaces of several novels (THE SPY, THE PIONEERS, LIONEL LINCOLN,
THE WING-AND-WING, AFLOAT AND ASHORE, THE PILOT, the L. S.
TALES), an excerpt from NOTIONS OF THE AMERICANS, part of his re-
view of Lockhart's LIFE OF SCOTT, and Parkman's review of his WORKS.

301 Barba, Preston A. "Cooper in Germany." GERMAN AMERICAN AN-
NALS 12 n.s. (January-February 1914):3-60. Also in his COOPER IN GER-
MANY. University of Indiana Studies, no. 21. Bloomington: University of
Indiana Press, 1914.

      C., whose writing was distinctly American, had a profound effect
on German literature, replacing Scott as that country's favorite foreign author.
Includes bibliographies of reviews from German periodicals and of German
translations of C's. novels.

302 Barnett, Louise K. THE IGNOBLE SAVAGE: AMERICAN LITERARY
RACISM, 1790-1890. Contributions in American Studies, no. 18. Westport,
Conn.: Greenwood Press, 1975. Scattered references.

303 Beard, James F. "Cooper and His Artistic Contemporaries." NEW YORK
HISTORY 35 (October 1954):480-95.

      On the artistic descriptions (painterly) and aesthetic effects of C's.
novels that set them apart from their European counterparts.

304 _____. "Cooper and the Revolutionary Mythos." EARLY AMERICAN
LITERATURE 11 (Spring 1976):84-104.

      Revolutionary War novels reflected ideas, values, and attitudes
possessed by the citizen of the early 1800s that had resulted in independence
and the creation of a new country.

305 _____. "James Fenimore Cooper, Craftsman of Democratic Fiction."
Ph.D. dissertation, Princeton University, 1949.

306 _____ and James P. Elliott. THE WRITINGS OF JAMES FENIMORE
COOPER: A STATEMENT OF EDITORIAL PRINCIPLES AND PROCED-
URES. Worcester: Clark University Press, 1977.

307 Beard, James F. et al., eds. The Writings of James Fenimore Cooper Series. Albany, N. Y.: State University of New York Press, 1980- .

      An important series with historical introductions and textual notes
by recognized scholars for each work. The following books have been published as of 1990:

    GLEANINGS IN EUROPE: SWITZERLAND, 1980
    THE PIONEERS, 1980
    GLEANINGS IN EUROPE: ENGLAND, 1981
    GLEANINGS IN EUROPE: ITALY, 1981
    THE PATHFINDER, 1981
    WYANDOTTE, 1981
    GLEANINGS IN EUROPE: FRANCE, 1983

THE LAST OF THE MOHICANS, 1983
LIONEL LINCOLN, 1984
THE PRAIRIE, 1985
GLEANINGS IN EUROPE: THE RHINE, 1986
THE PILOT, 1986
THE DEERSLAYER, 1987
NOTIONS OF THE AMERICANS, 1990
RED ROVER, 1990
SATANSTOE, 1990
THE TWO ADMIRALS, 1990

308 Beers, Henry A. AN OUTLINE SKETCH OF AMERICAN LITERA-
TURE. New York: Chautaugua Press, 1887. Pp. 104-08. Reprinted in IN-
ITIAL STUDIES IN AMERICAN LETTERS. New York: Chautaugua Press,
1891. Pp. 81-84.
        C. is the most successful novelist America has ever produced even
though his social novels were poorly done, he possessed little humor, he had
no ability to create characters, and he wrote in an unreadable style. Where he
excelled was in description (especially of the Indian) and plot.

309 _____. "James Fenimore Cooper, 1789-1889." THE CRITIC 12 (September 14, 1889):125-27.
        C. was a truly American writer, whereas Irving was as much En-
glish as American. Irving, however, was the superior of the two, at least stylistically, if not inventively.

310 Bender, Thomas. "James Fenimore Cooper and the City." NEW YORK
HISTORY 51 (April 1970):287-305.
        C's. attitude toward the landed gentry changed as they were slow-
ly replaced by an urban aristocracy. Thus, the locus of his social order was
not geographical, but depended upon stability and leadership, something that
by his death in 1851 he believed the city could best provide.

311 Benjamin, Nancy Berg. "Traditional Enclosed Gardens in Nineteenth-
Century American Fiction: The Constriction of Adamic Aspirations." Ph.D.
dissertation, University of Houston, 1984.
        Enclosed gardens as a symbol of everything the American Adam
rejected. In C's. case, the emphasis is on social and political factors.

312 Berbrich, Joan D. THREE VOICES FROM PAUMANOK: THE IN-
FLUENCE OF LONG ISLAND ON JAMES FENIMORE COOPER, WIL-
LIAM CULLEN BRYANT, AND WALT WHITMAN. Port Washington, N.
Y.: Ira J. Friedman, 1969. Pp. 5-58. Originally "The Influence of Long Island

on Three Major Writers." Ph.D. dissertation, New York University, 1964.

Recounts C's. life on Long Island during which he gained a knowledge of whaling techniques, navigation, and Revolutionary spy activities.
These were used for subject matter in fifteen novels, including THE SEA
LIONS and THE PILOT. He also patterned several characters in these novels
after inhabitants of the Island. Contains material on the C/Bryant relationship.

313 Bertone, Robert E. "The Development of the Hero-type in Fenimore
Cooper's Works." Master of Arts degree, Boston College, 1965.

314 Bewley, Marius James. THE COMPLEX FATE. London: Chatto &
Windus, 1952. Pp. 1-2.

C's. style was adequate when concerned with those events central
to the book, but deficient at other times.

315 _____. ECCENTRIC DESIGN; FORM IN THE CLASSIC AMERI-
CAN NOVEL. London: Chatto & Windus, 1959. Pp. 47-112. Pages 201-04
and pp. 110-12 reprinted as "James Fenimore Cooper: 'A Kind of Guardian
Spirit of the Wilderness'" in Rubin, Louis D., Jr. and John R. Moore, eds.
THE IDEA OF AN AMERICAN NOVEL. New York: Thomas Y. Crowell
Co., 1961. Pp. 197-200.

Three chapters are concerned with C. The first finds no contrast or
change of opinion in C's. political thought, but only continuity that illustrates
varying aspects of concern by the ruling class. The second considers action as
it relates to form in the novels. The third discusses C's. symbolism.

316 _____. "Fenimore Cooper and the Economic Age." AMERICAN LIT-
ERATURE 26 (May 1954):166-95.

C's. writings are characterized by a conflict that resulted from the
author's interpretation of society and history. This conflict is essentially a political one, but also manifests itself in social, economic, and international
spheres. It is especially evident in the European novels and the Littlepage Trilogy.

317 _____. MASKS AND MIRRORS: ESSAYS IN CRITICISM. New
York: Atheneum Publications, 1970. Pp. 226-54.

Views C's. fiction as national literature that sought to tell Americans how to think and act as Americans. Characterizes C. as a Democrat, a
Jacksonian toward the end of his life, a man who admired aristocratic values,
and one who encouraged agricultural, against commercial and urban, wealth.

318 _____. "Revaluations (XVI): James Fenimore Cooper." SCRUTINY 19
(Winter 1952-53):98-125.

Basically concerned with action in C's. novels, especially THE DEERSLAYER. Bewley blames the lack of attention C. received on the label "American Scott" which he was given early in his career. Reprinted in THE ECCENTRIC DESIGN, above, without many of the references to Scott.

319 Bier, Jesse. THE RISE AND FALL OF AMERICAN HUMOR. New York: Holt, Rinehart & Winston, 1968. Pp. 361-63.

C's. intended humor is poorly conceived for he had no real talent here. His inadequacies as a writer often create humor where none was intended.

320 Birss, John Howard. "A Letter of Herman Melville." NOTES AND QUERIES (London) 162 (January 16, 1932):39.

Letter from Herman Melville dated February 20, 1852, describing C. as "a great robust-souled man, all whose merits are not yet seen, yet fully appreciated."

321 Boake, Mary L. "The Development of Cooper's Political and Social Ideas in Relation to the Structure of His Novels." Master of Arts degree, University of Oklahoma, 1939.

322 Bobrova, Maria. JAMES FENIMORE COOPER: AN ESSAY ON HIS LIFE AND CREATIVE WORK. Saratov, U.S.S.R., 1967.

C's. novels went beyond their age in describing the developmental period in American history, for they realized the evils of capitalism and opposed the racist attitudes commonly directed toward the Indians. In Russia, his influence exceeded that of Scott.

323 Bowen, Ray P. "A Comparison of the Methods of Composition in Cooper and Balzac." FRENCH AMERICAN REVIEW 3 (October-December 1950):297-313.

C. and Balzac developed independently of each other, and similarities between the two are due to each authors' admiration for Scott. See item no. 999 which is in opposition to this interpretation.

324 Boyles, Mary P. "Sensibility in the Novels of James Fenimore Cooper." Ph.D. dissertation, University of North Carolina, 1977.

Sensibility, as used by C., is an index to a character's social and moral outlook on life. In his early writings C. often located this quality in those of the lower classes, but as he grew older and more disillusioned with society and politics, it came to reside almost exclusively in the upper classes. It was in this group that C. placed his hope for America's future.

325 Boynton, Percy H. LITERATURE AND AMERICAN LIFE. Boston: Ginn & Co., 1936. Pp. 254-72.

C., a democrat who rejected aristocracy, possessed great ability as a story teller and social critic. As such, his works are important today to the student of American history.

326 Bradfield, Scott Michael. "Dreaming Revolution: Transgression in Nineteenth-Century American Literature." Ph.D. dissertation, University of California, Irvine, 1987.

On language and law.

327 Bradsher, Frieda K. "Women in the Works of James Fenimore Cooper." Ph.D. dissertation, University of Arizona, 1979.

Contends that by tracing C's. treatment of women one can discover changes in his ideas of morality and truth.

328 Brady, Charles A. "James Fenimore Cooper, 1789-1851: Myth-maker and Christian Romancer." AMERICAN CLASSICS RECONSIDERED: A CHRISTIAN APPRAISAL. Edited by Harold C. Gardiner. New York: Charles Scribner's Sons, 1958. Pp. 59-97.

C., one of America's most religious novelists, gained his popularity from his orthodoxy and morality. It is, however, for this very reason that he is no longer read today. A Catholic viewpoint.

329 Breinig, Helmbrecht. "'Turn Your Mind on the Ways of the Inner Country': Cooper and the Question of Western Expansion." WESTERN EXPANSION IN AMERICA (1803-1860). Edited by Wolfgang Binder. Erlangen, FRG: Palm & Enke, 1987. Pp. 47-63.

Not seen.

330 Brevoort, Henry. LETTERS OF HENRY BREVOORT TO WASHINGTON IRVING. TOGETHER WITH OTHER UNPUBLISHED BREVOORT PAPERS. Edited by George S. Hellman. New York: G. P. Putnam's Sons, 1918. Pp. 160-61, 236-37, 268-69, 301.

Comments of a very general nature.

331 Bridgman, Richard. THE COLLOQUIAL STYLE IN AMERICA. New York: Oxford University Press, 1966. Pp. 66-69.

C's. use of dialogue, while possessing great variety, was often clumsy, especially where Natty Bumppo was concerned.

332 Brooks, Van Wyck. WORLD OF WASHINGTON IRVING. New York: E. P. Dutton & Co., 1944. Pp. 214-33, 315-36, 399-425.

Three chapters concern C.: 1. "Cooper: The First Phase"--the influence of the forest, sea, and Indians; 2. "Irving and Cooper Abroad"--the influence of Europe on C's. writings; 3. "New York: Cooper"--his feelings of distress for the changes he observed in America upon his return from abroad.

333 Brown, Herbert Ross. THE SENTIMENTAL NOVEL IN AMERICA, 1789-1860. Freeport, N. Y.: Books for Libraries Press, 1970. Originally Durham, N. C.: Duke University Press, 1940. Scattered references.

Religion, slavery, temperance, women, and sentimentality are among the subjects covered.

334 Brownell, William Crary. AMERICAN PROSE MASTERS: COOPER--HAWTHORNE--EMERSON--POE--LOWELL--HENRY JAMES. Edited by Howard Mumford Jones. Cambridge Mass.: Belknap Press of Harvard University Press, 1963. Pp. 5-42. Reprinted from THE LITERATURE OF AMERICA, VOL. I: FROM THE BEGINNING TO THE CIVIL WAR. Edited by Arthur Hobson Quinn et al. New York: Charles Scribner's Sons, 1938. Pp. 1088-98.

C. was a moral writer, following those convictions he possessed as a man. As a creator of excellent characters, his greatest fault was tedium.

335 _____. "Cooper." SCRIBNER'S MAGAZINE 36 (April 1906):455-68.

On C's. general literary talent, his indebtedness to Scott, his Indians, his descriptive ability, his characterizations (especially the female ones), and his role in creating a native literature.

336 Bryant, William Cullen. A DISCOURSE ON THE LIFE AND GENIUS OF JAMES FENIMORE COOPER. Works of William Cullen Bryant Series. Irvine, Cal.: Reprint Services Corp., 1989. Reprint of an 1852 edition.

337 _____. ORATIONS AND ADDRESSES. New York: G. P. Putnam's Sons, 1873. Pp. 43-91. Reprinted in "Introduction" to PRECAUTION. New York: D. Appleton & Co., 1881; PROSE WRITINGS OF WILLIAM CULLEN BRYANT. Vol. 1. Edited by Parke Godwin. New York: Russell & Russell, 1964 (originally 1884). Pp. 299-331; and HERITAGE OF AMERICAN LITERATURE. Vol. 1. Edited by Norman Richardson et al. Boston: Ginn, 1951. Pp. 444-49.

338 Burich, Keith Robert. "The Catholic Church and American Intellectuals: From Cooper to Santayana." Ph.D. dissertation, University of North Carolina at Chapel Hill, 1979.

C's. view of the Catholic Church was a more favorable one than many who had gone before him. He saw it as a bastion of permanence and moral direction.

339 Burke, Martin. "Cooper as an Exponent of American Romanticism." Master of Arts degree, Louisiana State University, 1935.

340 Burton, Richard. LITERARY LEADERS OF AMERICA; A CLASS-BOOK ON AMERICAN LITERATURE. New York: Charles Scribner's Sons, 1904. Pp. 42-65.

      Irving was superior to C. as a writer, but the latter will always be read because of his perceptiveness. His greatest defects were in style and technique. Includes biographical material.

341 _____. MASTERS OF THE ENGLISH NOVEL; A STUDY OF PRINCIPLES AND PERSONALITIES. New York: Henry Holt & Co., 1909. Pp. 313-21.

      C's. greatest achievement was his ability to take literature, at a time when it was a private experience, and make it a public one. He possessed a creative mind and must be considered one of the four great fiction writers in relation to the novel's evolution in America.

342 Bush, C. W. "The Treatment of Religion and Religious Character in the Nineteenth Century American Novel Through Selected Fiction by Cooper, Hawthorne, Melville, Harriet Beecher Stowe, Oliver Wendell Holmes and Mark Twain." Master of Philosophy degree, University of London, 1967.

343 Butterfield, Lyman H. "Cooper's Inheritance: The Otsego Country and Its Founders." NEW YORK HISTORY 35 (October 1954):374-411.

      A discussion of the settlement of Otsego County up to 1830. According to Butterfield these early years and the role that Judge Cooper had played in them, set the stage for C's. later paternalistic Christian view of society. For further information on William Cooper see Arndt, Karl J. "John Christopher Hartwick: German Pioneer of Central New York." NEW YORK HISTORY 18 (July 1937):293-303; Butterfield, Lyman H. "Judge William Cooper (1754-1809): A Sketch of His Character and Accomplishment." NEW YORK HISTORY 30 (October 1949):385-408; Cooper, William. A GUIDE TO THE WILDERNESS. Dublin: 1810; reprinted Rochester, N. Y., 1897; and Penney, A. Owen. "Leatherstocking Country." AMERICAS 11 (September 1959):25-28.

344 Byington, Steven T. "Some Linguistic Items from Cooper." AMERICAN SPEECH 20 (April 1945):115-17.

      C'.s use of language in THE PRAIRIE and THE WING-AND-WING.

345 Cady, Edwin Harrison. THE GENTLEMAN IN AMERICA: A LITERARY STUDY IN AMERICAN CULTURE. New York: Greenwood Press, 1969. Pp. 103-45.

To C., it was impossible that the gentleman and his society would not prevail. To struggle against him was only to unnecessarily delay the progress of civilization.

346 _____. ["Introduction"]. WHITTIER ON WRITERS AND WRITING. Edited by Edwin Harrison Cady and Harry Hayden Clark. Syracuse, N. Y.: Syracuse University Press, 1950. Pp. 3, 6-7.

Although Whittier believed that a combination of C. and Charles Brockden Brown would produce the perfect novelist, he was the first to criticize C. for his romantic Indians and female characters.

347 Cagidemetrio, Alide. " A Plea for Fictional Histories and Old-Time 'Jewesses.'" The Invention of Ethnicity. Edited by Werner Sollors. New York: Oxford University Press, 1989. Pp. 14-43.

Not seen.

348 Cairns, William B. A HISTORY OF AMERICAN LITERATURE. New York: Oxford University Press, 1930. Pp. 147-83. Reprinted New York & London: Johnson Reprint Corp., 1969.

While possessed of many faults, C. was the leader of his age and has not been equalled today.

349 Callow, James T. KINDRED SPIRITS: KNICKERBOCKER WRITERS AND AMERICAN ARTISTS, 1807-1855. Chapel Hill: University of North Carolina Press, 1967. Pp. 52-62, 158-63, 188-90, 192-215.

On relationships between the Hudson River school of painters and the Knickerbocker writers. Includes: friendships, literary influences exerted upon landscape painting, artistic influences in literary description, and C. and others as patrons of the arts.

350 Canby, Henry Seidel. CLASSIC AMERICANS: A STUDY OF EMINENT AMERICAN WRITERS FROM IRVING TO WHITMAN; WITH AN INTRODUCTORY SURVEY OF THE COLONIAL BACKGROUND OF OUR NATIONAL LITERATURE. New York: Russell & Russell, 1959. Pp. 97-142.

Emphasizes C's. background (e.g. Quakerism) and his role as a social critic.

351 _____. "James Fenimore Cooper." SATURDAY REVIEW OF LITERATURE 3 (April 23, 1927):747-49.

Concerned with Quaker influences in C's. writings, especially those exhibited by Natty Bumppo.

352 Candido, Ann Marie. "The Major Literary Artist as Biographer: Some 'Uses' of Biography in Nineteenth-Century England and America." Ph.D. dissertation, Indiana University, 1983.
Includes material on how C. viewed his subjects.

353 Cannon, Evelyn. "Cooper as a Social Critic." Master of Arts degree, Southern Methodist University, 1930.

354 "Century of Fenimore Cooper." NATION 112 (February 16, 1921):255-56.
C's. characters, especially Leatherstocking, Harvey Birch, and Long Tom Coffin, came to be identified as national types by a great portion of the European reading public, just as did their simplicity and prejudices. This simplicity of character in turn dictated that C's. novels be ones of action and not completely true to history or the real world.

355 Charvat, William. "Cooper as Professional Author." NEW YORK HISTORY 35 (October 1954):496-511.
On publishing in the nineteenth century and C's. attitude toward writing and the reading public.

356 Chase, Richard. THE AMERICAN NOVEL AND ITS TRADITION. Garden City, N. Y.: Doubleday Anchor Books, 1957. Pp. 43-65.
Largely concerned with SATANSTOE and THE PRAIRIE, this chapter concentrates on the novel as a study in manners, on Natty Bumppo as a mythical figure, and on C's. female characters.

357 Chislett, William. MODERN AND NEAR MODERNS: ESSAYS ON HENRY JAMES, STOCKTON, SHAW, AND OTHERS. Freeport, N. Y.: Books for Libraries Press, 1967; originally The Grafton Press, 1928. Pp. 103-06.
Deals with C's. prefaces and what they divulge about him as a man and a writer.

358 Clark, Harold Edward. "Fenimore Cooper's 'Leather-stocking Tales': A Problem in Race." Ph.D. dissertation, Indiana University, 1955.
Intermarriage, white/Indian friendship, and treatment of Indians.

359 Clark, Harry Hayden. "Fenimore Cooper and Science." Wisconsin Academy of Science, Arts and Letters, TRANSACTIONS 48, 49 (1959,

1960):179-204, 249-82.

        C's. knowledge and attitude toward science, his scientific interests (astronomy), his handling of environmental and hereditary (race) subjects, and his respect for practical applications of scientific discoveries (navigation, commerce).

360 _____, ed.. TRANSITIONS IN AMERICAN LITERARY HISTORY. Durham, N. C.: Duke University Press, 1953.

        Many significant references to C. in M. F. Heiser's article, "The Decline of Neo-classicism, 1801-1848" (pp. 91-159) and G. Harrison Orians' essay, "The Rise of Romanticism, 1805-1855" (pp. 161-244), concerning social and political beliefs, descriptive abilities, style, and treatment of the Indians.

361 Clark, Robert, ed. JAMES FENIMORE COOPER: NEW CRITICAL ESSAYS. London: Vision, 1985.

        Includes eight essays:

            Brotherston, Gordon. "'The Prairie'
                and Cooper's Invention of the West," pp. 162-86.
            Cheyfitz, Eric. "Literally White,
                Figuratively Red: The Frontier of Translation in 'The Pioneers.'" pp. 55-95.
            Clark, Robert. "Rewriting
                Revolution: Cooper's War of Independence," pp. 187-205. (LIONEL LINCOLN, THE SPY, WYANDOTTE)
            Godden, Richard. "Pioneer
                Properties, or 'What's in a Hut?'" pp. 121-42. (THE PIONEERS) Ickstadt, Heinz. "Instructing the American Democrat: Cooper and the Concept of Popular Fiction in Jacksonian America," pp. 15-37.
            McWilliams, John P. "Red Satan:
                Cooper and the American Indian Epic," pp. 143-61. (L. S. Tales)
            Swann, Charles. "Guns Mean
                Democracy: 'The Pioneers' and the Game Laws," pp. 96-120.
            Wallace, James D. "Cultivating an
                Audience: From 'Precaution' to 'The Spy.'" pp. 38-54.

362 Clavel, Marcel. A PROPOS DU CENTENAIRE DE LA MORT DE FENIMORE COOPER ET DU CONGRES DE COOPERSTOWN DE SEPTEMBRE 1951. A FRENCH TRIBUTE TO JAMES FENIMORE COOPER. [n.p., n.d.].

On Clavel's C. research, C's. twentieth century reputation, and suggestions for further research.

363 Coad, Oral Sumner. "The Gothic Element in American Literature Before 1835." JOURNAL OF ENGLISH AND GERMANIC PHILOLOGY 24 (First quarter 1935):87-88.

Although C. has not been classed as a Gothic writer, several of his novels contain characteristics common to this genre. Namely, THE PRAIRIE, THE WATER WITCH, THE PILOT, LIONEL LINCOLN, and THE HEIDENMAUER.

364 Cohen, Barbara K. "Plot and Characters in the Novels of James Fenimore Cooper: The First Decade." Master of Arts degree, Rutgers University, 1957.

365 Collins, Frank M. "Cooper and the American Dream." Modern Language Association of America, PUBLICATIONS 81 (March 1966):79-94.

Concerns C's. belief in man's inherent goodness, especially in America. Collins concludes that C. developed feelings of ambivalence toward this concept later in life as he found the depravity and evil of the old world creeping into the new.

366 _____. "The Religious and Ethical Ideas of James Fenimore Cooper." Ph.D. dissertation, University of Wisconsin, 1953. Examines C's. religious principles from his early attachment to the Episcopal Church to the mysticism of his later years.

367 Cooper, James Fenimore. EARLY CRITICAL ESSAYS (1820-1822). Edited by James F. Beard. Gainsville, Fla.: Scholars' Facsimiles and Reprints, 1955.

Book reviews by C. from 1820-22 appearing in THE LITERARY AND SCIENTIFIC REPOSITORY, with critical comment in the general introduction and in the introduction to each essay.

368 Cooper, Susan Fenimore. "A Glance Backward." ATLANTIC MONTHLY 59 (February 1887):199-206.

Reminiscences of C. by his daughter pertaining to the writing of PRECAUTION, the identity of Harvey Birch, and publication of THE SPY.

369 _____. PAGES AND PICTURES FROM THE WRITINGS OF JAMES FENIMORE COOPER. New York: W. A. Townsend Co., 1861. Reprinted as THE COOPER GALLERY; OR PAGES AND PICTURES FROM THE WRITINGS OF JAMES FENIMORE COOPER. New York: James Miller, 1865 and as revised and expanded "Introductions" to fifteen of C's. novels in

the 1876 Household Edition of his works published by Houghton, Mifflin & Co.

370 _____. "A Second Glance Backward." ATLANTIC MONTHLY 60 (October 1887):474-86.

        Susan Cooper's reminiscences of the years 1828-30 which were spent in Europe. Includes material on THE WEPT OF WISH-TON-WISH, THE WATER WITCH, and THE BRAVO. Further information on the career of Susan Cooper can be found in Kurth, Rosaly Torna. "Susan Fenimore Cooper: A Study of Her Life and Works." Ph.D. dissertation, Fordham University, 1974.

371 "Cooper and His Novels." AMERICAN QUARTERLY CHURCH REVIEW 14 (July 1861):243-57.

        C., as a great "Christian Moralist" who held faithfully to the tenets of the Church, will be remembered for his original characters and descriptive abilities. Contains some biographical information relating to the period that closely preceded his death.

372 THE COOPER VIGNETTES FROM DRAWINGS BY F. O. C. DARLEY. New York: James G. Gregory, 1862.

        Sixty-two engravings reproduced from C's. novels.

373 Cotora, C. "Literary Offenses, or the Revenge of Cooper." MARK TWAIN JOURNAL 21 (1983):19-20.

        Not seen.

374 Cowie, Alexander. THE RISE OF THE AMERICAN NOVEL. New York: American Book Co., 1948. Pp. 115-64.

        C. should not be judged on his technical faults, but rather on what he attempted to accomplish. The L. S. TALES, as an epic, cannot be evaluated by standard literary principles, but must be seen in the light of national literature. Discusses nearly all of C's. novels.

375 Cross, Wilbur L. THE DEVELOPMENT OF THE ENGLISH NOVEL. New York: Macmillan Co., 1899. Pp. 150-58.

        C. accomplished little as a writer of history, but was an excellent writer of romance.

376 Cunliffe, Marcus. THE LITERATURE OF THE UNITED STATES. 3d ed. Baltimore: Penguin Books, 1967. Pp. 60-70.

        On C's. social code in the L. S. TALES, his stylistic deficiencies, and his concept of democracy as depicted in the Littlepage Trilogy.

377 Cunningham, Richard Earle. "James Fenimore Cooper and the New England Mind." Ph.D. dissertation, University of Illinois, 1965.

C's. disdain for the Puritans caused him to trace undesirable social and political attitudes back to America's New England foundations. Views him as a Jacksonian democrat, but more conservative than the national party.

378 Curry, Patricia Elaine. "The American Experience Through a Looking Glass Darkly: Three Case Studies in the Political Thought of John Locke and the Novels of James Fenimore Cooper." Ph.D. dissertation, Indiana University, 1973.

Examines the convergence of C's. thought with that of Locke's in the areas of civil and natural law and property.

379 Darnell, Donald. "Cooper and Faulkner: Land, Legacy, and Tragic Vision." SOUTH ATLANTIC BULLETIN 34 (March 1969):3-5.

Comparison of Faulkner's and C's. tragic vision.

380 _____. "'Visions of Hereditary Rank': The Loyalist in the Fiction of Hawthorne, Cooper, and Frederic." SOUTH ATLANTIC BULLETIN 42 (May 1977):45-54.

C. sympathetically portrayed Loyalists as aristocratic, courageous, and unswerving in their devotion.

381 Dauber, Kenneth. "Cooper's Myth." THE IDEA OF AUTHORSHIP IN AMERICA: DEMOCRATIC POETICS FROM FRANKLIN TO MELVILLE. Madison: University of Wisconsin Press, 1990. Pp. 78-117.

Not seen.

382 Dekker, George. JAMES FENIMORE COOPER: THE NOVELIST. London: Routlege and Kegan Paul, 1967. American edition: JAMES FENIMORE COOPER: THE AMERICAN SCOTT. New York: Barnes & Noble, 1967.

On C's. debt to Scott, his development as a novelist, and his politics. Dekker finds no incompatibility with C. the writer of romances and C. the social critic. See also Cox, C. B. "Hawkeye and the Indians." SPECTATOR 219 (November 3, 1967):533-34, for a review of this book. Cox discusses Hawkeye, the L. S. TALES, and miscegenation.

383 Delbanco, Andrew. "Imagining America." NEW REPUBLIC 194 (June 9, 1986):38-41.

From a two volume, Library of America edition of the L. S. Tales. A general discussion that concludes that C. was a conservative whose political judgments are not presently in favor. As a conservative he searched in nature for a guide to the future and, although disillusioned with society, he always wrote of America with a sense of love for it.

384 Derby, J. C. FIFTY YEARS AMONG AUTHORS--BOOKS AND PUB-LISHERS. New York: G. W. Carleton, 1884.
        References to C's. relationship with several literary figures of his time, including John Wiley (pp. 293-95) and Daniel Bixby (pp. 591-93).

385 Dethier, Charles Brock. "I. Submission and Rebellion: The Religious Solution in Cooper's Late Novels. II. Teaching Difficult Classics: Pedagogy as Public Relations." Ph.D. dissertation, University of Virginia, 1978.
        Part I examines Christianity, women, Indians, heroes, symbolism, authority figures, and faith. Includes material on OAK OPENINGS, THE SEA LIONS, and THE PIONEERS.

386 Diffey, C. T. "Out of that Generous Land, a Study of the Scope of the Novel based on American Practice from Cooper to Faulkner." Ph.D. dissertation, Bristol University, 1964.

387 Dodd, William Horace. "The Classical American Hero and Women: Studies in Repression." Ph.D. dissertation, Union for Experimenting Colleges and Universities, 1989.
        Examines the male protagonist separated from women and society at the novel's end and the dark/sexual *vs.* the light/moralistic woman.

388 Donaldson, Scott and Ann Massa. "The New World and the Old World." AMERICAN LITERATURE: NINETEENTH AND EARLY TWENTIETH CENTURIES. New York: Barnes & Noble, 1978. Pp. 9-46.
        Not seen.

389 Duncan, Robert W. "The London 'Literary Gazette' and American Writers." PAPERS ON ENGLISH LANGUAGE AND LITERATURE 1 (Spring 1965):153-66.
        C's. novels, on the whole, were given favorable, although superficial treatment in the GAZETTE.

390 Dunn, M. V. "Nature as the Primary Teacher of Man in Cooper's Novels." Master of Arts degree, Boston College, 1937.

391 Duyckinck, Evert A. and George L. Duyckinck. CYCLOPEDIA OF AMERICAN LITERATURE. Vol. 1. Edited by M. Laird Simons. Philadelphia: Wm. Rutter & Co., 1875. Pp. 807-16.
        Commentary and plot summaries of each of C's. works. Includes

a biographical sketch.

392 Earnest, Ernest. EXPATRIATES AND PATRIOTS: AMERICAN ARTISTS, SCHOLARS, AND WRITERS IN EUROPE. Durham, N. C.: Duke University Press, 1968. Pp. 71-92.

     C's. return to America from Europe was characterized by descriptions of his native country that assumed many of the qualities of the British critics he had despised.

393 "Editorial Narrative--History of 'The Knickerbocker Magazine': Number 10." KNICKERBOCKER MAGAZINE 55 (February 1860):215-21.

     An analysis of C's. criticism of Lockhart's LIFE OF SCOTT that shows C. to be as aggressive and disagreeable as many have made him out to be.

394 Ekirch, Arthur A. THE IDEA OF PROGRESS IN AMERICA, 1815-1860. New York: Columbia University Press, 1944. Pp. 179-82.

     On C's. shift from optimism to pessimism in his writings.

395 Engell, John Frederick. "Brackenridge, Brown, Cooper, and the Roots of the American Novel." Ph.D. dissertation, University of North Carolina at Chapel Hill, 1982.

     Deals with form and content, C's. writing career, and foreign influences on him.

396 Erskine, John. LEADING AMERICAN NOVELISTS. New York: Henry Holt, 1910. Pp. 51-129.

     Praise of C. as a story teller and as a man. His best works are THE SPY, THE PILOT, and the L. S. TALES, novels in which he displayed no conscious purpose.

397 Erwin, Mary E. "Cooper's Novels on the Adelphi Stage, 1825-1835." Master of Arts degree, Columbia University, 1937.

398 Evans, Constantine. "James Fenimore Cooper: Young Man to Author." COURIER 23 (Spring 1988):57-77.

     Not seen.

399 Ewart, M. "The Constancy of Cooper: An Experiment in the Structuration of Ideology." Ph.D. dissertation, University of York, 1978.

400 "Fenimore Cooper." ECLECTIC MAGAZINE 26 (June 1852):207-13.

     C. was a genius at writing the romantic novel, but a failure when he wandered from this genre.

401 "Fenimore Cooper Today." THE LOOKOUT 69 (December 21, 1901):1037-39.
Generally favorable criticism. Some biography.

402 Ferguson, J. De Lancey. AMERICAN LITERATURE IN SPAIN. New York: Columbia University Press, 1916. Pp. 32-54.
C. was popular in Spain, even more so than Poe, but he was never taken as a serious writer.

403 Fields, Nadine E. "Portraiture of the American Indian in the Novels of Cooper, Bird, and Simms." Master of Arts degree, Oklahoma State University, 1957.

404 Fields, Wayne, ed. JAMES FENIMORE COOPER: A COLLECTION OF CRITICAL ESSAYS. Englewood Cliffs, N. J.: Prentice-Hall, 1979.
Fourteen essays, all having appeared elsewhere except Fields', "Beyond Definition: A Reading of 'The Prairie'", pp. 93-111. The prairie has no boundaries. It becomes a neutral ground, a place where one must not just survive, but create and order his world.

405 "The First American Teller of Tales." THE OUTLOOK 86 (August 17, 1907):807-08.
C. is revered as an author, but he remains unread except by children. This is because the young can overlook his excessive elegance of language and his failure to create realistic female characters, as they concern · themselves only with his action scenes.

406 Fitch, George Hamlin. GREAT SPIRITUAL WRITERS OF AMERICA. San Francisco: Paul Elder, 1916. Pp. 48-57.
C., best known for his descriptions of the Indian, also introduced America to Europe. Although he lacked literary style (he was careless and redundant), he was unequalled as a creator of adventure and mystery.

407 Fleischner, Jennifer Bryna. "Narrative Authority in Austen, Scott, Cooper and Hawthorne." Ph.D. dissertation, Columbia University, 1988.
On female sexuality and its connection to narrative interpretation.

408 Foerster, Norman. NATURE IN AMERICAN LITERATURE. New York: Macmillan, 1923; reprinted New York: Russell & Russell, 1958. Pp. 3-6.
Although C's. style was clumsy, his depiction of nature was

excellent, dwarfing both characterization and action. It was these settings that impressed his European readers.

409 Ford, Paul Leicester. "The American Historical Novel." ATLANTIC MONTHLY 80 (December 1897):721-27.

   Comments on the Littlepage Trilogy, the Revolutionary War novels, and C. as creator of the Indian character.

410 Fox Dixon Ryan. "James Fenimore Cooper, Aristocrat." NEW YORK HISTORY 22 (January 1941):18-24.

   C. considered himself a democrat and preached against those who would undermine the democratic way of life. In truth, he was an aristocrat who cared little for social equality or an increase in the common man's say in political matters.

411 Franklin, Wayne. THE NEW WORLD OF JAMES FENIMORE COOPER. Chicago: University of Chicago Press, 1982.

   A major author. C. should not be critiqued for his social and moral preachings, for these are not important and were espoused by others elsewhere. Rather, his imagination is what matters, for it shaped and gave energy to his writings.

412 Frederick, John T. THE DARKENED SKY: NINETEENTH-CENTURY AMERICAN NOVELISTS AND RELIGION. Notre Dame, Ind.: Notre Dame University Press, 1969. Pp. 1-26.

   C's. early fiction exhibited a deistic outlook, but near the end of his career he moved to a more orthodox Christianity.

413 French, Florence. "The Use of Proverbs in Selected Novels of James Fenimore Cooper." Master of Arts degree, Texas Technological University, 1967.

414 Fuller, Eunice. "Cooper Loved But Scolded America." NEW YORK TIMES, "Magazine," September 12, 1926, p. 12, 20. On the Bread and Cheese Club, C's. social and political beliefs, and relationships to New York City.

415 Gates, W. B. "Cooper's Indebtedness to Shakespeare." Modern Language Association of America, PUBLICATIONS 67 (September 1952):716-31.

   Gates considers incidents, characterizations, and plot in eighteen of C's. novels that had their origins in Shakespeare's dramas.

416 Gerlach, John. "James Fenimore Cooper and the Kingdom of God."

ILLINOIS QUARTERLY 35, Pp. 32-50.
  Not seen, citation taken from AMERICAN LITERARY SCHOLARSHIP, 1973, p. 211.

417 Gerould, Gordon Hall. THE PATTERNS OF ENGLISH AND AMERICAN FICTION: A HISTORY. Boston: Little, Brown & Co., 1942. Pp. 238-42.
  C's. inability to control his imagination or to enforce any measure of self-criticism on his writings is a major fault, but one that can be overlooked in his better novels. Compares his concern with social values to those expressed in Scott's fiction.

418 Gilbert, Susan Hull. "James Fenimore Cooper, the Historical Novel and the Critics." Ph.D. dissertation, University of North Carolina, 1974.
  Traces critical appraisals of C. from his lifetime to the present.

419 Gillespie, Vincent Elliott. "James Fenimore Cooper and the Concept of Civilization." Ph.D. dissertation, University of Kansas, 1970.
  C's. social criticism was based upon a belief that provincialism and materialism stood as a threat to desired social change. NOTIONS OF THE AMERICANS, THE AMERICAN DEMOCRAT, HOMEWARD BOUND, HOME AS FOUND, AFLOAT AND ASHORE, MILES WALLINGFORD, and the Littlepage Trilogy are examined in light of this philosophy.

420 Ginther, Mary L. "Charles Brockden Brown as a Novelist: His Type, Style and Influence upon Cooper, Hawthorne and Poe." Master of Education degree, Henderson State College, n.d.

421 Gladsky, Thomas S. "James Fenimore Cooper and the Genteel Hero of Romance." Ph.D. dissertation, University of North Carolina, 1975.
  C's genteel hero developed from a minor two-dimensional character in the first few novels, into a realistic, complicated American figure who stood at the center of the author's philosophy.

422 _____. "Jerzy Kosinski: The Polish Cooper." NOTES ON CONTEMPORARY LITERATURE 19 (March 1989):11-12.
  Not seen.

423 Graham, Louis Bertrand. "Expediency, Legality, and Morality: The Political Reactions of Irving, Cooper, and Emerson." Ph.D. dissertation, University of Utah, 1973.
  C., although a supporter of Jackson, never supported the

Jacksonian Party, for his only political loyalty was to the Constitution. As an outspoken critic of America's two greatest enemies (aristocracy and the press), C. was repeatedly attacked by his opponents who distorted his character. These distortions, repeated even in modern day biographies, have led writers to fail to see that he was a reasonable and astute political observer.

424 Grattan, Hartley. "A Note on Fenimore-Cooper." DOUBLE DEALER 7 (July 1925):219-22.

C. will continue to maintain a certain degree of popularity with juvenile readers, but will never again find and adult audience, for he completely lacks any intellectual value.

425 Green, Martin. "Cooper, Nationalism, and Imperialism." JOURNAL OF AMERICAN STUDIES 12 (April 1978):161-68.

C., an apprentice of Scott, became the American model for nationalistic/imperialistic fiction.

426 Greenfield, Bruce Robert. "The Rhetoric of Discovery: British and American Exploration Narratives, 1760-1845, and American Renaissance Writing." Ph.D. dissertation, Columbia University, 1985.

Investigates the means by which C. and others used exploration narratives to support the idea of continental destiny.

427 Griffin, Max L. "Cooper's Attitude Toward the South." STUDIES IN PHILOLOGY 48 (January 1951):67-76.

C's. attitudes toward the South were based upon three principles: property rights, moral (but practical solutions to problems), and a refusal to accept disunion. With these principles in mind he developed a philosophy that was fair to the South in its consideration of constitutional law and national interests.

428 Grossman, James. JAMES FENIMORE COOPER. American Men of Letters Series. New York: W. Sloan Associates, 1949.

A psychological interpretation of C. and his novels. Included is an explanation of the anti-rent controversy, C's. legal and political problems, his ideas on democracy, and his misanthropy.

429 _____. "James Fenimore Cooper: An Uneasy American." YALE REVIEW 40 (June 1951):696-709.

C. was an uneasy man living between two worlds: that of the imagination and that of every day reality. While he was able to escape the practical world with the invention of Natty Bumppo and others, his personality compelled him to return to the social and political activities of his day.

430 _____. "Fenimore Cooper: The Development of the Novelist." THE CHIEF GLORY OF EVERY PEOPLE: ESSAYS IN CLASSIC AMERICAN WRITERS. Edited by Matthew J. Bruccoli. Carbondale & Edwardsville: Southern Illinois University Press, 1973. Pp. 1-24.

A general analysis of C. as a writer (nearly every book is commented upon) that concludes that his greatest works are those dealing with society and manners (THE PIONEERS, HOMEWARD BOUND, THE TWO ADMIRALS, and SATANSTOE).

431 Guttman, Allen. THE CONSERVATIVE TRADITION IN AMERICA. New York: Oxford University Press, 1967. Pp. 51-59.

C's. support of the Old World idea of a landed aristocracy was tempered by his realization that a democratic order would prevail in America.

432 Haas, Inge M. "Two Interpretations of Democracy: A Comparison of Political Views of James Fenimore Cooper and Hugh Henry Brackenridge." Master of Arts degree, Smith College, 1934.

433 Hale, Edward Everett. "American Scenery in Cooper's Novels." SEWANEE REVIEW 18 (July 1910):317-32.

It was not until early in the nineteenth century that American writers expressed a love for nature and C., in the 1820s, expressed it best. The one underlying quality of these descriptions is that of realism.

434 Hales, John Richard. "Time's Last Offspring: Millennialism in America from John Cotton to James Fenimore Cooper." Ph.D. dissertation, State University of New York at Binghamton, 1985.

C. presented an optimistic look into the future in THE PIONEERS, but described the ruin of America in THE CRATER. He believed America's end would eventually lead to destruction of the rest of the world.

435 Hall, Wilma Bauer. "The Moral Significance of Land and Landscape in the Novels of James Fenimore Cooper." Ph.D. dissertation, University of Pennsylvania, 1967.

Advances the thesis that C. saw in property, not only the social basis for civilization, but a moral one as well.

436 Hartung, George Westebee. "James Fenimore Cooper's Attitude Toward England." Ph.D. dissertation, University of Wisconsin, 1957.

Examines C's. attitudes toward English life, manners, and traditions, and the way in which they influenced his writing and thought. Concludes that he was a spokesman for English ideas of respect for law, a paternal landed class, and morality based upon religion.

437 Hawthorne, Julian and Leonard Lemmon. AMERICAN LITERATURE: A TEXTBOOK FOR THE USE OF SCHOOLS AND COLLEGES. Boston: D. C. Heath, 1892. Pp. 46-52.

  Includes comments on C. as a person, his weak dialogue, his original characters, and his position in the literary world.

438 Haywood, Ralph S. "James Fenimore Cooper: Critic of American Society." Master of Arts degree, University of Texas, 1959.

439 Henderson, Harry Brinton, III. "The American Historical Novel from Cooper to Crane." Ph.D. dissertation, Yale University, 1968.

  Analyzes the imaginative aspects of nineteenth century historical fiction and historical narrative, including that of C.

440 _____. VERSIONS OF THE PAST: THE HISTORICAL IMAGINATION IN AMERICAN FICTION. New York: Oxford University Press, 1974. Pp. 50-90.

  On C's. holism and its effect upon his characterizations and social outlook.

441 Hewitt-Thayer, Harvey Waterman. AMERICAN LITERATURE AS VIEWED IN GERMANY, 1818-1861. Chapel Hill: University of North Carolina Press, 1958. Pp. 18-38.

  C. was being reviewed in Germany by 1824. He was highly praised when he kept his stories in, or on, the American side of the ocean.

442 Higginson, Thomas Wentworth. "James Fenimore Cooper." AMERICAN PROSE SELECTIONS. Edited by George Rice Carpenter. New York: Macmillan & Co., 1898. Pp. 147-71. Reprinted in CARLYLE'S LAUGH AND OTHER SURPRISES. Freeport, N. Y.: Books for Libraries Press, 1968. Originally, New York: Houghton Mifflin Co., 1909. Pp. 45-54.

  C., a conservative reformer, is second only to Scott in permanence as an author. He had little success with his main characters and suffered stylistic problems resulting from conformity to the writing of the period.

443 Hillard, G. S. "James Fenimore Cooper." ATLANTIC MONTHLY 9 (January 1862):52-68.

  Lengthy and laudatory review of the W. A. Townsend edition of C's. novels.

444 Hintz, Howard William. QUAKER INFLUENCE IN AMERICAN

LITERATURE. New York: Fleming H. Revell Co., 1940. Pp. 41-48.
Considers the Quaker influence of C's. early years and how it influenced his writing. Hintz links this religious training to C's. Jeffersonianism and liberalism.

445 Hogue, William L. "The Novel as a Religious Tract: James Fenimore Cooper--Apologist for the Episcopal Church." HISTORICAL MAGAZINE OF THE PROTESTANT CHURCH 40 (1971):5-26.
C. made Episcopalians of many of his heroic characters while attributing Puritanism to others who were less desirable individuals.

446 Holman, C. Hugh. "The Influence of Scott and Cooper on Simms." AMERICAN LITERATURE 23 (May 1951):203-18.
William Gilmore Simms attempted to do for southern fiction what C. had done for the novel of the North. For him, however, Scott was the master of the romance. His inability to see that C. had provided the proper model was his greatest failure.

447 House, Kay Seymour. COOPER'S AMERICANS. [Columbus]: Ohio State University Press, 1965.
C. used characters, of which there were two types, to convey his own ideas about society and politics. The first type was developed in relation to a social class and the conflicts therein. The second group escaped to the sea or frontier as it sought to avoid the problems of its native culture. House discusses C's women, the slavery issue, New England, Indians, and Natty Bumppo.

448 _____. "James Fenimore Cooper: Cultural Prophet and Literary Pathfinder." HISTORY OF LITERATURE IN THE ENGLISH LANGUAGE. Vol. 8. AMERICAN LITERATURE TO 1900. Edited by Marcus Cunliffe. London: Barrie & Jenkins, 1973. Pp. 106-29.
C., whose primary concerns were moral and cultural ones, enjoyed world-wide success due to his storytelling ability and knowledge of America. Foreign readers found his fiction not only exciting, but possessed of the European mythical ideals of the New World.

449 _____. "James Fenimore Cooper's American Characters." Ph.D. dissertation, Stanford University, 1963.
Discusses C's. characters as an expression of unity in community behavior patterns. It was through them he described and judged American culture.

450 _____ and Genevieve Belfiglio. "Fenimore Cooper's Heroines."

AMERICAN NOVELISTS REVISITED: ESSAYS IN FEMINIST CRIT-
ICISM. Edited by Fritz Fleischmann. Boston: G. K. Hall, 1982. Pp. 42-57.
The heroine as a linking figure and her influence on Natty
Bumppo.

451 Howard, Leon. LITERATURE AND THE AMERICAN TRADITION.
Garden City, N. Y.: Doubleday, 1960. Pp. 94-102.
C. failed to develop a national literature although he represents a
stage in its creation. His language does not appeal to readers of later years and
there is no desire to look beyond his surface meanings.

452 Howells, William Dean. "Heroines of Nineteenth-Century Fiction."
HARPER'S BAZAAR 33 (August 11, 1900):903-08. Reprinted in HER -
OINES OF FICTION. Vol. 1. New York: Harper & Bros., 1901. Pp. 111-12.
C. had no heroines, only women. Brockden Brown was much like
C. in this respect. For comments on the opinions expressed here see
Fortenberry, George. "The Unnamed Critic in William Dean Howells
'Heroines of Fiction.'" MARK TWAIN JOURNAL 16 (Winter 1971-72):7-8.
The unnamed critic is Mark Twain, from whom Howells got his opinions.

453 Hughes, Rupert. "Pioneers of American Literature." PETERSON
MAGAZINE 6 n.s. (December 1896):1223-25.
As a pioneer in American literature C. is immortal, but there are
many faults with his work (e.g. moralizing, dialogue).

454 Hyland, John Lewis. "Comic Characters in James Fenimore Cooper's
Fiction." Ph.D. dissertation, University of Wisconsin, 1979.
Most of C's. comic characters play minor roles, are little more
than caricatures, have only one dimension, possess little psychological depth,
and react in a predictable manner.

455 Ignoto. "Fenimore Cooper: Two Queries." NOTES AND QUERIES
(London). 177 (July 1, 1939):66.
On Harper, from THE SPY, who is really George Washington.
The author asks if the English were not in fact aware of Washington's
appearance, and if it was not unusual for him to venture off as he did in C's.
novel. Also includes a comment on Natty Bumppo who, according to this
author, is the most "amply exhibited' fictional hero, having appeared in five
novels, assumed five different names, and who rejected two beautiful girls.

456 Ingraham, Charles Anson. WASHINGTON IRVING AND OTHER
ESSAYS. Cambridge, Mass.: The Author, 1922. Pp. 53-74.
C. was one of America's greatest authors who, although he was

more popular than Hawthorne or Irving, was also inferior to them.

457 "J. Fenimore Cooper." APPLETON'S JOURNAL 7 (May 18, 1872):549-51.
        C., as the founder of American literature, should be read for the moral qualities of his works.

458 Jacobs, Wilbur R. "Some of Parkman's Literary Devices." NEW ENGLAND QUARTERLY 31 (June 1958):244-52.
        Parkman possessed great admiration for C., especially for his descriptions of nature.

459 Jaffe, Mary F. "James Fenimore Cooper: The Pioneer Portrayer of the American Spirit as Revealed by His Major Works." Master of Education degree, Temple University, 1937.

460 James, Oliver Lawrence, Jr. "Kinesthetic Imagery and the Nightmare of Falling in the Fiction of Brown, Cooper, Poe, and Melville." Ph.D. dissertation, Pennsylvania State University, 1981.
        C's. images of falling go hand-in-hand with ideas of man's dependence on God. It is never the morally upright character who finds himself at the edge of an abyss, but the one who is evil.

461 "James Fenimore Cooper." CHAMBER'S EDINBURGH JOURNAL 17 n.s. (January 3, 1852):3-6.
        Biographical sketch with criticism of each novel. Considers C. the greatest American novelist who will be best remembered for his sea and frontier novels.

462 "James Fenimore Cooper." READER MAGAZINE 5 (December 1904):127-29.
        C. was possessed of faulty and excessive moralizing, but he was a gifted storyteller.

463 Johnson, Manley. "The Visual and the Visionary in the Work of James Fenimore Cooper." Ph.D. dissertation, University of Minnesota, 1957.
        C's novels were a philosophical means of looking at truth. His descriptions of nature and landscape were not merely embellishments, but served to aid plot and characterization.

464 Jones, Howard Mumford. BELIEF AND DISBELIEF IN AMERICAN LITERATURE. Chicago: Chicago University Press, 1967. Pp. 24-47.
        C's. complete belief in the trinity is unique among American

novelists. His interpretation of man in light of this view is best expressed in THE SEA LIONS, but is also evident in THE CRATER and other novels. Concurrent with this concept is that of natural religion (especially in the L. S. TALES) in which the man of the forest is found to be superior to that of the city.

465 _____. 'Introduction' to "James Fenimore Cooper: A Reappraisal." NEW YORK HISTORY 35 (October 1954):369-73.

466 _____. JEFFERSONIANISM AND THE AMERICAN NOVEL. Studies in Culture & Communication. Edited by Martin S. Dworkin. New York: Teachers College Press, Teachers College, Columbia University, 1966. Pp. 28-30.

      C. exhibits the unselfish principles associated with the typical Jeffersonian: action based upon the absence of passion and moral righteousness guided by reason.

467 _____. "Prose and Pictures: James Fenimore Cooper." TULANE STUDIES IN ENGLISH 3 (1952):133-54. Reprinted in "James Fenimore Cooper and the Hudson River School." MAGAZINE OF ART 45 (October 1952):243-41 and HISTORY AND THE CONTEMPORARY: ESSAYS IN NINETEENTH CENTURY LITERATURE. Madison: University of Wisconsin Press, 1964. Pp. 61-83.

      C. has been neglected in the United States due to Twain's criticism and the resulting belief that his novels were meant only for boys. His writing, however, should be seen as a cultural record of early America that patterned itself after the Hudson River School of landscape painters. While he was definitely a moralist, C. was also involved in the aesthetic developments and happenings around him.

468 _____. THE PURSUIT OF HAPPINESS. Cambridge, Mass.: Harvard University Press, 1953. Pp. 105-13.

      As C. approached the end of his life he defined happiness, not in terms of social class or position, but in terms of a contemplative life that considered God and His works.

469 Jones, Julia Elizabeth. "The Problem of Time in the Novels of James Fenimore Cooper, Nathaniel Hawthorne, and Herman Melville." Ph.D. dissertation, University of North Carolina at Chapel Hill, 1983.

      C. saw America as a country that selfishly acted upon its own immediate desires. This would eventually lead to instability. Stability could be achieved only through the establishment of social institutions or through man's harmony with nature. C. was never sure which means was the answer.

470 Kasson J. S. "Templeton Revisited: Social Criticism in 'The Pioneers' and 'Home as Found.'" STUDIES IN THE NOVEL 9 (Spring 1977):54-64.
  Concerned with C's. changing ideas of society.

471 Kennedy, J. Gerald. "Anti-intellectualism: The Comic Man of Learning." STUDIES IN AMERICAN HUMOR 3 (October 1976):69-75.
  On C's. use of the educated man as a ridiculous, awkward, ill-clothed, verbose, and impractical character, contrasted with the simple, decisive, wise, and less educated one.

472 Kirk, Russell. THE CONSERVATIVE MIND FROM BURKE TO SANTAYANA. Chicago: Henry Regnery Co., 1953. Pp. 171-78.
  C. possessed democratic principles that sought to find a middle road between northern capitalism and southern separatism. Within this framework, he espoused political equality, progress, freedom, property rights, and gentility.

473 Kligerman, Jack. "Style and Form in the Fiction of James Fenimore Cooper." Ph.D. dissertation, University of California, Berkeley, 1967.
  Having placed C. in his proper historical perspective, the author argues that the language of expression of the nineteenth century severely restricted the novelist. Discusses THE PIONEERS, THE PILOT, THE BRAVO, THE DEERSLAYER, HOME AS FOUND, and HOMEWARD BOUND.

474 Koehnline, Phyllis G. "The Theory of the Picturesque as Seen in Landscape Art and in the Works of Cooper, Irving, and Bryant. Master of Arts degree, Ohio State University, 1952.

475 Kolodny, Annette. "The Pastoral Impulse in American Writing, 1590-1850: A Psychological Approach." Ph.D. dissertation, University of California, Berkeley, 1969.
  C's. novels form part of the tradition that sought to dominate nature, but at the same time they illustrate a desire to withdraw from the struggle and return to a period of greater tranquility. Seen in psycho-sexual terms.

476 Kurtz, Kenneth. "Emerson and Cooper: American Versions of the Heroic." EMERSON SOCIETY QUARTERLY, no. 42 (1st Quarter 1966):1-8.
  The primitive American society supplied C. with the material to create a truly American hero. These characters are generally subordinate ones who exhibit intelligence, skill, endurance, self-control, loyalty, and integrity.

477 Lamb, Susan R. "James Fenimore Cooper and His Uses of Quotations."

Master of Arts degree, Columbia University, 1936.

478 Lanier, Sterling. "The Moral, Social, and Political Theories of James Fenimore Cooper." Ph.D. dissertation, Harvard University, 1955.

        C. should be remembered as a social critic, rather than a literary figure. His view of society rested upon a moral law which was, in turn, based upon religion (Episcopalism, Quakerism, and Deism) and nature. This law called for the landed gentry to provide the nation's leaders as a barrier against commercial forces. They were, however, and aristocracy of ability, not of birth, who sought to minimize the influences of commerce and leveling by a system of checks and balances and factionalism. The Whig party, in which the wealth of the mercantile class resided, was greatly distrusted by C.

479 Lawton, William Cranston. A STUDY OF AMERICAN LITERATURE. New York: Globe School Book Co., 1907. Pp. 85-91.

        Textbook. Lawton places C. above Bryant and Parkman in his ability to impress upon the mind of America the enormity and beauty of nature. Consequently, he made a significant contribution to the nationalist literature of the nineteenth century.

480 Leisy, Ernest E. THE AMERICAN HISTORICAL NOVEL. Norman: University of Oklahoma Press, 1950. Scattered references.

        C's. knowledge of recent American history and his penchant for action made him particularly suited to write the romantic adventure novel.

481 _____. AMERICAN LITERATURE: AN INTERPRETIVE SURVEY. New York: Thomas Y. Crowell Co., 1929. Pp. 53-60.

        C. represents the epitome of early American pioneer fiction.

482 Letterman, Henry L. "Realism *Vs.* Romance: Aesthetic Distance and Symbolic History in the Novels of James Fenimore Cooper." Ph.D. dissertation, Loyola University, 1974.

483 Levy, Walter. "Thomas Cole and James Fenimore Cooper: A Study of Contrasting Attitudes Toward the Use of American History in Literature and Art." Ph.D. dissertation, Fordham University, 1978.

        Develops the thesis that, in spite of C's. and Cole's similar descriptions of landscape, they chose opposite sides in the debate over subjects best suited to aid the creation of an American cultural identity.

484 Lewis, R. W. B. THE AMERICAN ADAM: INNOCENCE, TRAGEDY, AND TRADITION IN THE NINETEENTH CENTURY. Chicago: Chicago University Press, 1955. Pp. 98-105.

C's. genius resided in his ability to create a setting and then develop a wholly alive character within it.   This creation of the "Adamic myth" is the determining factor in C's. works.

485 Lindroth, James Richard. "The Comic Perspective of James Fenimore Cooper." Ph.D. dissertation, New York University, 1969.
Places C. in the American comic tradition.   Investigates humor's function in the L. S. TALES, HOME AS FOUND, THE SEA LIONS, and SATANSTOE.

486 Lofgren, Hans B. "Democratic Skepticism: Literary-Historical Point of View in Cooper, Hawthorne, and Melville." Ph.D. dissertation, University of California, 1977.
C. adopted European forms to promote his ideas of democratic possibilities.

487 Lomando, Anna Emma "A Checklist of Literary References in Critical Editions of the Writings of James Fenimore Cooper and His Letters and Journals." Ph.D. dissertation, University of Pittsburgh, 1987.
A list of C's. readings showing his interests, awareness, and, perhaps, their relationship to his writing.

488 Long, Robert Emmet. JAMES FENIMORE COOPER. New York: Continuum Publishing Co., 1990
Examines most of C's. writings and concludes that he was not equal to Henry James, Hawthorne, or Melville, but still must be considered a major nineteenth century author.   While often flawed and posssessed of religiuos orthodoxy, he was a writer with a keen imagination upon whose foundations American literature was built.

489 Longino, Maranda Mazur Hunter. "Action in Fenimore Cooper's Tales." Ph.D. dissertation, University of Florida, 1987.
Concerned with type, structuring, and the significance of action.

490 Loshe, Lillie Deming. THE EARLY AMERICAN NOVEL. Columbia University Studies in English, Series II, Vol. II, no. 2. New York: Columbia University Press, 1907. Pp. 85-105.   Originally as a Ph.D. dissertation, Columbia University, 1907.
A discussion of C's. novels and the effect they had upon those who followed him (Neal, McHenry, Sedgwick, Paulding, etc.).   Also includes material on characterization.

491 Lukacs, Paul Braddock. "Against the Current: A Historical Perspective in

Ante-Bellum American Fiction." Ph.D. dissertation, Johns Hopkins University, 1986.

Uses THE PIONEERS, HOME AS FOUND, and THE DEER-SLAYER to show that writers of the early 1800s often searched for an individual and national identity that was out of character with American culture.

492 Lyman, Susan E. "'I Could Write You a Better Book Than That Myself'--Twenty-five Unpublished Letters of James Fenimore Cooper." New York Historical Society, QUARTERLY BULLETIN 29 (October 1945):213-41.

Letters written by C. to his publisher from May to October 1820 about the printing of THE SPY and PRECAUTION.

493 Lynen, John F. THE DESIGN OF THE PRESENT: ESSAYS ON TIME AND FORM IN AMERICAN LITERATURE. New Haven, Conn.: Yale University Press, 1969. Pp. 169-204.

C's. ethical and social beliefs were his justification for writing and cannot be separated from his settings.

494 McAfee, Annie K. "Cooper's Characterization of American Life." Master of Arts degree, George Peabody College for Teachers, 1937.

495 McCormick, John. CATASTROPHE AND IMAGINATION: AN INTERPRETATION OF THE RECENT ENGLISH AND AMERICAN NOVEL. London: Longman's, Green & Co., 1957. Pp. 183-86.

C. was able to take elements of English Romanticism, place them in an American setting, and create a truly American tradition.

496 McNeer, Marietta W. "The Boy as a Character in American Fiction by Standard Authors from Cooper to Twain." Master of Arts degree, University of North Carolina, 1934.

497 McWilliams, John P. "A Law for Democracy: Cooper and the American Frontier." Ph.D. dissertation, Harvard University, 1967.

C. attempted to create an acceptable mode of life in a young country by interjecting personal principles into his novels. His was a national literature in which he saw himself as the preserver of democracy.

498 _____. POLITICAL JUSTICE IN A REPUBLIC: JAMES FENIMORE COOPER'S AMERICA. Berkeley: University of California Press, 1972.

C. possessed an intense belief in democracy and its political rights. This belief, however, did not include social and economic equality, for its maintenance depended upon those of superior ability and position.

499 _____ . "Red Achilles, Red Satan." THE AMERICAN EPIC: TRANSFORMING A GENRE, 1770-1860. Cambridge: Cambridge University Press, 1989. Pp. 123-57.
　　　　Not seen.

500 Madson, Arthur Leon. "The Scapegoat Story in the American Novel." Ph.D. dissertation, University of Oklahoma, 1966.
　　　　Examines nine novels, including THE BRAVO. Sees the scapegoat story as one in which individualism is sacrificed to community ideals. C. is placed in opposition to that literature which emphasizes American opportunity and freedom of action.

501 Malin, Irving. "The Authoritarian Family in American Fiction." MOSAIC 4 (1971):153-73.
　　　　Considers C's. sense of family order as expressed in THE AMERICAN DEMOCRAT, THE PRAIRIE, and THE LAST OF THE MOHICANS.

502 Mani, Lakshmi. "The Apocalypse in Cooper, Hawthorne, and Melville." Ph.D. dissertation, McGill University, 1972.
　　　　C. drew upon the apocalyptic myths found in both the Christian and Indian heritages to attack the popular expansionist viewpoints of his day.

503 Marshall, Sarah Latimer. "The Concept of History in Cooper's Fiction." Ph.D. dissertation, University of Mississippi, 1970.
　　　　C. envisioned history as the fulfillment of God's divine purpose. Man acted as His agent and progressed, not due to intellect, but by carrying out the duties appointed him by God.

504 Martin, Terence. "Telling the World Over Again: The Radical Dimension of American Fiction." AMERICAN LETTERS AND THE HISTORICAL CONSCIOUSNESS: ESSAYS IN HONOR OF LEWIS P. SIMPSON. Edited by Gerald Kennedy and Daniel Mark Fogel. Baton Rouge: Louisiana State University Press, 1987. Pp. 158-76.
　　　　The "pristine" as found in C., Cather, and Faulkner.

505 Matlack, T. Chalkey. MANUSCRIPT DICTIONARY OF CHARACTERS IN THE NOVELS OF COOPER, SUMMARIES OF PLOTS, EXCERPTS FROM CONTEMPORARY CRITICISMS, DRAWINGS FROM DARLEY, AND MAPS OF THE SCENES OF THE NOVELS. Historical Societies of Pennsylvania and Burlington, N. J., 1914.

506 Matthews, Brander. AMERICANISMS AND BRITICISMS WITH

OTHER ESSAYS ON OTHER ISMS. New York: Harper & Bros., 1892. Pp. 89-102.

On C's. popularity abroad, with favorable comments on several of the sea and frontier tales.

507 _____. "The Centenary of Fenimore Cooper." THE CENTURY 16 (September 1889):796-98. Partially reprinted in THE CRITIC 12 (September 14, 1889):127.

C. created wooden female characters and possessed little humor, but he excelled in depicting people and nature as they existed in the wilderness and on the oceans.

508 _____. "Fenimore Cooper." ATLANTIC MONTHLY 100 (September 1907):329-41.

C., America's foremost novelist, was also the first to reveal the American character. Done with sympathy, these portraits are realistic portrayals by a great patriot. The critics, who are wont to point out his defects, have failed to see beyond them to the far more significant merits of his works.

509 Maulsby, D. L. "Fenimore Cooper and Mark Twain." THE DIAL 22 (February 16, 1897):107-09.

Maulsby claims that Twain's criticisms of C. were unjust. See item nos. 653, 1052.

510 Metcalf, John Calvin. AMERICAN LITERATURE. Richmond: B. F. Johnson Publishing Co., 1914. Pp. 119-29.

General assessment of C. as a man and a writer. He is important because he was the first to describe the American frontier and to work from native materials.

511 Meyers, Marvin. "The Great Descent: A Version of Fenimore Cooper." PENSIERO E SCUOLA 10, pp. 367-81.

Not seen. Citation from Modern Language Association, BIBLIOGRAPHY, 1956, p. 247.

512 Mikkelsen, Hubert Aage. "James Fenimore Cooper's Fiction: Theory and Practice." Ph.D. dissertation, St. John's University, 1976.

Chapters on influences upon C. (society and religion), his ideas on instruction and entertainment, his characterizations, and his craftsmanship, style, and descriptive abilities.

513 Miller, Cecil John. "The Theme of Social Decay in the Last Five Novels

of James Fenimore Cooper." Ph.D. dissertation, University of the Pacific, 1968.

Each novel (JACK TIER, THE CRATER, OAK OPENINGS, THE SEA LIONS, and WAYS OF THE HOUR) deals with an important social problem in an intellectual manner. They all foresee a millennium based upon Christianity and divine guidance that will overcome the social decay of the author's day.

514 Miller, Wayne Charles. AN ARMED AMERICA; ITS FACE IN FICTION: A HISTORY OF THE AMERICAN MILITARY NOVEL. New York: New York University Press, 1970. Pp. 29-52. Originally as "The American Military Novel: A Critical and Social History." Ph.D. dissertation, New York University, 1968.

C. made use of caricature as he failed to seriously consider social problems in THE SPY and THE PILOT. His works set the precedent for later writers of the military novel.

515 Mills, Nicolaus. "The Crowd in the Classic American Novel." THE CENTENNIAL REVIEW 26 (Winter 1982):61-85.

Compares and contrasts the treatment of crowds in C., Hawthorne, Melville, and Twain.

516 Milne, Gordon. THE AMERICAN POLITICAL NOVEL. Norman: University of Oklahoma Press, 1966. Pp. 12-18.

C. attacked both European and American politics. He disliked Europe for its system of privilege, but also distrusted Jacksonian democracy. He favored the United States Constitution and the safeguards it provided, while finding that it often failed in actual practice.

517 _____. THE SENSE OF SOCIETY: A HISTORY OF THE AMERICAN NOVEL OF MANNERS. Teaneck, N. J.: Farleigh Dickinson University Press, 1977. Pp. 20-34.

An attack upon C's. novels of manners for their lack of proper focus, style, and tone.

518 Mitchell, Donald G. AMERICAN LAND AND LETTERS, THE MAYFLOWER TO RIP-VAN-WINKLE. New York: Charles Scribner's Sons, 1907. Pp. 161-84.

Biographical and critical material on C. and his works (THE SPY, THE PIONEERS). Sees Lounsbury's biography (item no. 114) as honest and fair. C. is described as brilliant, but arrogant and easily irritated. His best work was his sea fiction because it was personal in approach.

519 Monson, Arthur Douglas. "Social Structure and Property in Selected Novels of James Fenimore Cooper." Ph.D. dissertation, University of Nebraska, 1976.

  THE SPY, THE BRAVO, HOME AS FOUND, THE PATHFINDER, and SATANSTOE are used to illustrate the relationships between property, social structure, and democracy.

520 Mooney, D. N. "Social Principles and Criticism in the Novels of James Fenimore Cooper After 1830." Master of Arts degree, Ohio State University, 1940.

521 Morse, David. "Fenimore Cooper: The Excessive Pathfinder." AMERICAN ROMANTICISM. Vol. I. New York: Barnes & Noble, 1988. Pp. 30-87.

  Not seen.

522 Morse, James Herbert. "The Native Element in American Fiction." CENTURY ILLUSTRATED MONTHLY MAGAZINE 4 n.s. (1883): 288-98.

  C. was inferior to European romancers in style and technique, but he far outdistanced other American novelists as a writer of sea and frontier fiction.

523 Mott, Frank Luther. GOLDEN MULTITUDES: THE STORY OF BEST SELLERS IN THE UNITED STATES. New York: Macmillan Co., 1947. Pp. 73-76.

  On the publication of C's. novels and his popularity over the course of a century.

524 Murray, Hazel G. "James Fenimore Cooper's Literary Treatment of the American Negro." Master of Arts degree, University of Tennessee, 1956.

525 NATIONAL QUARTERLY REVIEW, September 1860, pp. 283-314.

  Not seen, citation taken from Clavel, p. 153 (item no. 5).

526 Nelson, John Herbert. THE NEGRO CHARACTER IN AMERICAN FICTION. Humanistic Studies no. 15. Lawrence: University of Kansas Press, 1926. Pp. 32-34.

  C's, characterizations of blacks were not without fault, but did possess sympathy.

527 Neuhauser, Rudolph "James Fenimore Cooper and Russia." Pacific Northwest Conference on Foreign Languages, PROCEEDINGS 17, pp. 75-85.

Not see.   Citation taken from Publications of the Modern Language Association, BIBLIOGRAPHY, 1966, P. 190.

528 Nevius, Blake. COOPER'S LANDSCAPES: AN ESSAY ON THE PICTURESQUE VISION. Berkeley & Los Angeles: University of California Press, 1976.
    Focuses on C's. aesthetics in relation to his knowledge and interest in landscape art and gardening. The author contends that too little attention has been paid to this aspect of C's. fiction.

529 Newby, P. N. "The Sea and the Savage." LISTENER, September 20, 1951, pp. 457-58.
    Not seen.

530 Nichol, John. AMERICAN LITERATURE: AN HISTORICAL SKETCH, 1620-1880. Edinburgh: Adam & Charles Black, 1882. Pp. 175-77.
    The greatest American novelist. He was undoubtedly influenced by Scott.

531 Nicholson, Virginia. "Cooper's Novels as Source Material for the History of American Culture." Master of Arts degree, Texas Women's University, 1938.

532 Nilon, Charles H. "Cooper, Faulkner, and the American Venture." 'A COSMOS OF MY OWN': FAULKNER AND YOKNAPATAWPHA. Edited by Doreen Fowler and Ann J. Abadie. Jackson: University of Mississippi Press, 1981. Pp. 168-98.
    A comparison of the two writers' treatment of civilization, colonists, and aristocrats.

533 _____. "Some Aspects of the Treatment of Negro Character By Five Representative Novelists: Cooper, Melville, Tourgee, Glasgow, Faulkner." Ph.D. dissertation, University of Wisconsin, 1952.
    C's. stereotypical black characters have been copied in fiction until very recent times. The physical and mental characteristics he created helped C. to illustrate his political and social theories.

534 Nirenberg, Morton. "The Reception of American Literature in German Periodicals, 1820-1850." JAHRBUCH FÜR AMERIKASTUDIEN 29 (1970):54-74.
    As long as C. continued to write of the frontier and sea, he was well received by German literary critics. Although these themes had been popular in that country before C. came on the scene, it was his novels that

gave the ring of authenticity to the American adventure romance.

535 Noble, Charles. STUDIES IN AMERICAN LITERATURE. New York: Macmillan, 1907. Pp. 132-40.

C's. style was characterized by the rapid movement of action (especially in THE PIONEERS) through the skillful use of conversation. Dialogue added variety, moved the story along, created dramatic situations, and made long descriptive narration unnecessary.

536 NORTH AMERICAN REVIEW 74 (January 1852):147-61.

Review of the revised Putnam edition of C'.s works. Original and an excellent example of national literature. While C. is inferior to Scott, he is worthy of comparison to his predecessor.

537 _____ 89 (July 1859):279-80.

Comments on the 1859 Townsend edition of five C. novels (THE PIONEERS, THE LAST OF THE MOHICANS, RED ROVER, THE SPY, and WYANDOTTE). C. is praised as a pioneer to whom American literature is deeply indebted.

538 O'Donnell, Charles. "The Mind of the Artist: Cooper, Thoreau, Hawthorne, Melville." Ph.D. dissertation, Syracuse University, 1957.

These four writers possessed similar attitudes toward conflicts within the human condition. They used literary creation to define this condition and then to reconcile it.

539 Ossoli, Sarah Margaret (Fuller). LITERATURE AND ART. New York: Fowlers and Wells, 1852. Pp. 129. Reprinted in "American Literature." ART, LITERATURE, AND THE DRAMA. Edited by Arthur B. Fuller. New York: The Tribune Association, 1869. P. 305.

In spite of C's. inability to create either characters or plot, his sea and forest scenes have rescued a lost way of life from oblivion.

540 Overton, Grant. AN HOUR OF THE AMERICAN NOVEL. Philadelphia: J. B. Lippincott Co., 1929. Pp. 18-24.

An evaluation of those novels that would be of interest to the reader of 1929.

541 Paine, Gregory. "Cooper and 'The North American Review.'" STUDIES IN PHILOLOGY 28 (October 1931):799-809.

In their desire to promote a native American literature and new American authors, the editors of THE NORTH AMERICAN REVIEW responded to C's. early novels in a favorable manner. From 1838-50, however, he was denounced in the periodical.

542 _____. "James Fenimore Cooper as an Interpreter and Critic of America." Ph.D. dissertation, University of Chicago, 1925.
        The success of C's. fiction can be attributed to his knowledge of setting, careful character development, accuracy of historical detail, and familiarity with Indian customs. Paine claims that he was not anti-English and was a conservative democrat who trusted institutions rather than majorities.

543 _____. "Realism in the Novels of James Fenimore Cooper." Master of Arts degree, University of Chicago, 1920.

544 Painter, F. V. N. INTRODUCTION TO AMERICAN LITERATURE. Boston: Sibley & Ducker, 1897. Pp. 122-33.
        C's. style possessed little real art. His genius was in his ability to describe and create detail for the reader.

545 Pancoast, Henry S. AN INTRODUCTION TO AMERICAN LITERATURE. New York: Henry Holt, 1898. Pp. 130-40.
        C. was freer of European influences than was Irving. Although he possessed many faults, he was a nationalist who carried the American West to European readers.

546 Parker, Hershel. "The Writings of James Fenimore Cooper: An Essay Review." UNIVERSITY OF MISSISSIPPI STUDIES IN ENGLISH 5 (1984-87):110-19.
        Review article on the Beard edition of C's. novels.

547 [Parkman, Francis]. "James Fenimore Cooper." NORTH AMERICAN REVIEW 74 (January 1852):147-61.
        Review of THE WORKS OF JAMES FENIMORE COOPER, Putnam, 1851. C. is the most original and national of all American writers. While he was unsurpassed as a portrayer of action and describer of nature, his characterizations were often poorly conceived, with the exception of Hawkeye in THE LAST OF THE MOHICANS.

548 Parrington, Vernon Louis. MAIN CURRENTS IN AMERICAN THOUGHT. Vol. 2. THE ROMANTIC REVOLUTION IN AMERICA, 1800-1860. New York: Harcourt, Brace, 1927. Pp. 222-37.
        Parrington saw C. as a Jeffersonian defender of the republic attempting to reconcile his ideas of aristocracy with democracy. He was an idealist who desired the best for the country, as well as an individual who

recognized democracy's shortcomings.

549 Partridge, Eric. "Fenimore Cooper's Influence on the French Romantics." MODERN LANGUAGE REVIEW 20 (April 1925):174-78.

      C's. sea and western fiction was popular in France from 1826-43, and it influenced several of the French romantic dramatists and novelists during this period. This article includes several references to French reviews of C's. works.

550 Pates, Adaline S. "Social Theory in the Fiction of Cooper and Melville." Master of Arts degree, Smith College, 1935.

551 Pattee, Fred Lewis. THE FIRST CENTURY OF AMERICAN LITERATURE, 1770-1870. New York: Appleton Century, 1935. Pp. 314-45.

      A short biographical sketch with a story line for each novel. The critical material considered here deals with C's. style. He wrote too quickly, chose his words poorly, forced his characters to respond unnaturally, and failed to unify plot and events. All this is forgiven, however, for his action writing and descriptive abilities were unsurpassed.

552 _____. A HISTORY OF AMERICAN LITERATURE WITH A VIEW TO THE FUNDAMENTAL PRINCIPLES UNDERLYING ITS DEVELOP-MENT. Boston: Silver, Burdett, 1896. Pp. 135-46.

      Textbook for high schools and colleges. Mini-assessments of most of C's. novels with suggested readings and a biographical sketch.

553 _____. "James Fenimore Cooper." AMERICAN MERCURY 4 (March 1925):289-97.

      Part biographical and part critical. C's. literary life is divided into three phases: the 1820s, a period of experimentation; the 1830s, characterized by the use of European themes; and the 1840s, described as a decade of social criticism and comment.

554 Patterson, Mark R. "Myth from the Perspective of History: James Fenimore Cooper and Paternal Authorities." AUTHORITY, AUTONOMY, AND REPRESENTATION IN AMERICAN LITERATURE, 1776-1865. Edited by M. R. Patterson. Princeton, N. J.: Princeton University Press, 1988. Pp. 81-136.

      Not seen.

555 Paul, Jay S. "Actions and Agents: Cooper's Evolving Aesthetic." Ph.D. dissertation, Michigan State University, 1971.

THE SPY, THE BRAVO, THE DEERSLAYER, and SATAN-
STOE are investigated from the viewpoints of structure, relationships among
the various fictional components, the use made of each fictional component
individually, the relationship of form to purpose, and the place of each book in
C's. artistic growth.

556 _____. "Home as Cherished: The Theme of Family in Fenimore
Cooper." STUDIES IN THE NOVEL 5 (Spring 1973):39-51.
       C's. anti-utopian outlook caused him to create characters and
situations that threatened the security of the family, thus denying them the
peace of mind that derives from a settled existence.

557 Peck, H. Daniel. "An American Poetics of Space: Applying the Work of
Gaston Bacheland." MISSOURI REVIEW 3 (Summer 1980):77-91.
       Not seen.

558 _____. "The Pastoral Vision: A Study of the Aesthetic Space of James
Fenimore Cooper's Fiction." Ph.D. dissertation, University of Iowa, 1974.
Reprinted as A WORLD BY ITSELF: THE PASTORAL MOMENT IN
COOPER'S FICTION. New Haven & London: Yale University Press, 1977.
       Peck relates C's. pastoral vision to the author's (and the nation's)
long past childhood--a past of peace and innocence whose delicate balance has
since been upset.

559 Perry, Bliss. THE AMERICAN SPIRIT IN LITERATURE. Chronicles
of America Series. New Haven, Conn.: Yale University Press, 1920. Pp. 95-
101.
       C. spent too little time in plot development and his reputation
suffered because of it. He is remembered mainly for his descriptive abilities
(landscape and nature) and for the action his novels contained.

560 Phelps, William Lyon. "Fenimore Cooper and His Writings." NEW
YORK HISTORY 22 (January 1941):27-35.

561 _____. "Makers of American Literature: The Spirit of Romance--James
Fenimore Cooper." LADIES HOME JOURNAL, January 1923, pp. 18-19,
115-18.
       C., who wrote too much, is remembered, not for his stylistic
errors, but for his action and suspense. These qualities made it possible for his
novels to be extremely successful in translation.

562 _____. SOME MAKERS OF AMERICAN LITERATURE. Boston:
Jones, Marshall, 1923. Pp. 34-64.

Phelps claims that C's. popularity outlasted that of many other technically better writers because he was truly American and concerned only with action. Consequently, the reader had no time to consider style or language.

563 Phillips, Jeanette Nichols. "On the Trail of Cooper's Novels." MIDLAND MONTHLY 9 (June 1898):483-92.

On C's. use of the geography of east-central New York in his novels.

564 Phinit-Akson, Helen. "James Fenimore Cooper: A Critical Study of His Religious Vision." Ph.D. dissertation, University of Pittsburgh, 1972.

Eight novels written from 1829-49 illustrate that C. believed in specific Christian spiritual and ethical principles. These principles dictated his solutions to problems and the code of conduct followed by his characters. Includes THE WEPT OF THE WISH-TON-WISH, THE BRAVO, THE HEIDENMAUER, MERCEDES OF CASTILE, THE WING AND WING, THE SEA LIONS, and THE OAK OPENINGS.

565 Pickering, James H. "James Fenimore Cooper and the History of New York State Novels." Ph.D. dissertation, Northwestern University, 1964.

An examination of eight novels with New York settings. Illustrates that C. was aware of the state's historical backgrounds and the advantages of historical romance as a literary technique. Includes the L. S. TALES, THE SPY, WYANDOTTE, SATANSTOE, and THE CHAINBEARER.

566 Pollock, George Willard. "The Yankee as Scapegoat in Cooper's Fiction." Ph.D. dissertation, Texas Technological University, 1974.

C's. attitude toward the New Englander shifted from that of hero in the 1820s, to that of scapegoat later in his career. With the exception of the spy, Harvey Birch, C. possessed a better opinion of the Yankee at sea than he did of him on land.

567 Postell, William Dosite. "Medicine and Physicians of James Fenimore Cooper." Medical Library Association, BULLETIN 47 (April 1959):165-69.

C. had little to say about the prevalent diseases of his day, although he often described the character and training of the nineteenth century physician. While he had great respect for those who had been trained in England, he pointed out that medical care in the United States was equal to that of Europe.

568 Price, Lawrence Marsden. THE RECEPTION OF ENGLISH LITERATURE IN GERMANY. Berkeley: University of California Press,

1932. Pp. 426-29.
   C's. portrayal of the Indian, if not new, seemed realistic to the German reader. Consequently, German authors often copied directly from him.

569 Pudaloff, Ross J. "Cooper's Genres and American Problems." ELH (formerly JOURNAL OF ENGLISH LITERARY HISTORY) 50 (Winter 1983):711-27.
   Considers plot, ideology, democracy, and aristocracy.

570 _____. "The Gaze of Power: Cooper's Revision of the Domestic Novel, 1835-1850." GENRE 17 (Fall 1984):275-95.
   Concerns the novels that followed THE LAST OF THE MOHICANS and C.'s. increasing political and cultural disillusionment.

571 Quinn, Arthur Hobson. AMERICAN FICTION: AN HISTORICAL AND CRITICAL SURVEY. New York: D. Appleton, 1936. Pp. 53-76. Reprinted in Quinn, ed. LITERATURE OF THE AMERICAN PEOPLE: AN HISTORICAL AND CRITICAL SURVEY. New York: Appleton-Century Crofts, 1951. Pp. 428-32.
   C's. fiction and nonfiction is best understood in the light of Jeffersonian democracy which required individual responsibility on the part of the aristocracy.

572 _____. "American Literature and American Politics." American Antiquarian Society, PROCEEDINGS 54 (April 19, 1944):59-112.
   C's. philosophy of leadership recognized the land owner as the true aristocrat to whom rights were owed by the rest of society, but who was also obligated to rule wisely. The novels, which expounded this viewpoint in their positive picture of democracy, were translated into thirty-four languages and certainly must have colored foreign impressions of America.

573 _____. THE SOUL OF AMERICA: YESTERDAY AND TODAY. Philadelphia: University of Pennsylvania Press, 1932. Pp. 45-46.
   C., a Jeffersonian democrat with a feudal concept of society, was both a realist as an author and an astute observer of the national character.

574 Railton, Stephen. FENIMORE COOPER: A STUDY OF HIS LIFE AND IMAGINATION. Princeton, N. J.: Princeton University Press, 1978.
   A Freudian interpretation.

575 _____. "James Fenimore Cooper: A Psychological Study." Ph.D. dissertation, Columbia University, 1975.

C's. novels can be interpreted in light of his life long struggle to find his own identity as the son of William Cooper. THE PIONEERS is closely examined.

576 Rans, Geoffrey. "The Origin and History of the Idea of Corruption in American Writing, and Its Expression in James Fenimore Cooper, Edgar Allan Poe, and Ralph Waldo Emerson." Ph.D. dissertation, Leeds, 1964.

577 Read, Helen Appleton. "Karl May, Germany's James Fenimore Cooper." AMERICAN GERMAN REVIEW, June 1936, pp.4-7.
        Discussion of the influence of C. on the German novelist Karl May and of the American West on German youth.

578 Record, Verna S. "Syntactic Patterns in the Writing of Irving, Cooper, and Hemingway." Master of Arts degree, San Diego State College, 1964.

579 Redekop, Ernest Henry. "Land and Landscape in the Travel Books and Selected Novels of James Fenimore Cooper." Ph.D. dissertation, University of Toronto, 1974.

580 _____. "Picturesque and Pastoral: Two Views of Cooper's Landscapes." CANADIAN REVIEW OF AMERICAN STUDIES 8 (Fall 1977):184-205.

581 Reed, Barbara Loraine. "James Fenimore Cooper: Experiments Within Form." Ph.D. dissertation, Indiana University, 1970.
        C. experimented with setting (as a moral background against which judgments were made), with the romantic hero as a social critic (in the form of the outsider, alien, or returned heir), and with disguise (especially in his fiction of adventure), as means of exploring conflicting ideas and values.

582 Reed, Glenn Martin. "Humor in the Early Novels of James Fenimore Cooper." Ph.D. dissertation, University of Nebraska, 1970.
        Examines C's. first seven novels and concludes that the quality of his humor improved with time, just as his interest in its use increased.

583 Richardson, Charles F. AMERICAN LITERATURE, 1607-1885. Vol. 2. AMERICAN POETRY AND FICTION. New York: G. P. Putnam's Sons, 1893. Pp. 297-329.
        C's. novels are not examples of great literature, but he did possess considerable ability to describe events involving action. While he exhibited many faults, he created a field of literature.

584 Ringe, Donald A. "Chiaroscuro as an Artistic Device in Cooper's

Fiction." Modern Language Association of America, PUBLICATIONS 78 (September 1963):349-57.

Chiaroscuro, or the arrangement of light and shadow, is a technique often associated with the Hudson River school of painters. C's. use of these elements in his landscape descriptions merits its discussion as literary device as well.

585 _____. "Cooper's Last Novels, 1847-1850." Modern Language Association of America, PUBLICATIONS 75 (December 1960):583-90.

C's. last five novels, written within a social context, possess moral viewpoints that are more clearly identified here than in his earlier works. Includes THE CRATER, JACK TIER, OAK OPENINGS, THE SEA LIONS, and WAYS OF THE HOUR.

586 _____. JAMES FENIMORE COOPER. U. S. Authors Series, no. 11. New York: Twayne, 1962. Updated edition, 1988.

Ringe focuses on the themes used by C. and the modes by which he chose to give them expression. In general, they were more alike than different, failing as social commentary, but succeeding in several of the moral tales.

587 _____. "James Fenimore Cooper and Thomas Cole: An Analogous Technique." AMERICAN LITERATURE 30 (March 1958):26-36.

Thomas Cole, one of the Hudson River painters, and C. exhibit similarities in form and content in their portrayal of the landscape. Both men make use of moral themes, mountain peaks, lighting, and contrasts between scenes to communicate like ideas.

588 _____. "Painting as a Poem in the Hudson River Aesthetic." AMERICAN QUARTERLY 12 (Spring 1960):71-83.

Includes C's. comments on Cole as an artist.

589 _____. THE PICTORIAL MODE: SPACE & TIME IN THE ART OF BRYANT, IRVING, & COOPER. Lexington: University of Kentucky, 1971.

A thorough study of the influence of the Hudson River school of painters (especially Cole and Durand) on the Knickerbocker writers.

590 Ross, John F. THE SOCIAL CRITICISM OF FENIMORE COOPER. University of California Publications in English, vol. 3, 1932-44. Berkeley & Los Angeles: University of California Press, 1944. Pp. 17-117. Reprinted by Kraus Reprint Co., 1977. Originally as "James Fenimore Cooper as Social Critic." Ph.D. dissertation, University of California at Berkeley, 1929.

C's. chief reason for writing was to indulge in social criticism.

Whether this criticism was right or wrong, he must be considered a forerunner of many present-day social critics.

591 Ross, Morton L. "The Rhetoric of Manners: The Art of James Fenimore Cooper's Social Criticism." Ph.D. dissertation, State University of Iowa, 1964.

On the relationship of C's. concern with social problems to that of the romantic novel as a medium of expression.

592 Rourke, Constance. AMERICAN HUMOR: A STUDY OF THE NATIONAL CHARACTER. New York: Harcourt, Brace & Co., 1931. Pp. 114-15.

Stage adaptations of C's. novels depicted a legendary Indian whose stature and tragic end was remote from reality.

593 Sandy, Alan F., Jr. "The Sublime, the Beautiful, and the Picturesque in the Natural Description of James Fenimore Cooper." Ph.D. dissertation, University of California at Berkeley, 1965.

On C's. use of the aesthetic elements of description as thematic devices to criticize manners and promote values.

594 Schauble, Roman John. "James Fenimore Cooper's Use of and Attitudes Toward Time Schemes, History and Tradition in His European, Pre-Revolutionary, and Leatherstocking Novels." Ph.D. dissertation, University of Wisconsin, 1966.

Examines C's. adherence to the belief in a ruling class of enlightened, paternalistic landed gentry who had earned leadership positions through ability rather than birth.

595 Schlesinger, Arthur M., Jr. THE AGE OF JACKSON. Boston: Little, Brown & Co., 1946. Pp. 375-80.

C., a Jeffersonian democrat, believed that the nation's future must be firmly grounded in the agricultural community. Although he had little faith in the people as a whole, he possessed even less faith in the aristocratic commercial class. This belief was altered in his later years, however, as a result of the anti-rent problems in New York. His realization that property needed to be protected drove him toward the commercial interests, but his faith in them or the future was never strong.

596 Schriber, Mary Suzanne. "James Fenimore Cooper: The Point of Departure." GENDER AND THE WRITER'S IMAGINATION: FROM COOPER TO WHARTON. Lexington: University of Kentucky Press, 1987. Pp. 16-44.

C. created the first distinctly American women and they are as important as the male characters.

597 _____. "Toward Daisy Miller: Cooper's Idea of 'The American Girl.'" STUDIES IN THE NOVEL 13 (Fall 1981):237-49.
Henry James's concept of the American girl (intelligent, spirited, experienced) was first created by C.

598 Sears, Lorenzo. AMERICAN LITERATURE IN THE COLONIAL AND NATIONAL PERIODS. Boston: Little, Brown, 1902. Pp. 211-23.
When C. wrote of primitive life and the sea it was of the highest quality. It is here that his ability to disassociate himself from the present and to write good literature in the middle of the bad is best exemplified.

599 Seaton, Beverly Gettings. "James Fenimore Cooper's Historical Novels: A Study of His Practice as Historical Novelist." Ph.D. dissertation, Ohio State University, 1968.
Examines characterization, plot, style, and theme in twenty-five novels.

600 Seelye, John. "Buckskin and Ballistics: William Leggett and the American Detective Story." JOURNAL OF POPULAR CULTURE 1 (1967):52-57.
Leggett's detective stories were inspired by C.

601 _____. "If at First You Don't Secede, Try, Try, Again: Southern Literature from Fenimore Cooper to Faulkner." American Antiquarian Society, PROCEEDINGS 98 (1988):51-68.
C., a great influence on Simms and Kennedy, can be considered a Southern novelist due to his plantation-like scenes, depiction of Virginians, comic blacks, and meddling Yankees.

602 Sheppard, Alfred Tresidder. THE ART & PRACTICE OF HISTORICAL FICTION. London: Hymphrey Toulmin, 1930. Pp. 57-59.
C. was admired in his own day, but later critics have been less kind. Although not a great writer he possessed both imagination and descriptive ability, while remaining truthful to historical fiction.

603 Shulenberger, David. COOPER'S THEORY OF FICTION: HIS PREFACES AND THEIR RELATION TO HIS NOVELS. Humanistic Studies, no. 32. Lawrence: University of Kansas, 1955. Originally as a Ph.D. dissertation, University of Chicago. Reprinted, New York: Octagon Books, 1972.

Through an examination of the "Prefaces", Shulenberger shows that C. was concerned with the realistic depiction of his characters and settings in the early novels, but as he grew older, moral principle became his most important concern. Character and setting were then idealized to aid in defining morality.

604 Sikes, Herschel M. "William Howard Gardiner and the American Historical Novel." New York Public Library, BULLETIN 66 (May 1962):290-96.

On Gardiner's reviews of THE SPY and THE LAST OF THE MOHICANS in the NORTH AMERICAN REVIEW. See item nos. 982 an 1224.

605 Sixbey, George L. "James Fenimore Cooper, Frontier Churchman." HISTORICAL MAGAZINE OF THE PROTESTANT EPISCOPAL CHURCH 35 (December 1966):373-85.

C's. novels often become apologies for the older, conservative religious thought of his day.

606 Smiley, James B. A MANUAL OF AMERICAN LITERATURE. New York: American Book Co., 1905. Pp. 88-100.

A general assessment of C's. life and writings.

607 Smith, Aleck. L. "The Indian and Black in Cooper: A Study in Racist Stereotypes." ANNUAL REPORT OF STUDIES. Vol. 20. Kyoto: Doshisha Women's College of Liberal Arts, 1969.

Not seen. Citation from Publications of the Modern Language Association, BIBLIOGRAPHY, 1970. p. 105.

608 Smith, Margaretta Caroline. "James Fenimore Cooper's Female Characters." Master's degree, Southern Methodist University, 1941.

Attacks the commonly held idea that C's. female characters were one dimensional and did not vary. It was only in the sea novels, or in those where women played a small part, that he failed to give them individualized personalities.

609 Smith, Scott Hallett. "British Periodical Criticism of James Fenimore Cooper, 1821-1851: An Annotated Checklist." Ph.D. dissertation, University of Georgia, 1985.

Contains references to 358 British criticisms, information on British reviewing media, the state of British book reviewing, and an evaluation of C's. reception in England.

610 Smyth, Albert H. AMERICAN LITERATURE. Philadelphia: Eldredge & Bro., 1897. Pp. 48-55.

        An analysis of several novels, taking into account style, plot, use of language, storytelling ability, and descriptive ability.

611 Snell, George. THE SHAPERS OF AMERICA. New York: Cooper Square Publishers, 1961. Pp. 15-27. Originally New York: E. P. Dutton, 1947.

        General discussion of C's. works, including his failures when dealing with contemporary themes in historical novels, his attitude toward Sir Walter Scott, his descriptive abilities, his social observations, and a psychological analysis of his characters.

612 Snook, Donald Gene. "Leadership and Order in the Border Novels of James Fenimore Cooper." Ph.D. dissertation, University of North Carolina, 1974.

        The Border novels (THE PIONEERS, THE WEPT OF WISH-TON-WISH, HOMEWARD BOUND, HOME AS FOUND, WYANDOTTE, THE CRATER, and the Littlepage Trilogy), which encompass nearly twenty-five years of writing, deal with progressively changing ideas on leadership and order. In spite of C's. overriding concern with these two themes, he was never able to resolve the dilemmas they created for him.

613 _____. "The Shaper of American Romance." YALE REVIEW 34 (March 1945):482-94.

        While C's. technical and artistic abilities were not of the highest quality, he possessed an imagination that still demands to be read and imitated.

614 Spann, Edward K. IDEALS AND POLITICS: NEW YORK INTELLECTUALS AND LIBERAL DEMOCRACY, 1820-1880. Albany: State University of New York Press, 1972. Pp. 132-41.

        C's. sense of isolation from society derived from an early belief that he belonged to a small elite from which most people rising to the top were excluded. His repudiation of the "nouveau riche" and the "nouveau grande" at a time when these classes were gaining power, only served to isolate him further and to strengthen his conservative views.

615 Spencer, Benjamin T. THE QUEST FOR NATIONALITY: AN AMERICAN LITERARY CAMPAIGN. Syracuse, N. Y.: Syracuse University Press, 1957. Scattered references.

        Includes many references to C. and his role in the development of a national literature.

616 Spengemann, William C. THE ADVENTUROUS MUSE: THE POETICS OF AMERICAN FICTION, 1789-1900. New Haven & London: Yale University Press, 1977. Pp. 107-16.

        C. sensed that civilization had destroyed an essential party of man's nature. It was through destruction of the Indian that it became possible for white society to reestablish contact with a baser, but indispensable, part of instinct.

617 Spiller, Robert E. "Cooper's Notes on Language." AMERICAN SPEECH 4 (April 1929):294-300.

        Although C. was often inconsistent in the use of dialogue in his novels, he was well aware of language in its everyday use. As a critic he studied English and New England dialects, scorned the language of the press, and summarized his views in THE AMERICAN DEMOCRAT.

618 _____. CYCLE OF AMERICAN LITERATURE: AN ESSAY IN HISTORICAL CRITICISM. New York: Macmillan, 1955. Pp. 39-46.

        C. was the first to see that both traditional and foreign literary models must be cast aside in favor of something distinctly American. Although he remained an amateur as a novelist, he was aware of what needed to be done.

619 _____. FENIMORE COOPER: CRITIC OF HIS TIMES. New York: Minton, Balch, 1931.

        An attempt to illustrate that C. was a profound social critic. He took up what Irving refused to consider and that which others seems incapable of.

620 _____. "Fenimore Cooper: Critic of His Times: New Letters from Rome and Paris, 1830-31." AMERICAN LITERATURE 1 (May 1929):131-48.

        A series of C. letters that illustrate the conflict between the author's aristocratic social attitudes and his Jacksonian politics.

621 _____. "Fenimore Cooper's Defense of Slave-owning America." AMERICAN HISTORICAL REVIEW 35 (April 1930):575-82.

        Although C. did not approve of slavery as an institution, he failed to condemn it. Rather, he attempted to explain the circumstances of its existence as he predicted its eventual end due to natural forces.

622 _____. JAMES FENIMORE COOPER. Pamphlets on American Writers, no. 48. Minneapolis: University of Minnesota Press, 1965. Reprinted as "James Fenimore Cooper: 1789-1851." AMERICAN WRITERS:

A COLLECTION OF LITERARY BIOGRAPHIES. Vol. 1. Edited by Leonard Unger. New York: Charles Scribner's Sons, 1974. Pp. 335-57.

        Spiller calls for the reader to consider C's. novels in the context of the times in which they were written, the circumstances surrounding their development, and the author's point of view, before he considers them as literary or historical creations.

623 _____. JAMES FENIMORE COOPER: REPRESENTATIVE SELECTIONS. New York: American Book Co., 1936. Pp. ix-lxxxiii.

        C. developed the novel of manners which sought to create principles that were compatible with his own self-concept and the nations's ideals.

624 _____. "James Fenimore Cooper." SIX AMERICAN NOVELISTS OF THE NINETEENTH CENTURY: AN INTRODUCTION. Edited by Richard Foster. Minneapolis: University of Minnesota Press, 1968. Pp. 10-44.

        C., who gave expression to the spirit of his age, became the father of American literature. As such, it is not the form, but the subject of his novels that is important today. For a complete understanding of the man as author, one must follow him from his early position of observer to the later one of social critic.

625 _____. "War With the Book Pirates." PUBLISHERS' WEEKLY 132 (October 30, 1937):1736-38.

        To avoid having their works pirated in Europe, C. and Irving often had them published first in London, then in America.

626 _____ et al. LITERARY HISTORY OF THE UNITED STATES: HISTORY. 3d ed., rev. New York: Macmillan Co., 1963. Pp. 253-69.

        C. the social critic will never outlive C. the romancer, yet these novels of adventure depend greatly on the author's examination of society and manners.

627 Stanford, A. B. "Cooper." AMERICAN WRITERS ON AMERICAN LITERATURE, BY THIRTY-SEVEN CONTEMPORARY WRITERS. Edited by John Macy. New York: Liveright, 1931. Pp. 72-80.

        C. achieved much as a writer, but was an author of many contradictions. He wrote as a poet when describing nature, but lacked the same feelings for the people he portrayed.

628 Steele, Thomas J. "Literate and Illiterate Space: The Moral Geography of Cooper's Major American Fiction." Ph.D. dissertation, University of New Mexico, 1968.

For C., the land was the source of all values and he judged men on their relationship to it. Good men were those who acted as responsible landowners and tenants or those who dwelled in the forest beyond civilization. Bad men were represented by those who did not possess legal title to their land or who failed as stewards of it (speculators, squatters, etc.).

629 Stein, Paul. "Cooper's Later Fiction: The Theme of Becoming." SOUTH ATLANTIC QUARTERLY 70 (Winter 1971):77-87.

It was not until after 1838 that C. moved beyond standard nineteenth century styles to those that more satisfactorily served his own sense of moral obligation. With this change came a renewed sense of creativity.

630 _____. "In Defense of Truth: Structure and Theme in James Fenimore Cooper's Novels." Ph.D. dissertation, Case Western Reserve University, 1968.

All of C's. novels investigated the role of truth, from the early ones, which emphasized confusion when it was not found, to the later ones that saw it as a moral principle.

631 Steinbrink, Jeffrey. "James Fenimore Cooper and the Limits of History." HISTORICAL REFLECTIONS 3 (Winter 1976):25-33.

C. failed as an historical novelist. This failure led him to turn to romances as a means of expressing his social views and judging his contemporaries.

632 Stenger, Lorna. "American Manners and Customs as Shown by the Novels of James Fenimore Cooper." Master of Arts degree, University of Tulsa, 1940.

633 Stout, Janis P. "The City Evaluated: Cooper and Others." SODOMS IN EDEN: THE CITY IN AMERICAN FICTION BEFORE 1860. Contributions to American Studies, no. 19. Westport, Ct.: Greenwood Press, 1976. Pp. 67-90.

634 Streeter, Robert E. "'WASP'S' and Other Endangered Species." CRITICAL INQUIRY 3 (Summer 1977):725-39.

A mention of C. as a writer who successfully used his familiarity with time and place. (p.738)

635 Stubbs, John Caldwell. "The Theory of the Prose Romance: A Study in the Background of Hawthorne's Literary Theory." Ph.D. dissertation, Princeton University, 1964.

Explores the literary theory of the romantic novel in America using Hawthorne as its culminating figure. C's. historical romances are credited for eliciting discussion of purpose and method among the critics, and for increasing the popularity of the genre.

636 Summerlin, Mitchell Eugene. "A Dictionary to the novels of James Fenimore Cooper." Ph.D. dissertation, University of Georgia, 1983.
    C's. concern was with an American class system, but one based not upon social hierarchy, but on differences in culture, race, and religion.

637 Sutton, Walter. "American Literature Re-examined: Cooper as Found--1949." UNIVERSITY OF KANSAS REVIEW 16 (Autumn 1949):3-10.
    Readers and critics have overlooked C's. many faults (plot, dialogue, characterization) in favor of his ability to create suspense. They have also justified his worth on the basis of his social and political commentary. The truth is, however, that C. never achieved a high level of imaginative literary creation, nor did his social and political criticism provide a true look at nineteenth century America.

638 Tanner, Tony. SCENES OF NATURE, SIGNS OF MEN. Cambridge: Cambridge University Press, 1987. Pp. 1-24.
    Not seen.

639 Taylor, Archer. "To Face the Music." AMERICAN NOTES AND QUERIES 7 (April 1969):120.
    Three varying derivations of C's. phrase "to face the music" are presented.

640 Taylor, Walter Fuller. A HISTORY OF AMERICAN LETTERS. New York: American Book Co., 1936. Pp. 101-11.
    THE SPY was the first American novel with merit and it led the way for Melville and Conrad. THE L. S. TALES were the closest American literature had come to a national theme up to that point. C. exhibited great imagination and ability for suspense, reality, and improvisation.

641 Test, George A., ed. JAMES FENIMORE COOPER AND HIS COUNTRY, OR GETTING UNDER WAY. Papers from the 1978 Conference at State University of New York at Oneonta and Cooperstown, N. Y. [Oneonta: Department of English, State University of New York], 1979.
        Contains seven essays:
        Larkin, F. Daniel, "Cooper Country," pp. 4-6.
        Philbrick, Thomas, "Cooper Country in Fiction," pp. 7-14.
        Williams, Merril Kennedy, Jr., "Cooper's Use of American History," pp. 15-25.

Ringe, Donald A., "Cooper's Mode of Expression," pp. 26-34.

House, Kay Seymour, "Cooper's Females," pp. 35-44.

Madison, Robert D., "Getting Under Way With James Cooper," pp. 45-54.

Elliott, James P., "Editing Cooper's Works," pp. 55-61.

642 _____. JAMES FENIMORE COOPER: HIS COUNTRY AND HIS ART. Papers from the 1979 Conference at State University College of New York, Oneonta and Cooperstown. Oneonta: Department of English, State University College [1980?].

    Not seen.

643 _____. JAMES FENIMORE COOPER: HIS COUNTRY AND HIS ART. Papers from the 1980 Conference at State University of New York, Oneonta and Cooperstown. Oneonta: Department of English, State University of New York, 1981.

    Contains seven essays:

Philbrick, Thomas, "Cooper in Europe: The Travel Books," pp. 1-8.

Denne, Constance Ayers, "Cooper in Italy," pp. 9-23.

Walker, Warren S., "Cooper's Fictional Use of the Oral Tradition," pp. 24-39. (Thematic and narrative use of folk elements)

Ashley, Leonard R. N., "The onomastics of Cooper's Verbal Art in 'The Deerslayer' and Elsewhere," pp. 40-51. (Use of place names).

Denne, Constance Ayres, "Cooper's Use of Setting in the European Trilogy," pp. 52-70.

Walker, Warren S., "Cooper's Yorkers and Yankees in the Jeffersonian Garden," pp. 71-80.

Mani, Lakshmi, "James Fenimore Cooper and the Apocalypse," pp. 81-92. (Apocalyptic and millennial references)

644 _____. JAMES FENIMORE COOPER: HIS COUNTRY AND HIS ART. Papers from the 1984 Conference at the State University of New York, Oneonta and Cooperstown. Oneonta: State University of New York, 1985.

    Contains eight essays:

Madison, Robert D., "Cooperstown's Contribution to Cooper Scholarship," pp. 1-9.

Schachterle, Lance, "Textual Editing and the Cooper Edition," pp. 10-23.

Alpern, Will, "Indian Sources, Critics," pp. 25-33.

Egger, Irmgard, "Cooper and German Readers," pp. 35-40.

Egger, Irmgard, "'The Leatherstocking Tales' as Adapted for German Juvenile Readers," pp. 41-48.

Adams, Charles H., "'The Guardian of the Law': George Washington's Role in 'The Spy,'" pp. 49-59.

Kowaleski, Michael, "Fictions of Violence in 'The Deerslayer,'" pp. 60-74.

Madison, Robert D., "Cooper's Columbus," pp. 75-85.

645 [Thackeray, William Makepeace]. "On a Peal of Bells. Roundabout Papers, no. XXIV." CORNHILL MAGAZINE 6 (September 1862):425-32.

C's. heroes are equal to those of Scott and Leatherstocking is probably superior. (p. 428)

646 Thorp, William. "Cooper Beyond America." NEW YORK HISTORY 35 (October 1954):522-39.

C., whose works could be found for sale in every major European city, was not only widely read, but had a profound influence upon the fiction of European novelists.

647 Tichi, Cecelia. "Questioning and Chronicling: Thoreau, Cooper, Bancroft." NEW WORLD, NEW EARTH: ENVIRONMENTAL REFORM IN AMERICAN LITERATURE FROM THE PURITANS THROUGH WHITMAN. New Haven: Yale University Press, 1979. Pp. 151-205.

C. saw society's survival in terms of its governance by a few gentleman-democrats. They alone could tip the balance that existed between civilization and savagery. This attitude did not leave room for the eventual education and enlightenment of the public at large.

648 Timpe, Eugene F. AMERICAN LITERATURE IN GERMANY, 1861-1872. Chapel Hill: University of North Carolina Press, 1964. Pp. 26-29.

Little attention was paid to C. during this decade although he had been popular in Germany prior to this time. He was, however, admired as an author of children's books.

649 Trent, William Peterfield. A HISTORY OF AMERICAN LITERATURE, 1607-1865. New York & London: D. Appleton, 1920. Pp. 233-49.

A general discussion of several C. novels.

650 _____ and John Erskine. GREAT AMERICAN WRITERS. New York: Henry Holt, 1912. Pp. 38-57. Reprinted 1917.

C. used his own experiences in his writings rather than building on the work of others. Discusses the L. S. TALES, the European novels, THE PILOT, and THE SPY.

651 Tucker, Martin, gen. ed. THE CRITICAL TEMPER: A SURVEY OF MODERN CRITICISM ON ENGLISH AND AMERICAN LITERATURE FROM BEGINNINGS TO THE TWENTIETH CENTURY. New York: Frederick Unger, 1979. Vol. IV, pp. 490-93, Vol. V, pp. 482-86.

652 [Tuckerman, Henry Theodore]. "James Fenimore Cooper." NORTH AMERICAN REVIEW 89 (October 1859):289-316.
Although possessed of stylistic faults, unartistic plots, poorly drawn characters, and personal prejudices, C's. novels are significant for he was the first truly American writer.

653 Twain, Mark. "Fenimore Cooper's Literary Offenses." NORTH AMERICAN REVIEW 161 (July 1895):1-12. Reprinted in Babcock, Clarence Merton, ed. AN ANTHOLOGY OF READINGS IN COMMUNICATION. New York: Harper, 1958. Pp. 333-48; Brown, Clarence Arthur. ACHIEVEMENT OF AMERICAN CRITICISM: REPRESENTATIVE SELECTIONS FROM THREE HUNDRED YEARS OF AMERICAN CRITICISM. New York: Ronald Press, 1954. Pp. 475-81; DeVoto, Bernard, ed. PORTABLE MARK TWAIN. New York: Viking Press, 1946. Pp. 541-56; Jameson, Robert U., ed. ESSAYS OLD AND NEW, 3d ed. New York: Harcourt, Brace, 1955. Pp. 83-98; Leary, Lewis, ed. AMERICAN LITERARY ESSAYS. Vol. 1. Readers Bookshelf of American Literature. New York: Crowell, 1960. Pp. 80-88; Locke, Louis Glen et al., eds. READINGS FOR A LIBERAL EDUCATION. New York: Rinehart, 1948. Pp. 274-83, rev. ed., pp. 352-61; "Mark Twain Has Fun With Fenimore Cooper." LITERARY DIGEST 11 (August 10, 1895):10-11; Mayberry, George, ed. LITTLE TREASURY OF AMERICAN PROSE: THE MAJOR WRITERS FROM COLONIAL TIMES TO THE PRESENT DAY. New York: C. Scribner's Sons, 1949. Pp. 540-54; Perkins, George. THE THEORY OF THE AMERICAN NOVEL. New York: Holt, Rinehart & Winston, 1970. Pp. 116-29; Smithberger, Andrew Thomas, ed. ESSAYS: BRITISH AND AMERICAN. Boston: Houghton Mifflin, 1953. Pp. 264-76; Stewart, John Lincoln, ed. THE ESSAY: A CRITICAL ANTHOLOGY. New York: Prentice-Hall, 1952. Pp. 208-19; Targ, William, ed. READER FOR WRITERS: WITH AN INTRODUCTION AND NOTES. New York: Hermitage House, 1951. Pp. 245-62; Walter, Erich Albert, ed. TOWARD TODAY: A COLLECTION OF ENGLISH AND AMERICAN ESSAYS PRESENTING THE EARLIER DEVELOPMENT OF IDEAS FUNDAMENTAL IN MODERN LIFE AND LITERATURE. Atlanta, etc.:

Scott Foresman & Co., 1938. Pp. 438-46; and Wilson, Edmund, ed. SHOCK OF RECOGNITION: THE DEVELOPMENT OF LITERATURE IN THE UNITED STATES, RECORDED BY THE MEN WHO MADE IT. New York: Doubleday & Co., 1943. Pp. 582-94, reprint ed. New York: Farrar, Strauss, 1955.

A satirical and humorous attack on C.   Listed among the criticisms are the lack of invention, the failure to be a good observer, dull dialogue, poorly drawn characters, and a lack of excitement.

654 Van Antwerp, Richard Fenn. "The Design of Cooper's Fiction." Ph.D. dissertation, University of Pittsburgh, 1975.

On C's. characters, plots, and his means of utilizing contrast and opposition in them to place his theme before the reader.

655 Vandiver, Edward P., Jr. "James Fenimore Cooper and Shakespere [sic]." SHAKESPEARE ASSOCIATION BULLETIN 15 (April 1940):110-17.

C. quoted more than 1,100 lines from thirty-six Shakespeare plays in his novels.   Most of these appear as chapter headings or as mottoes for introductions or for the entire book.   It is evident from the obscure nature of many of these references that C. possessed a wide knowledge of the English playwright's work.

656 Van Doren, Carl. AMERICAN NOVEL, 1789-1939, rev. ed. New York: Macmillan, 1940. Pp. 21-42.

It was C's. ability to create a true rendering of the American experience that established his work as valuable history and raised him above inadequacies in style and characterization.

657 _____. "Fiction I: Brown, Cooper." THE CAMBRIDGE HISTORY OF AMERICAN LITERATURE, Vol. 1. Edited by William Peterfield Trent et al. New York: G. P. Putnam's Sons, 1917. Pp. 293-306.

On C's. creative powers and sense of history.

658 Van Santvoord, C. "Cooper, Extent to Which He is Read." NEW YORK TIMES, "Book Review Section," November 30, 1900, p. 756.

Discusses C's. readability in 1900.   Written in response to "The Paying Qualities of Books" by John Bell (September 8, p. 598).

659 Vincent Leon Henry. AMERICAN LITERARY MASTERS. Boston: Houghton, Mifflin & Co., 1960. Pp. 65-97.

C's. best stories are those of the sea and frontier. A democrat in theory and an aristocrat in practice, he possessed no skill when he attempted to deal with modern themes.

660 Wagenknecht, Edward Charles. CAVALCADE OF THE AMERICAN NOVEL, FROM THE BIRTH OF THE NATION TO THE MIDDLE OF THE TWENTIETH CENTURY. New York: Henry Holt, 1952. Pp. 14-30.

C's. greatest asset was his ability to portray action. His weakest one was his style, where he became no more than an imitator.

661 Walker, George W. "A Study of the Personal and Literary Relationships of Sir Walter Scott and James Fenimore Cooper." Ph.D. dissertation, University of North Carolina, 1948.

The relationship between C. and Scott can be divided into three periods: up to 1826 C. felt great admiration for Scott and the novels of the two authors show many similarities; from 1826-1838 is a transitional period which is characterized by C's. social novels that differ somewhat from those of Scott; from 1838 until his death C. made little mention of Scott and the novels of the two show wide differences.

662 Walker, Warren S. "Elements of Folk Culture in Cooper's Novels." NEW YORK HISTORY 35 (October 1954):457-67.

C's. novels make extensive use of the folklore of his day, much of it found there in written form for the first time. The Indian, the black, the frontiersman, and the seaman are all examples of the folk-type. The supernatural, the use of proverbs, and the employment of dialect to strengthen characterization represent additional elements of folk culture in his work.

663 _____. JAMES FENIMORE COOPER: AN INTRODUCTION AND INTERPRETATION. New York: Barnes & Noble, 1962.

C's. importance as a novelist lies in two areas. In the first, he preserved, somewhat romantically, two ways of life that were quickly passing from the American scene, but which were desired by the reading public. In the second, are found his political and social protestations, less popular themes, but of equal importance.

664 _____. PLOTS AND CHARACTERS IN THE FICTION OF JAMES FENIMORE COOPER. Hamden, Ct.: Shoe String Press, 1978.

Plot summaries, listing and identification of each character.

665 _____. "Proverbs in the Novels of James Fenimore Cooper." MIDWEST FOLKLORE 3 (Summer 1953):99-107.

A listing of over 200 proverbs with their origin if known. Walker concludes that C. used the greatest number of proverbs in those works that were closest to him in time and locale.

666 _____. "Selected Name Lore in the Fiction of James Fenimore Cooper."

NEW YORK FOLKLORE QUARTERLY 5 (Summer 1979):33-41.
     Indian, slave, seaman, and Yankee characters examined as sources for naming practices in the early 1800s.

667 Wallace, James D. "Early Cooper and His Audience." New York: Columbia University Press, 1986. Originally, Ph.D. dissertation, Columbia University, 1983.
     Techniques C. used to create an audience: publishing and commercialization, literary experiments, and fictional theory. Also considers the reception of C's. works.

668 Waples, Dorothy. THE WHIG MYTH OF JAMES FENIMORE COOPER. Yale Studies in English, vol. 88. New Haven, Conn.: Yale University Press, 1938. Originally as "The American Reputation of James Fenimore Cooper, 1821-1841." Ph.D. dissertation, Yale University, 1932.
     An explanation of the means by which C. became highly disliked as a person during his lifetime. Waples attributes his unpopularity to the Whig newspapers who opposed his affiliation with the Democratic Party. See Outland, item no. 201, for an opposing viewpoint.

669 Warren, Joyce W. "Solitary Man and Superfluous Woman: James Fenimore Cooper." THE AMERICAN NARCISSUS: INDIVIDUALISM AND WOMEN IN NINETEENTH CENTURY FICTION. New Brunswick, N. J.: Rutgers University Press, 1984. Pp. 91-113.
     C's strong and independent women were always flawed. Those who were dependent (the majority of them) were feminine, spirited, and modest. In general, C. viewed women, not as individuals with rights, but as a sex totally dependent upon the male.

670 Warren, Robert Penn. "James Fenimore Cooper." ATLANTIC BRIEF LIVES: A BIOGRAPHICAL COMPANION TO THE ARTS. Edited by Louis Kronenberger. Boston: Little, Brown & Co., 1971. Pp. 180-82.
     Contrasts the social criticism utilized by C. in his social and political fiction with that in the L. S. TALES. Comparisons are made to William Faulkner.

671 Watkins, Mildred C. AMERICAN LITERATURE. New York: American Book Co., 1894. Pp. 43-46.
     C's. works worth remembering are THE SPY, the L. S. TALES, THE RED ROVER, and THE PILOT.

672 Webster, Clara M. "Agrarianism of James Fenimore Cooper." Master of Arts degree, Boston University, 1952.

673 Wendell, Barrett and Chester Noyes Greenough. A HISTORY OF LIT-ERATURE IN AMERICA. New York: Charles Scribner's Sons, 1904. Pp. 148-57.

C's. work is characterized by skillfully conceived plots and backgrounds, but lacks well drawn characters. While not an especially significant writer, for his novels do not have the power and intellect of great literature, he nevertheless wrote "wholesome fiction."

674 Wettengel, LeDelle. "Cooper's French Characters." Ph.D. dissertation, University of Maryland, 1975.

C's. disapproving portrayals of Frenchmen was meant to serve as a means of instructing Americans in the proper way to behave.

675 Whipple, Edwin Percy. AMERICAN LITERATURE AND OTHER PAPERS. Boston: Ticknor & Co., 1887. Pp. 45-50.

C's. success, which was often marred by excessive detail, was due largely to his portrayal of manhood and his closeness to nature.

676 White, Clara M. "A Study of James Fenimore Cooper's Social Teachings on American Democratic Culture." Master of Arts degree, Texas Arts and Industries University, 1946.

677 Williams, J. Gary. "James Fenimore Cooper and Christianity: A Study of the Religious Novels." Ph.D. dissertation, Cornell University, 1973.

An examination of C's. treatment of the Puritans (admiration), his attitude toward Catholicism (positive), and of his own religious beliefs.

678 Williams, Merril Kennedy, Jr. "Fenimore Cooper's Use of the American Past." Ph.D. dissertation, University of Kentucky, 1978.

C. employed a statistical viewpoint in his nonfiction that was developed by gathering and evaluating large masses of evidence. He showed greater skill in utilizing history in his fiction, for here he was able to join historical and imaginative aspects in his narrative.

679 Williams, Stanley T. THE LIFE OF WASHINGTON IRVING. Vol. 2. New York: Oxford University Press, 1935. Scattered references.

Discusses several of C's. novels.

680 Wilson, James Grant. "Cooper Memorials and Memories." THE INDEPENDENT 53 (January 31, 1901):251-53.

Includes letters and information on C's. request for a consulship, his years in Europe, the acceptance of HOMEWARD BOUND and HOME AS FOUND, the libel suits, and various estimates of him as an author.

681 Wilson, Jennie Lee. "The Heroes of James Fenimore Cooper." Ph.D. dissertation, University of Kansas, 1975.

C. never became truly skillful at characterization, although his later heroes illustrate a complexity that his earlier ones did not. Natty Bumppo is emphasized.

682 Winter, William. OLD SHRINES AND IVY. New York: Macmillan & Co., 1892. Pp. 281-84.

The essence of C's. novels--his flights of fancy and suspenseful moods--does not lend itself to criticism nor should one expect it to.

683 Winters, Arthur Yvor. MAULE'S CURSE; SEVEN STUDIES IN THE HISTORY OF AMERICAN OBSCURANTISM. Norfolk, Conn.: New Directions, 1939. Pp. 25-50. Reprinted in Winters. IN DEFENSE OF REASON. New York: Swallow Press, 1947. Pp. 176-99.

C's. attempt to perpetuate an ideal that was nearing its end cost him his reputation, but he remains an astute critic, even if his social novels were poorly executed.

684 Wittmer, G. B. "James Fenimore Cooper, M*A*S*H and the Origins of TV Drama." TEACHING ENGLISH IN THE TWO-YEAR COLLEGE 14 (May 1987):93-97.

685 "The Works of James Fenimore Cooper." ECLECTIC REVIEW 3 n.s. (April 1852):410-22.

C. faithfully portrayed both manners and nature. His European novels gave him the opportunity to interject a freshness into his writings that prevented one from tiring of them.

686 Wright, Henrietta Christian. AMERICAN MEN OF LETTERS, 1660-1860. London: David Nutt, 1897. Pp. 51-68.

C., the greatest American novelist next to Hawthorne, is best measured by his L. S. TALES and sea fiction.

687 Wright, Nathalia. AMERICAN NOVELISTS IN ITALY; THE DISCOVERERS: ALLSTON TO JAMES. Philadelphia: University of Pennsylvania Press, 1965. Pp. 115-37.

During C's. European period his protagonists became more sophisticated, whereas his antagonists remained narrow-minded and unscrupulous. Civilization, as portrayed in these years, acquired many of the values exhibited by the frontier of his earlier works.

688 Yasuna, Edward Carl. "The Power of the Lord in the Howling

Wilderness: The Achievement of Thomas Cole and James Fenimore Cooper."
Ph.D. dissertation, Ohio State University, 1976.

Cole and C., applying theories of associationism and sublimity, were the first to create a truly American art that held out an optimistic hope for the future.

689 Zagarell, Sandra A. "Expanding 'America': Lydia Sigourney's 'Sketch of Connecticut', Catharine Sedgewick's 'Hope Leslie.'" TULSA STUDIES IN WOMEN'S LITERATURE 6 (1987):225-45.

Sigourney and Sedgewick moved far beyond C. in their interpretation of the role of women and Indians in American society.

690 Zoellner, Robert H. "Fenimore Cooper: Alienated American." AMERICAN QUARTERLY 13 (Spring 1961):55-66.

C. possessed little understanding of the American temperament that was so necessary for the gentleman leader. Consequently, he experienced increasing alienation from his own country as he imperfectly tried to play the role that he had assumed from his father.

4

FRONTIER AND INDIAN NOVELS

GENERAL STUDIES

Articles and Reviews Contemporary with Cooper

691 [Cass, Lewis.] "Structure of the Indian Languages. A Vindication of the Rev. Mr. Heckewelder's 'History of the Indian Nations'". NORTH AMERICAN REVIEW 26 (April 1828):366-403.
    It is unfortunate that C., who had great powers of observation and description, relied upon Heckewelder and other misinformed writers for his knowledge of the Indian. (pp. 373-76)

692 NEWCASTLE MAGAZINE 3 (January 1824):35-37.
    A comparison of THE SPY and THE PIONEERS in which the latter is highly praised as being more American.

693 SOUTHERN REVIEW 4 (November 1829):498-522.
    From a review of Scott's ANNE OF GEIERSTEIN. C's. genius lies in his ability to create excitement by means of action, incident, and character. This power is completely lost when he turns to polite society. (pp. 520-22)

694 "Tales of Indian Life." NEW MONTHLY MAGAZINE 20 (July 1827):77-82. Reprinted in PORT FOLIO 2, Hall's 2d series (August 1827):128-35.
    C's fiction belongs in the same class as that of the Waverly Tales, but he should not be considered an imitator of them. While inferior to Scott

overall, he has exceeded his predecessor in descriptive ability and has written truly American fiction.

695 "Traits of Indian Characters." NEW-YORK MIRROR 18 (July 4, 1840):12-14.
>   On C's. Indians and their inability to ever display love, fear, or affection.

Articles from Cooper's Death to the Present

696 Beeton, Beverly. "Frontiersmen Before Leatherstocking." MARKHAM REVIEW 7 (Fall 1977):1-5.
>   Of limited concern with C.

697 Bird, Robert Montgomery. NICK OF THE WOODS OR THE JIBBE-NAINOSAY: A TALE OF KENTUCKY, rev. ed. New York: Redfield, 1853. P. iv.
>   Depictions of Indians, including C's., are reminiscent of the shepherds of old pastoral poetry and romances.

698 Blake, Margaret M. "The Noble Indian of James Fenimore Cooper." Master of Arts degree, Boston College, 1951.

699 Bleasby, George. "James Fenimore Cooper: Frontier Novelist." MICHIGAN ALUMNUS QUARTERLY REVIEW 60 (May 22, 1954):257-65.
>   C. sought to describe the conflict between good and evil in his interpretation of the frontier. To this end he created authentic characters, many of them women. Although a devoted aristocrat, he had less success when delineating the men and women of the upper classes. Neither an able historian, nor an artist, C. nevertheless should be read by the student of social history and American literature.

700 Boynton, Percy H. THE REDISCOVERY OF THE FRONTIER. Chicago: University of Chicago Press, 1931. Pp. 70-72.
>   C. possessed a vastly romanticized view of the frontier. He failed to see it in terms of either democratic development or the advance of civilization. Rather, he sought to examine the plight of the Indian and the pioneer who escaped polite society to live a less oppressed existence.

701 Darnell, Donald. "Cooper, Prescott and the Conquest of Indian America." AMERICAN TRANSCENDENTAL QUARTERLY 30 (Spring 1976):7-12.

Comparison of Prescott's and C's. romantic conceptions of the Indian and his relationship to the white man. Concludes that their viewpoints are identical.

702 _____. "Visions of Hereditary Rank: The Loyalist in the Fiction of Hawthorne, Cooper, and Frederic." SOUTH ATLANTIC BULLETIN 42 (May 1977):45-54.
C. was ambivalent toward Tories. He usually portrayed them as Anglican gentlemen whom he could not quite make out to be villains, but whom he could never wholly accept.

703 Davie, Donald. "The Legacy of Fenimore Cooper." ESSAYS IN CRITICISM 9 (July 1959):222-38.
C's. portrayal of the Indian has been so widely accepted that writers, especially novelists, must take note of his work.

704 Enlow, Ruth E. "Comparison and Contrast of the Oklahoma Indian With the Indian Portrayed in Longfellow, Cooper and Neilhardt." Master of Arts degree, Oklahoma State University, 1926.

705 Folsom, James K. THE AMERICAN WESTERN NOVEL. New Haven, Conn.: College & University Press, 1966. Pp. 36-59.
A discussion of C's. influence on other western writers in the areas of law, justice, and property rights. Includes comments on C's. ability to move beyond the theme of pioneering to that of its social and moral implications--an idea largely ignored by those who followed him.

706 Francis, I. K. "A Critical Study of James Fenimore Cooper's Indian Novels." Ph.D. dissertation, University of Exeter, 1977.

707 Franklin, Wayne. THE NEW WORLD OF JAMES FENIMORE COOPER. Chicago: University of Chicago Press, 1982.
C., a major writer, was imaginative and fueled by the tensions created from westward migration.

708 Frederick, John T. "Cooper's Eloquent Indians." Modern Language Association of America, PUBLICATIONS 71 (December 1956):1004-17.
A comparison of C's. Indians with published records of Indian speech shows that he did not idealize their use of the language, for they possessed an eloquence overlooked by other critics.

709 Fríden, Georg. JAMES FENIMORE COOPER AND OSSIAN. Essays and Studies on American Language and Literature, no. 8. Uppsala:

Lundequitska Bokhandeln, 1949.
    The Ossian influences upon C.   His romantically developed Indians possessed the poetic speech and outlook on life similar to that of the Celt. They typify European romanticism as it influenced American fiction.

710 Gill, Katharine Tracy. "Frontier Concepts and Characters in the Fiction of Fenimore Cooper." Ph.D. dissertation, University of Illinois, 1956.
    C's. frontier novels exhibit a conflict between the conquest of the West (patriotism) and the greed and violence that attended it (morality).

711 Gleason, G. Dale. "Attitudes Toward Law and Order in the American Western." Ph.D. dissertation, Washington State University, 1978.
    Examines three types of law (statutory, natural, and moral) and how man relates to each.

712 Grünzweig, Walter. "'Where Millions of Happy People Might Live Peacefully': Jackson's West in Charles Sealsfield's 'Tokeah; or the White Rose,'" AMERIKASTUDIEN/AMERICAN STUDIES 28 (1983):219-36.
    Sealsfield's indebtedness to C.

713 Hamilton, Wynette L. "The Correlation Between Societal Attitudes and Those of American Authors in the Depiction of American Indians, 1607-1860." AMERICAN INDIAN QUARTERLY 1 (September 1974):1-26.
    Places C., Simms, Schoolcraft, Longfellow, and J. Miller in the same school--that of the romantic who depicted Indians as noble savages. C. and others are contrasted to those who viewed native Americans as evil savages.

714 Hand, Harry E. "Frontiers: Dilemmas of the American Spirit." LAUREL REVIEW 5 (1965):13-17.

715 Hawthorne, Julian. "James Fenimore Cooper." THE COLUMBIA UNIVERSITY COURSE IN LITERATURE. Vol. 16. Edited by John W. Cunliffe et al. New York: Columbia University Press, 1928-29. Pp. 383-89. Originally in WARNER LIBRARY. Vol. 7. Edited by John W. Cunliffe and Ashley H. Thorndike. New York: By the Knickerbocker Press for the Warner Library Co., 1917. Pp. 3985-92.
    C's. frontier novels, while lacking in realism, exhibit a superior imagination. This fact should not be viewed in negative terms, for it shows that he was greater than the complaining critic that so often emerges from his fiction.

716 House Kay Seymour. "Cooper's Indians After Yet Another 'Century of

Dishonor.'" LETTATURE D'AMERICA REVISTA TRIMESTRALE 4 (Autumn 1983):91-112.
     Not seen.

717 Howell, Elmo. "William Faulkner and the Mississippi Indians." GEORGIA REVIEW 21 (Fall 1967):386-96.
     C. lamented the passing of the frontier and its Indians at the same time that he supported the progress that civilization brought. By the twentieth century, however, there was little virgin country remaining in Mississippi and Faulkner viewed the passing of the Indians as wholly desirable.

718 Irving, Donald Charles. "James Fenimore Cooper's Alternatives to the Leatherstocking Hero in the Frontier Romances." Ph.D. dissertation, Indiana University, 1969.
     On C's. handling of the problems of social order *vs.* individualism and the love of another *vs.* independence. In addition to the L. S. TALES, THE WEPT OF WITH-TON-WISH, WYANDOTTE, and OAK OPENINGS are discussed.

719 Kaul, A. N. THE AMERICAN VISION: ACTUAL AND IDEAL SOCIETY IN NINETEENTH CENTURY FICTION. Yale Publications in American Studies, no. 7. New Haven, Conn.: Yale University Press, 1963. Pp. 84-138.
     The L. S. TALES and the Littlepage Trilogy as social fiction are not limited to C's. age, but present moral and historical precepts of value today.

720 Keiser, Albert. THE INDIAN IN AMERICAN LITERATURE. New York: Oxford University Press, 1933. Pp. 101-43.
     C's. portraits of the Indian were accurate and showed extensive knowledge. He did not, however, hesitate to enhance his realistic portrayals with imaginative colorings. He, more that any other writer, imprinted a concept of the American Indian on the American mind.

721 Kesterton, David B. "Milton's Satan and Cooper's Demonic Chieftains." SOUTH CENTRAL BULLETIN 29 (1969):138-42.

722 Koppell, Kathleen Sunshine. "Early American Fiction and the Call of the Wild: Nature and the Indian in Novels Before Cooper." Ph. D. dissertation, Harvard University, 1968.
     Although not concerned with an analysis of C's. novels, Koppell's study shows that C's. use of nature and the Indian was based upon those American writers who preceded him. He represents the end of a transitional

period that, while it failed to begin a whole new tradition, did move beyond the British style of writing to one of greater sophistication.

723 LADIES REPOSITORY 29 (March 1869):238.
      Discussion of STORIES OF THE PRAIRIE, AND OTHER ADVENTURES OF THE BORDER, a selection of C's. writings with simplified plots aimed at the juvenile reader.

724 Lindstrom, June L. "A Comparison of Two Novels by James Fenimore Cooper: 'The Pioneers' and 'Satanstoe.'" Master of Arts degree, 1967.

725 Lutz H. "Indians Through German *vs.* U. S. Eyes." INTERRACIAL BOOKS FOR CHILDREN BULLETIN 12 (no. 1, 1981):3-8.
      Not seen.

726 Melada, Ivan. "'Poor Little Talkative Christian': James Fenimore Cooper and the Dilemma of the Christian on the Frontier." STUDIES IN THE NOVEL 18 (Fall 1986):225-37.
      On C's. belief that Christianity could not exist on the frontier without compromises.

727 Mishler, Craig W. "'The Prairie': A Study in Romantic American Landscape as Reflected in the Writings of Cooper, Bryant, Irving, Melville and Whitman, 1827-1888." Master of Arts degree, Washington State University, 1967.

728 Montgomery, Esther Dean. "A Study of the Indian in American Fiction, 1820-1850." Master of Arts degree, University of Iowa, 1927.

729 Motley, Warren. THE AMERICAN ABRAHAM: JAMES FENIMORE COOPER AND THE FRONTIER PATRIARCH. Cambridge: Cambridge University Press, 1987.
      Focuses on C's. tales of patriarchal settlement. Allows the author to examine C's. views on familial and societal authority and responsibility. THE WEPT OF THE WISH-TON-WISH, THE PRAIRIE, and SATANSTOE are emphasized.

730 Movalli, Charles Joseph. "Pride and Prejudice: James Fenimore Cooper's Frontier Fiction and His Social Criticism." Ph.D. dissertation, University of Connecticut, 1972.
      Deals with C's. religious morality and political principles as they are illustrated in his frontier novels. In all instances his moral precepts form the basis for man's actions and reactions within a democratic society.

731 Murphy, John J. "Cooper, Cather, and the Downward Path to Progress." PRAIRIE SCHOONER 55 (Spring/Summer 1981):168-84.
    Sees C. as a pessimist who reacted to the loss of the wilderness and the materialism and wealth that resulted from its destruction.

732 Newcomber, Alphonso G. AMERICAN LITERATURE. Chicago: Scott Foresman, 1906. Pp. 77-93.
    Despite C's. many faults, without him the history and legend of westward settlement in the United States would have remained largely unrecorded.

733 Newtown, George Allyn. "Images of the American Indian in French and German Novels of the Nineteenth Century." Ph.D. dissertation, Yale University, 1979.
    C's. influence on European writers. A portion of one chapter deals with Balzac's criticism of C.

734 Peck, H. Daniel. "James Fenimore Cooper and the Writers of the Frontier." COLUMBIA LITERARY HISTORY OF THE UNITED STATES. Edited by Elliott Emory et al. New York: Columbia University Press, 1987. Pp. 240-61.
    Frontier comparisons of C., Bird, and Simms.

735 Pilkington, John "Nature's Legacy to William Faulkner." THE SOUTH AND FALUKNER'S YOKNAPATAWPHA: THE ACTUAL AND THE APOCRYPHAL. Edited by Evans Harrington and Ann J. Abadie. Jackson: University of Mississippi Press, 1977. Pp. 104-27.
    A review of the Edenic metaphor in American literature. Concludes that C. and Faulkner sought to make their readers sympathetic to the passing of the frontier.

736 Rans, Geoffrey. "Inaudible Man: The Indian in the Theory and Practice of White Fiction." CANADIAN REVIEW OF AMERICAN STUDIES 8 (Fall 1977):103-15.
    A comparison of C's. Indians to those of Irving, Faulkner, and others.

737 Sequeira, Isaac. "The Frontier Attack on Cooper, 1850-1900." INDIA JOURNAL OF AMERICAN STUDIES 8 (1978):25-35.
    On C's. Indian portraits, especially those put forth by his frontier characters. Sequeira claims that C's. Indians must be considered in light of the writer's goals, which emphasize theme, not historical fact.

738 Steele, Cynthia. "The Fiction of National Formation: The 'Indigenista' Novels of James Fenimore Cooper and Rosario Castellanos." REINVENTING THE AMERICAS: COMPARATIVE STUDIES OF LITERATURE OF THE UNITED STATES AND SPANISH AMERICA. Edited by Bell Gale Chevigny. New York: Cambridge University Press, 1986. Pp. 60-67.
    Compares Indian/white relations between the two authors.

739 Steinbrink, Jeffrey. "Attitudes Toward History and Uses of the Past in Cooper, Hawthorne, Mark Twain, and Fitzgerald." Ph.D. dissertation, University of North Carolina, 1974.
    C., who was unsuited to writing historical fiction, took advantage of the novelist's freedom to create a society which could deal with social and political problems according to the author's own ideals. Discusses the L. S. TALES and the Littlepage Trilogy.

740 Sullivan, Cecille G. "The Indian as Treated by Cooper and Simms." Master of Arts degree, Yale University, 1925.

741 Turner, Betty D. "Frontier Characters in Writings of Cooper." Master of Education degree, Henderson State College, n.d.

742 Walker, Warren S. "Cooper's Wooden Indians." CHICAGO JEWISH FORUM 20, pp. 157-60.
    Not seen. Citation from Modern Language Association, BIBLIOGRAPHY, 1961, p. 218.

743 Wallace, Paul A. "John Heckewelder's Indians and the Fenimore Cooper Tradition." American Philosophical Society, PROCEEDINGS 96 (1952):496-504.

744 Wasserman, Renata R. Mautner. "Re-Inventing the New World: Cooper and Alencar." COMPARATIVE LITERATURE 36 (Spring 1984):130-45.
    Illustrates how each author created a national literature that differed from that of Europe.

745 Williams, Owen D. "James Fenimore Cooper's 'Bad' Indians: A Study of Magua, Mahtoree and Wyandotte." Master of Arts degree, University of North Carolina, 1970.

746 Yoder, R. A. "The First Romantics and the Last Revolution." STUDIES IN ROMANTICISM 15 (Fall 1976):493-529.
    C. viewed the Revolution as a civil war in which neither side was completely right or wrong. As such, it was a period of moral trial, requiring

man to preserve those virtues upon which society rested, but which were seriously threatened by divided loyalties. Discusses THE SPY, LIONEL LINCOLN, THE PRAIRIE, and THE PILOT.

THE LEATHERSTOCKING TALES

Articles and Reviews Contemporary with Cooper

747 BROTHER JONATHAN 2 (July 16, 1842):325.
        The most American of C.'s novels and deserve to be published and circulated widely.

748 HOLDEN'S DOLLAR MAGAZINE 6 (November 1850):695.
        On the new edition--"handsome and uniform."

749 LITERARY WORLD 8 (February 8, 1851):113.
        On the new edition--possessed of a sincerity and freshness that should be a model for writers of the 1850s.

Articles from Cooper's Death to the Present

750 Allen, Walter. THE URGENT WEST: THE AMERICAN DREAM AND MODERN MAN. New York: E. P. Dutton, 1969. Pp. 110-15.
        C., neither a great nor a good writer, attempted to compare a world gone by with a vastly inferior present-day America.

751 Altherr, Thomas Lawson. "'Best of All Breathing': Hunting as a Mode of Environmental Perception in American Literature and Thought from James Fenimore Cooper to Norman Mailer." Ph.D. dissertation, Ohio State University, 1976.
        C., through Natty Bumppo, showed an ambivalent attitude toward hunting.

752 Askew, Melvin W. "The Pseudonymic American Hero." BUCKNELL REVIEW 10 (March 1962):224-31.
        Examines the sociological reasons for the changes in the names of characters within novels, and from novel to novel, in the works of C., Fitzgerald, Poe, Hawthorne, Twain, and Dreiser.

753 Aslinger, Annabel. "Customs and Characteristics of 'The Leatherstocking Tales.'" Master of Arts degree, Peabody College for Teachers, 1931.

754 Axelrad, Allen M. "Order of 'The Leatherstocking Tales': D. H. Lawrence, David Noble, and the Iron Trap of History." AMERICAN LITERATURE 54 (May 1982):189-211.

Makes a case for reading the L. S. TALES in the order of Leatherstockings's life rather than in order of publication.

755 Bach, Bert C. "A Reconsideration of Natty Bumppo." CIMARRON REVIEW no. 5 (September 1968):60-66.

Examines Natty Bumppo as both a philosophical and an artistic creation. In the former terms, he moves from optimism in his youth to pessimism as an aged frontiersman. Artistically, C's. success is more limited, for he seeks to defend, in the later novels, the end of Natty's life which he had presented earlier in the series.

756 Balk, Mary McArdle. "A Joint Stock Company of Two: The Bonded Pair in the Work of Cooper, Melville, Twain, Faulkner, Kesey, Herr, and Stone." Ph.D. dissertation, University of Manitoba, 1984.

An investigation of male bonding as it relates to male literary heroes--Natty Bumppo in C's. case. American literature is seen as an expression of acculturation resulting from the white European society's contact with a primitive New World one.

757 Ball, Lee Hampton, Jr. "James Fenimore Cooper's Artistry in the Characterization of Leather-stocking." Ph.D. dissertation, University of Wisconsin, 1958.

An attempt to account for Leatherstocking's appeal through time by considering both his universal and popular characteristics. Concludes that C's. idea of the character changed in successive novels, while still exhibiting great continuity.

758 _____. "Leather-Stocking's Simplicity of Mind as a Key to His Psychological Character." SOUTH CENTRAL BULLETIN 22 (1962):11-15.

759 Baym, Nina. "Women of Cooper's 'Leatherstocking Tales.'" AMERICAN QUARTERLY 23 (December 1971):696-709.

C's. female characters do assume an important place in his fiction, although they are often poorly drawn or play only minor roles. This was due to a conservative view of society that did not allow women a major role in events.

760 Beaumont, Edith. VALLEY SAMPLER, July 24, 31, 1969. Bennington, Vt.

On the disputes between those who favor Nathaniel Shipman as

the model for Natty Bumppo and those who favor David Shipman. Not seen.
Citation from Beard, FIFTEEN AMERICAN AUTHORS, p. 78.

761 "Believe Ancient Skeleton Is That of 'The Deerslayer.'" NEW YORK
TIMES, January 13, 1933, p. 13.
       Excavations near Hoosick, N. Y., yielded a skeleton purported to
be that of Natty Bumppo's real life counterpart.

762 Bewley, Marius James. "The Cage and 'The Prairie': Two Notes on
Symbolism." HUDSON REVIEW 10 (Autumn 1957):403-14.
       Although critics have claimed that C. was not interested in sym-
bols, his best works can be symbolically interpreted. Natty Bumppo, for instance, should be seen in terms of C's. love/hate response to a changing American society.

763 BLACKWOOD'S MAGAZINE 72 (December 1853):680-92.
       From a review of Sullivan's RAMBLES IN NORTH AND
SOUTH AMERICA. While C's. tales were both fascinating and moral, he
misled the world in regard to Indian life and lore.

764 Bleasby George. "The Frontier in Cooper's 'Leatherstocking Tales.'"
Ph.D. dissertation, University of Pittsburgh, 1952.
       C., a man who held to ideas of class and property distinction,
viewed the frontier, not as an expression of democracy, but as an area of conflict between those outside the law and those who believed in man-made rules.
It was a land that, by necessity, was learning to accept government and submission to authority.

765 Boewe, Charles. "Cooper's Doctrine of Gifts." TENNESSEE STUDIES
IN LITERATURE 7 (1962):27-35.
       C. used his concept of the "doctrine of gifts" to explain away
many barbaric acts of the Indians, to account for racial and social differences
in human behavior, and to defend his idea of a class society.

766 Bold, Christine. "How the Western Ends: Fenimore Cooper to Frederic
Remington." WESTERN   AMERICAN   LITERATURE   17   (Summer
1982):117-35.
       Remington's use of C. as a model.

767 Buchholz, Douglas Bernard. "Stages in the Development of American
Realism: A Lukacsian Persepective." Ph.D. dissertation, University of Pennsylvania, 1990.
       Expands upon Georg Lukàcs' discussion of the L. S. TALES in

THE HISTORICAL NOVEL (item no. 821). Concludes that C's. importance
as an historical realist has been underestimated.

768 Bunce, O. B. "To the Editors of the Critic." THE CRITIC 12 (September
14, 1889):126-27.
     Claims that C. had decided to write a Revolutionary War novel
with Natty Bumppo as the hero, but he was turned down by his publishers.
They feared that if the book was not a success, it would detract from the rest
of the highly profitable series.

769 Burkhardt, Peggy Craven. "Fenimore Cooper's Literary Defenses."
Ph.D. dissertation, University of Iowa, 1972.
     C., a literary realist, anticipated much of the fictional realism that
was to follow him. As a close follower of both English and American society,
he made use of characterization, dialect, plot, theme, and setting to present his
views of man and nature.

770 Burrell, Wesley R. "James Fenimore Cooper and the 'Long Rifle.'"
MICHIGAN ALUMNUS QUARTERLY REVIEW 40 (Winter 1949):140-51.
     Comments on C's. use of the rifle in the L. S. TALES and on
rifles in general during C's. lifetime.

771 Butler, Michael D. "Sons of Oliver Edwards; or, the Other American
Hero." WESTERN AMERICAN LITERATURE 12 (May 1977):53-66.
     The heroes of popular western fiction are in contrast to Natty
Bumppo, for they, rather than finding themselves torn between a primitive
society and advancing civilization, develop a mode of living that allows them
to cross comfortably from one way of life to the other.

772 Byron, John E. "Military Tactics and Techniques in the Leatherstocking
Series of James Fenimore Cooper." Master of Arts degree, University of Florida, 1961.

773 Cawelti, John G. "The Western: A Look at the Evolution of a Formula."
ADVENTURE, MYSTERY AND ROMANCE: FORMULA STORIES AS
ART AND POPULAR CULTURE. Chicago: University of Chicago Press,
1976. Pp. 192-259.
     The western began with THE PIONEERS and was essentially a
novel of manners. By the time the L. S. TALES were completed, however,
the western formula had become one of adventure as it is today.

774 Clark, Robert. "The Aesthetic Ideology: History, the Novel and Romance
in Cooper." HISTORY, IDEOLOGY, AND MYTH IN AMERICAN

FICTION, 1823-1852. New York: St. Martins Press, 1984. Pp. 48-50.
C. did not see himself as a writer of romance, but as an historical novelist, thus giving is work the legitimacy of truth.

775 Cooke, John Estes. "Cooper's Indians." APPLETON'S JOURNAL 12 (August 29, 1874):264-67.
C's. Indian descxriptions may be criticized on a few occasions, but overall they rank with his excellent sea and frontier characterizations.

776 THE CRITIC 15 (November 30, 1889):270.
Poorly printed, but the young should enjoy it.

777 Darkenwald, Gordon G. "The Evolution of Archetypes in Cooper's 'Leatherstocking Tales.'" Master of Arts degree, Hunter College, 1966.

778 Davie, Donald. THE HEYDAY OF SIR WALTER SCOTT. London: Routledge & Keegan Paul, 1961. Pp. 101-28.
An analysis of each of the five novels in the series that makes use of recent C. criticism.

779 Davis, David Brion. "The Deerslayer, A Democratic Knight of the Wilderness." TWELVE ORIGINAL ESSAYS ON GREAT AMERICAN NOVELS. Edited by Charles Shapiro. Detroit: Wayne State University Press, 1958. Pp. 1-22.
C's. use of fiction to convey a specific moral code to nineteenth century America.

780 Downs, Robert B. FAMOUS AMERICAN BOOKS. New York: Mc-Graw-Hill Book Co., 1971. Pp. 75-81.
Plot summaries with comments on C's. originality, Indians, women, and popularity.

781 Duncan, Jeffrey L. "Nature and Society in Cooper's 'Leatherstocking Tales.'" Masters thesis, University of Virginia, 1962.

782 Elliott, Karen Sue. "The Portrayal of the American Indian Woman in a Select Group of American Novels." Ph.D. dissertation, University of Minnesota, 1979.
C's. Indian women become more important as the L. S. TALES progress. They are usually characterized as either good or bad. If bad, they are likeable or non-thinking. Heckewelder had great influence on these portraits.

783 Evans, Constantine. "'The Origin of the Nation': Time and History in Cooper's 'Leatherstocking Tales.'" Ph.D. dissertation, Syracuse University, 1981.

784 "Fenimore Cooper's Home." NEW-YORK TRIBUNE, July 4, 1897, Supp., p. 10.
        Otsego Hall, its environs, and the discovery of Leatherstocking's cave, proving C's. attention to detail.

785 Fick, Thomas Hale. "An American Dialectic: Power and Innocence from Cooper to Kosinski." Ph.D. dissertation, Indiana University, 1985.
        Natty Bumppo as an early example of the American contradiction between innocence and power.

786 Fieldler, Leslie, LOVE AND DEATH IN THE AMERICAN NOVEL. New York: Criterion Books, 1960. Pp. 170-212.

787 _____. THE RETURN OF THE VANISHING AMERICAN. New York: Stein & Day, 1968. Pp. 117-18, 121-23.
        Natty Bumppo as American myth and Mark Twain's criticism of C's. handling of Indian characters.

788 Fiorelli, Edward A. "The American Hero: Natty Bumppo and Mythology of America." Master of Arts degree, Brooklyn College of City University of New York, 1967.

789 Fishwick, Marshall W. "Daniel Boone and the Pattern of the Western Hero." FILSON CLUB HISTORY QUARTERLY 27 (April 1953):119-38.
        C. raised the stature and popularity of Daniel Boone when basing Natty Bumppo on the real-life frontiersman. (pp. 128-29)

790 Franklin, Rosemary F. "The Cabin By the Lake: Pastoral Landscapes of Poe, Cooper, Hawthorne, and Thoreau." ESQ: A JOURNAL OF THE AMERICAN RENAISSANCE 22 (2d quarter 1976): 59-70.
        See pp. 61-64 for C. material.

791 Franz, Eleanor. "Hunting the Hunter: Nat Foster Today." NEW YORK FOLKLORE QUARTERLY 20 (December 1964):270-75.
        Nat Foster, an eighteenth century New York trapper and hunter who was known as "Leatherstocking," was undoubtedly the prototype for Natty Bumppo.

792 Freeman, Emily L. "Iroquois and Ojibway Legends in Cooper's 'The

Last of the Mohicans' and 'The Deerslayer,' and in Longfellow's 'Hiawatha.'"
Ph.D. dissertation, Columbia Teachers College, 1941.

793 Fussell, Edwin Sill. FRONTIER: AMERICAN LITERATURE AND
THE AMERICAN WEST. Princeton, N. J.: Princeton University Press, 1965.
Pp. 27-28.
        C. was not a great artist, for he often rambled and lacked a
distinctive style.   American literature up to Whitman, however, is merely a
footnote to him.   His best subject was the frontier.

794 Gelpi, Albert. "Emily Dickinson and 'The Deerslayer': The Dilemma of
the Woman Poet in America." SAN JOSE STUDIES 3 (1977):80-95.
        A comparison of selected Dickinson poems with several C. novels.
Natty Bumppo is emphasized.

795 Girgus, Sam B. "The Perverted Self in American Literature and Culture."
MIDWEST QUARTERLY 19 (Winter 1978):160-75.
        Sees the L. S. TALES as a struggle between individualism and
freedom (the heart) and civilization and wilderness (reality).

796 Harms, Tina C. "Dictionary of Characters in Cooper's 'Leatherstocking
Tales.'" Master of Arts degree, University of Kansas, 1927.

797 Harris, Laura V. "A Biographical Character Analysis of Nathaniel
Bumppo and Other Characters of the Leatherstocking Series". Master of Arts
degree, Auburn University, 1944.

798 Harte, Bret. "Muck-a-Muck: A Modern Indian Novel After Cooper."
THE WRITINGS OF BRET HARTE. Vol. 1. Standard Library Edition.
Boston & New York: Houghton, Mifflin & Co., 1896. Pp. 78-85.
        A satire.

799 Hayne, Barrie. "'Ossian', Scott and Cooper's Indians." JOURNAL OF
AMERICAN STUDIES 3 (July 1969):73-87.
        James Macpherson, Scott, and C. have many elements in common
(thematically, stylistically, and in terms of mood) that require them to assume
similar forms and methods of handling subject matter.

800 Hazard, Lucy Lockwood. THE FRONTIER IN AMERICAN
LITERATURE. New York: Barnes & Noble, 1941. Pp. 97-116.
        Refutes the idea that C. idealized his Indians, had characters carry
out superhuman feats, and that his female characters were poorly drawn.
Concludes that Leatherstocking is the epitome of the epic American hero.

801 Hocks, Richard A. "Thoreau, Coleridge and Barfield: Reflections on the Imagination and Laws of Polarity." CENTENNIAL REVIEW 17 (Spring 1973):175-98.

> Literary representation of the struggle between nature and society, and between a simple society and a complex civilization, which was illustrated by Natty Bumppo, was later transferred to real life by Thoreau.

802 Howard, David. "James Fenimore Cooper's 'Leatherstocking Tales': Without a Cross." TRADITION AND TOLERANCE IN NINETEENTH CENTURY FICTION: CRITICAL ESSAYS ON SOME ENGLISH AND AMERICAN NOVELS. Edited by David Howard, John Lucas, and John Goode. New York: Barnes & Noble, 1967. Pp. 9-54.

> C's use of fatalism and his sense of the ironic carry the L. S. TALES beyond mere social and political criticism toward a philosophy of history.

803 Johnson, Robert L. "The Road Out in Australian and American Fiction: A Study of Four Spokesmen." SOUTHERN REVIEW 1 (1965):20-31.

> The progress of Natty Bumppo is characteristic of much early American fiction and not dissimilar to the later western hero. As a man of the wilderness he emerges from the forest at the novel's beginning, moves within society for a time, but eventually rejects it, returning to the safety of the forest at the book's end.

804 Jones, Howard Mumford. THE FRONTIER IN AMERICAN FICTION: FOUR LECTURES ON THE RELATION OF LANDSCAPE TO LITERATURE. Jerusalem: Magness Press, 1956. Pp. 26-50.

> Wisdom, not economic determinism, was the directing force for C. in development of the frontier. Closely tied to this concept were the ideas of religion and tradition.

805 Jones, Virgil L. "Gustave Aimard." SOUTHWEST REVIEW 15 (Summer 1930):452-68.

> A comparative study of C. and Olivier Gloux (Gustave Aimard), C's. French imitator.

806 Jordan, Howell H., Jr. "The Changing Character of Natty Bumppo in the 'Leatherstocking Tales.'" Master of Arts degree, Columbia University, 1966.

807 Jorns, Effie E. "Uncas, Red Cloud, and Laughing Boy: The American Indian as Portrayed By the Romanticist Cooper, the Scholar-poet Neihardt and the Anthropologist LaFarge." Master of Arts degree, Oklahoma State University, 1930.

808 Kaplan, Harold. "Beyond Society: The Idea of Community in Classic American Writing." SOCIAL RESEARCH 42 (Summer 1975):204-29.

        C. made use of Natty Bumppo's relationship with the Indians to develop his idea of community.

809 _____. DEMOCRATIC HUMANISM AND AMERICAN LITERATURE. Chicago & London: University of Chicago Press, 1972. Pp. 103-13.

        Suggests that C's. fiction is representative of, not only created myth, but myth that has been poorly told. It lacks excitement and possesses awkward narrative, but provides pleasure to the reader.

810 Kaye, Francis W. "Cooper, Sarmiento, Wister, and Hernández: The Search for a New World Literary Hero." CLA JOURNAL 19 (March 1976):404-11.

        C's. attempt to create a national hero (Natty Bumppo) and, thus, a national literature, was not entirely successful. Having been raised, not in a frontier situation, but in a cultured environment, what he new of the West came from his imagination. Consequently, he neither empathized, nor had emotional identification with his creations.

811 Kebbel, T. E. "Leather-stocking." MACMILLAN'S MAGAZINE 79 (January 1899):191-201.

        Although C. created weak plots, he exhibited amazing powers of description and drew interesting characters who illustrated knowledge of human nature.

812 Kelly William P. "Inventing American History: Cooper and 'The Leatherstocking Tales.'" CUNY ENGLISH FORUM. Vol. 1. Edited by Saul N. Brody. New York: AMS, 1985. Pp. 359-79.

        On C's. historical imagination and use of American language.

813 _____. "'The Leatherstocking Tales': Fiction and the American Historical Experience." Ph.D. dissertation, Indiana University, 1977.

        Explores the development of C's. historical vision. Includes material on his use of Scott as a model and the difficulty American writers had adapting the British model to the New World situation.

814 _____. PLOTTING AMERICA'S PAST: FENIMORE COOPER AND 'THE LEATHERSTOCKING TALES'". Carbondale: Southern Illinois University Press, 1983.

        Not seen.

815 Kolodny, Annette. LAY OF THE LAND: METAPHOR AS EXPERIENCE AND HISTORY IN AMERICAN LIFE AND LETTERS. Chapel Hill: University of North Carolina Press, 1975. Pp. 89-115.

On theme in the L. S. TALES: Natty Bumppo's struggle to maintain an existence in a pastoral setting that had been either condemned or was in the process of being changed by others of his race. A psychological study.

816 Krause, Sydney J. "Cooper's Literary Offenses: Mark Twain in Wonderland." NEW ENGLAND QUARTERLY 38 (September 1965):291-311.

Mark Twain, who emphasized C's. technical faults, failed to take note of the symbolic and mythic elements that are of far greater importance.

817 Kuhlmann, Susan. KNAVE, FOOL, AND GENIUS. Chapel Hill: University of North Carolina Press, 1973. Pp. 11-13.

On Natty Bumppo.

818 Lawrence, David Herbert. "Studies in Classic American Literature. (V): Fenimore Cooper's Leatherstocking Novels." ENGLISH REVIEW 28 (March 1919):204-19. Reprinted in Arnold, Armin, ed. SYMBOLIC MEANING: THE UNCOLLECTED VERSIONS OF 'STUDIES IN CLASSICAL AMERICAN LITERATURE.' London: Centaur Press, 1962. Pp. 91-111; Beal, Anthony, ed. SELECTED LITERARY CRITICISM. New York: Viking Press, 1956. Pp. 314-29; Rahv, Philip, ed. LITERATURE IN AMERICA: AN ANTHOLOGY OF LITERARY CRITICISM. New York: Meridian, 1957, Pp. 35-48; STUDIES IN CLASSICAL AMERICAN LITERATURE. New York: Thomas Seltzer, 1923. Pp. 67-92; and Wilson, Edmund, ed. SHOCK OF RECOGNITION: THE DEVELOPMENT OF LITERATURE IN THE UNITED STATES, RECORDED BY THE MEN WHO MADE IT. Garden City, N. Y.: Doubleday, Doran & Co., 1943. Pp. 949-66.

Compares C. to the Effingham's socially (over-cultured) and to Natty Bumppo emotionally (crude and naive). This polarization is evident throughout C's. life.

819 Lewisohn, Ludwig. EXPRESSION IN AMERICA. New York: Harper & Bros., 1932. Pp. 55-57.

C. possessed no proper literary style, nor could he create a character with sufficient depth to be memorable. All he offered was an ability to invent and develop action. Thus, intelligent people cannot read him with any satisfaction.

820 Liljegren, S. B. THE CANADIAN BORDER NOVELS OF J. F.

COOPER. Upsala University Canadian Studies, no. 7. Upsala: Lundequistska Bokh., 1968.

C's. treatment of the Indian, the French, war, and scenery as they relate to areas near the Canadian border. Liljegren concludes that C. was not historically accurate, for he was too much of a Romantic. Includes some comments on THE OAK OPENINGS and THE WEPT OF WITH-TON-WISH.

821 Lukács, Georg. THE HISTORICAL NOVEL. Translated by Hannah and Stanley Mitchell. London: Merlin Press, 1962. Pp. 64-65.

C. made use of an essentially mediocre person (Natty Bumppo), not only to portray the moral and physical destruction of the Indians, but to show how the European search for freedom in the New World was destroyed by man's economic and moral shortcomings.

822 Lyndenberg, John. "American Novelists in Search of a Lost World." REVUE DES LANGUES VIVANTES 27 (1961):306-21.

Presents Natty Bumppo and Huckleberry Finn as the only two real, non-tragic American heroes in American fiction. Emphasizes the innocence possessed by both characters.

823 McAleer, John J. "Biblical Analogy in the 'Leatherstocking Tales.'" NINETEENTH CENTURY FICTION 17 (December 1962):217-35.

C's. cautious use of Biblical analogies, which were really early experiments with symbolism, always sought to place Calvinism in an unfavorable light.

824 McNulty, Robert. "Leatherstocking and the American Spirit." NEW YORK HISTORY 22 (January 1941):46-51.

As the winning essay in the Cooper Essay Contest, McNulty's article attributes to Leatherstocking those traits that best define the American character: justice and equality, courage, democracy, belief in God, and the love of truth.

825 MacPhee, Laurence Edward. "Patterns of Action and Imagery in 'The Leatherstocking Tales.'" Ph.D. dissertation, Rutgers University, 1967.

C's. use of the figurative in support of theme and characterization. An attempt to add to C's. reappraisal as a major literary figure.

826 McWilliams, Wilson Carey. "Fenimore Cooper: Natty Bumppo and the Godfather." THE ARTIST AND POLITICAL VISION. Edited by Benjamin R. Barber and Michael J. Gargas McGrath. New Brunswick, N. J.: Transaction Books, 1982. Pp. 233-44. Originally "Natty Bumppo and the

Godfather." COLORADO QUARTERLY 24 (Autumn 1975):133-44.

     While Natty Bumppo is destined to be destroyed by civilization due to his innate sense of morality, the Corleone family, modern day barbarians, manage to survive in an alien civilization through deceit and treachery.

827 Macy, John. THE SPIRIT OF AMERICAN LITERATURE. New York: Boni & Liveright, 1913. Pp. 35-44.

     Although critics consistently condemn C. for his stylistic imperfections, the reader disregards them, finding that the action alone creates a work of art.

828 Marder, Daniel. "Exiles at Home in American Literature." MOSAIC 8 (Spring 1975):49-75.

     The L. S. TALES depict a struggle between nature and society. Eventually Leatherstocking sees the futility of this struggle and surrenders himself to the inevitable.

829 Martin, Terence. "Beginnings and Endings in 'The Leatherstocking Tales.'" NINETEENTH CENTURY FICTION 33 (June 1978):69-87.

     On the order of the writing of the L. S. TALES, what this order means in terms of life, death and rebirth, and what C. saw as connections between the novels.

830 _____. "The Negative Character in American Fiction." TOWARD A NEW AMERICAN LITERARY HISTORY: ESSAYS IN HONOR OF ARLIN TURNER. Edited by Louis J. Budd, Edwin Harrison Cady, and Carl L. Anderson. Durham, N. C.: Duke University Press 1980. Pp. 230-43.

     Natty Bumppo as the classic negative figure in literature.

831 _____. "Surviving on the Frontier: The Doubled Consciousness of Natty Bumppo." SOUTH ATLANTIC QUARTERLY 75 (Autumn 1976):447-59.

     Martin explores relationships between Natty Bumppo and Chingachgook, concluding that introduction of the latter character allowed C. to protect and vindicate Natty's innocence.

832 Matthews, Brander. "Introduction." COOPER'S LEATHERSTOCKING-TALES. New York: T. Y. Crowell, 1895.

     A review of this edition is found in THE CRITIC 29 (November 21, 1896):326.

833 Maxwell, Desmond Ernest Stuart. AMERICAN FICTION; THE INTELLECTUAL BACKGROUND. New York: Columbia University Press,

1963. Pp. 97-140.
        C., who intellectually was a liberal democrat, but emotionally an aristocrat, used action and character to express his social and political ideas.

834 May, Judith Stinson. "Family Aggression in the Leatherstocking Series." Ph.D. dissertation, University of Illinois at Urbana-Champaign, 1976.

835 Merlock, Raymond James. "From Flintlock to Forty-five: James Fenimore Cooper and the Popular Western Tradition in Fiction and Film." Ph.D. dissertation, Ohio University, 1981.
        Examination of those who preceded C., C's. sources, and writers and film makers who followed him. Conclusions on C. as inventor of the western novel and the legacy left to other artists.

836 Meyer, William Claus. "The Development of Myth in 'The Leatherstocking Tales' of James Fenimore Cooper." Ph.D. dissertation, Ball State University, 1972.
        C's. mythic imagination is important, not only because it occupies a primary place in the history of American literature, but for its literary merit as well.

837 Mills, Gordon. "The Symbolic Wilderness: James Fenimore Cooper and Jack London." NINETEENTH CENTURY FICTION 13 (March 1959):329-40.
        C. was unable to condemn either the wilderness or uncivilized society. He did, however, acknowledge that Leatherstocking was inferior to the leaders of the nineteenth century.

838 Minor, Dennis E. "The Epic Qualities of the Early American Frontier Novel: Cooper's 'Leatherstocking Tales.'" Master of Arts degree, Texas Agricultural and Mechanical University, 1968.

839 Mossberg, Christer Lennart. "Notes Toward an Introduction to Scandanavian Immigrant Literature on the Pioneer Experience." PROCEEDINGS OF THE PACIFIC NORTHWEST CONFERENCE ON FOREIGN LANGUAGES 28 (Part 1, 1977):112-17.
        Scandanavians immigrating to America had read C. and their concepts of forest and prairie came from him. They possessed visions of vast, open areas where one would be out of reach of grasping landowners, where they could be individuals, and where their destiny could be self-controlled.

840 Mulqueen, James E. "Three Heroes in American Fiction." ILLINOIS QUARTERLY 36, pp. 44-50.

Comparisons between Natty Bumppo, the Virginian, and Lew Archer. Not seen. Citation from Modern Language Association, BIBLIOGRAPHY, 1974, p. 147.

841 Nevins, Allan, ed. "Introduction." THE LEATHERSTOCKING SAGA. New York: Pantheon Books, 1954. Pp. 1-34.

Suggests that much C. criticism should be ignored and that the L. S. TALES be read as the fine example of romance they are, and as an American epic which they nearly are. Reviews of this edition are found in the following sources: BOOKLIST 51 (November 15, 1954):132; CHICAGO TRIBUNE, October 10, 1954, p. 4; CHRISTIAN SCIENCE MONITOR, December 2, 1954, p. 17; GEORGIA REVIEW 10 (Summer 1956):237-40; KIRKUS REVIEW 22 (September 15, 1954):635; NEW YORKER 30 (November 27, 1954):200; NEW YORK HERALD TRIBUNE, "Book Review Section," November 14, 1954, part I, p. 8, part II, p. 34; NEW YORK TIMES, "Book Review Section," October 3, 1954, p. 5; SAN FRANCISCO CHRONICLE, November 29, 1954, p. 25; SATURDAY REVIEW OF LITERATURE 42 (November 20, 1954):22-23; SPRINGFIELD REPUBLICAN, November 7, 1954, p. 9c; and TIME 64 (December 27, 1954):66.

842 Nevius, Blake. "Landscapes of Leatherstocking." TIMES (London), "Literary Supplement," November 4, 1977, p. 1290.

843 Noble, David W. "Cooper, Leatherstocking and the Death of the American Adam." AMERICAN QUARTERLY 16 (Fall 1964):419-31. Reprinted in Cohen, Henny, ed. THE AMERICAN EXPERIENCE: APPROACHES TO THE STUDY OF THE UNITED STATES. Boston: Houghton MIfflin Co., 1968. Pp. 169-82.

In opposition to Lewis's THE AMERICAN ADAM (item no. 484). Noble agrees that C. was writing about the American myth, but rather than celebrating the concept of the American Adam, he sought to destroy it.

844 _____. THE EXTERNAL ADAM AND THE NEW WORLD GARDEN; THE CENTRAL MYTH IN THE AMERICAN NOVEL SINCE 1830. New York: George Brazillier, 1968. Pp. 1-47.

Noble takes the position that C's. novels do not celebrate the myth of the American dream held by the Jacksonians, but rather sought to illustrate its total futility.

845 Noble, Donald R. "James Fenimore Cooper and the Environment." CONSERVATIONIST 26 (October 1971):3-7.

C. tried, through such characters as Natty Bumppo, Judge Temple, Judith Hutter, and Richard Temple, to make his early nineteenth century readers aware of the need for forest management, wildlife preservation, and the conservation of other natural resources.

846 Paine Gregory. "The Indians of 'The Leather-stocking Tales.'" STUDIES IN PHILOLOGY 23 (January 1926):16-39.
      C., who had little first-hand knowledge of the Indians, took advantage of many sources of information available to him that he believed to be accurate. The Indians in the early L. S. TALES are based largely on Hecke-welder, but later he allowed his imagination to take over as he created his epic hero Chingachgook.

847 Parker, Arthur C. "Sources and Range of Cooper's Indian Lore." NEW YORK HISTORY 35 (October 1954):447-56.
      C. gained his information on the Indian from local legend, the factual and fictional literature of his day, and occasional acquaintances with Indians of the area. Although much of what he wrote was taken as fact, C. was a novelist whose first concern was the plot, not the recording of truth.

848 Pearce, Roy Harvey. "Civilization and Savagism: The World of 'The Leatherstocking Tales.'" ENGLISH INSTITUTE ESSAYS. Vol. 4. Edited by Alan S. Downer. New York: Columbia University Press. Pp. 92-116.
      The L. S. TALES are an attempt to understand the westward movement and the progress of the civilized world that accompanied it. Consequently, Indian society is portrayed as greatly inferior to that of the advancing white man.

849 _____. HISTORICISM ONCE MORE: PROBLEMS & OCCASIONS FOR THE AMERICAN SCHOLAR. Princeton, N. J.: Princeton University Press, 1969. Pp. 109-36.
      The L. S. TALES (and specifically Natty Bumppo) present a struggle between civilization and a more natural environment. Natty, who was potentially good, had to be destroyed in the necessary and inevitable advancement of civilization. For C., the loss of the independent frontier type was not necessarily bad, but it did signify that something unique in American life was being destroyed and that some people would suffer in the process. This essay is a combination of the SOUTH ATLANTIC QUARTERLY article below, other Pearce essays, and some new material.

850 _____. "'The Leatherstocking Tales' Re-examined." SOUTH ATLANTIC QUARTERLY 46 (October 1947):524-36.
      The L. S. TALES can be appreciated on two levels: that of action and that of ideas. As novels of action they are highly successful, but C. has failed entirely as a novelist of ideas.

851 _____. THE SAVAGES OF AMERICA: A STUDY OF THE INDIAN AND THE IDEA OF CIVILIZATION. Baltimore: Johns Hopkins Press, 1953. Pp. 159-60, 196-97, 200-12. Reprinted as SAVAGISM AND CIVILIZATION. Baltimore: Johns Hopkins Press, 1965.

The symbol of the Indian as savage was a necessary one if Americans were to continue to subscribe to ideas of westward progress. C. was the first novelist to incorporate this idea into his fiction.

852 Pease, Donald. "Visionary Compacts and the Cold War Consensus." VISIONARY COMPACTS: AMERICAN RENAISSANCE WRITINGS IN CULTURAL CONTEXT. Madison: University of Wisconsin Press, 1987. Pp. 3-48.

Hawkeye, having divorced himself from a past and a locality, became free to assume a national identity. This national identity theme justified, for C., the white man's assumption of control of the frontier which, in turn, opened up possibilities for mobility while creating a threat to social and political institutions.

853 Person, Leland S. "Cooper's 'The Pioneers' and Leatherstocking's Historical Function." ESQ: A JOURNAL OF THE AMERICAN RENAISSANCE 25 (1st quarter, 1979):170-80.

THE PIONEERS ends with Indian and white views and needs being fused. C's. further TALES illustrate that this situation did not exist in reality, but only as a literary promise.

854 Peyton, Robert Louis. "Western Justice: The Politics of Fenimore Cooper, Owen Wister and the Western Movies." Ph.D. dissertation, University of California, Berkeley, 1980.

Concludes that political statements made in the fiction of C. and Wister found their way into film adaptations.

855 Pieschel, Bridget Smith. "The Rhetoric of Degeneration from Bradford to Cooper." Ph.D. dissertation, University of Alabama, 1989.

C. and his fear of miscegenation.

856 Poirier. Richard. A WORLD ELSEWHERE: THE PLACE OF STYLE IN AMERICAN LITERATURE. New York: Oxford University Press, 1966. Pp. 71-77.

C. wrote his best fiction when he dealt with situations involving action (physical forces), rather than those displaying social concerns common to the manneristic novel.

857 Porte, Joel. THE ROMANCE IN AMERICA: STUDIES ON COOPER,

POE, HAWTHORNE, MELVILLE, AND JAMES. Middletown, Conn.: Wesleyan University Press, 1969. pp. 3-52.

The L. S. TALES, which celebrate an American myth, are important for their ideas, often presented in the form of conflict (e.g. civilization *vs.* nature). A psychological study.

858 Pound, Louise. "The Dialect of Cooper's Leather-stocking." AMERICAN SPEECH 2 (September 1927):479-88. Reprinted in Wimberly, Lowry C., ed. SELECTED WRITINGS OF LOUISE POUND. Lincoln: University of Nebraska, 1949. Pp. 164-77.

C's. dialect was composed largely of archaisms. It therefore possessed simplicity, lacked slang, and will remain intelligible for a long period of time.

859 Pratt, Linda Ray. "The Abuse of Eve By the New World Adam." IMAGES OF WOMEN IN FICTION FEMINIST PERSPECTIVES. Edited by Susan Koppelman Cornillon. Bowling Green, Ohio: Bowling Green University Popular Press, 1972. Pp. 155-74.

Considers several female characters, both "pure and impure", and Natty Bumppo's reaction to them. (pp. 157-60)

860 Prentiss, Mark O. "Cooper Memorial." SATURDAY REVIEW OF LITERATURE 15 (February 29, 1936):9.

The L. S. TALES are the most popular, and often the only, American literature known in parts of Persia, Turkey, Russia, and the Orient.

861 Rans, Geoffrey. "'But the Penalty of Adam': Cooper's Sense of the Subversive." CANADIAN REVIEW OF AMERICAN STUDIES 3 (Spring 1972):21-32.

C., while not always skeptical, expressed a social philosophy that doomed the Natty Bumppo's of the world while it called for the eventual destruction of the civilization that replaced them.

862 Rawe, Lucy R. "The Ambiguities of James Fenimore Cooper's Doctrine of Gifts and Its Effects Upon the Literary Success of 'The Leatherstocking Tales.'" Master of Arts degree, St. Louis University, 1967.

863 "The Real 'Natty' an Elder Brother." New York Historical Society, PROCEEDINGS 16 (1917):187-92. Reprinted from THE OTSEGO FARM, July 19, 1912.

Contends that Nathaniel Shipman, not David Shipman, was the real life model for Natty Bumppo.

864 Routh, James. "The Model of 'The Leather-stocking Tales.'" MODERN LANGUAGE NOTES 28 (March 1913):77-79.

      Routh claims that all five of the TALES are essentially the same in plot and characterization. The use of the same formula for the first three, which were produced in quick succession, is not surprising. Thirteen years elapsed before the fourth was written, however, and it is evident that C. had earlier devised a formula and that he was adhering to it even at this late date.

865 Russell, Jason Almus. "Cooper: Interpreter of the Real and the Historical Indian." JOURNAL OF AMERICAN HISTORY 23 (1st quarter 1929):41-71.

      Russell concludes that C's. Indian descriptions were historically accurate, that he was the first in American fiction to give serious treatment to Indian women, and that he drew his knowledge from the best sources available (personal contacts with Indians and from traditions and stories of the New York frontier).

866 Salamon, Lynda Brown. "Two Nineteenth Century American Views of History: James Fenimore Cooper and Francis Parkman." Ph.D. dissertation, University of Maryland, College Park, 1989.

      Examination of the L. S. TALES shows that C. viewed history as both static and cyclical. This pessimistic outlook was due, in part, to his Episcopal background.

867 Scharnhorst, Gary. "Had Their Mothers Only Known: Horatio Algier, Jr., Rewrites Cooper, Melville, and Twain." JOURNAL OF POPULAR CULTURE 15 (Winter 1981):175-82. Also in JOURNAL OF AMERICAN CULTURE 5 (Summer 1982):91-95.

      Algier often caricatured Leatherstocking and specific action scenes from the L. S. TALES.

868 Seed, David. "The Concept of Chivalry in Fenimore Cooper's 'Leatherstocking Tales.'" DUTCH QUARTERLY REVIEW 12 (1982):82-98.

      Not seen.

869 Sheppard, Keith Salisbury. "Natty Bumppo: Cooper's Americanized Adam." Ph.D. dissertation, Wayne State University, 1973.

      Natty Bumppo's racism, vanity, and hypocrisy have been seen by others as merely surface details. In reality, these characteristics point out America's national shortcomings and make Natty a truly American hero.

870 Siedlecki, Peter Anthony. "The Two Paths in Cooper's 'Leatherstocking Tales.'" Ph.D. dissertation, State University of New York at Buffalo, 1981.

      C. saw white expansion into the wilderness as immoral, but

unavoidable. Natty Bumppo, while never able to become a member of this society, was able to influence it and lessen its inherent evil.

871 Slotkin, Richard. REGENERATION THROUGH VIOLENCE: THE MYTHOLOGY OF THE AMERICAN FRONTIER, 1660-1860. Middletown, Conn.: Wesleyan University Press, 1973. Pp. 467-513.

    C. used the wilderness not only to illustrate the superiority of certain racial and cultural forces, but to aid in the establishment of social values and identity.

872 Smith, Burley G. "An Analysis of the Female Characters in Cooper's 'Leatherstocking Tales.'" Master of Arts degree, Bowling Green State University, 1960.

873 Smith, Henry Nash. "Consciousness and Social Order: The Theme of Transcendence in 'The Leatherstocking Tales.'" WESTERN AMERICAN LITERATURE 5 (Fall 1970):177-94.

    C was unable to accept Leatherstocking as the best that America had to offer. While the frontiersman may have embodied positive elements that could be found within both civilization and the savage existence, C. could not overlook the importance of order that was an integral part of a stratified society.

874 _____. VIRGIN LAND: THE AMERICAN WEST AS SYMBOL AND MYTH. Cambridge, Mass.: Harvard University Press, 1950. Pp. 59-70.

    The L. S. TALES do not form a major literary production, but they are symbolic of America's national expansionist adventure. C's. failure to resolve the conflict between his view of the social order and his ideas of freedom and nature created an ambiguity in his writing that he was unable to resolve.

875 Smith, Lewis. "History and Race in 'The Leatherstocking Tales.'" HIROSHIMA STUDIES IN ENGLISH LANGUAGE AND LITERATURE 20 (1975):1-12.

876 Stearns, Bertha Monica. "Nineteenth-Century Writers in the World of Art." ART IN AMERICA 40 (Winter 1952):29-41.

    Concerns paintings of scenes from the L. S. TALES by William Dunlap, Thomas Cole, Henry Inman, George Loring Brown, Alvan Fisher, and others.

877 Steeves, Edna. "'No Time for Fainting': The Frontier Woman in Some Early American Novels." AMERICAN EXPLORATION AND TRAVEL.

Edited by Steven E. Kagle. Bowling Green, Ohio: Bowling Green University Popular Press, 1979. Pp. 191-205.

C. was a Victorian and so are his women. They faint, are home bodies, and are moral inspirations. They also have courage, are resourceful, and act as a lady should.

878 Steinberg, Alan L. "James Fenimore Cooper: The Sentimental Frontier." SOUTH DAKOTA REVIEW 15 (Spring 1977):94-108.

Steinberg, in an attempt to correct the imbalance that has favored "psychological and archetypal criticism," evaluates the L. S. TALES as sentimental literature. He considers conflicts between good and evil and between morality and social class, as well as C's. attempt to create mythic and epic elements in his fiction.

879 Stern, Milton R. "American Values and Romantic Fiction." STUDIES IN AMERICAN FICTION 5 (Spring 1977):13-33.

Natty Bumppo possessed the ideals of a conservative pre-Jacksonian democrat. He functioned as the expresser of eighteenth century manners and property rights while subordinating himself to those persons of a higher social station.

880 Stockton, Edwin L., Jr. "The Influence of the Moravians Upon 'The Leather-stocking Tales.'" Ph.D. dissertation, Florida State University, 1960. Also in Moravian Historical Society, TRANSACTIONS, 1964.

C's. portrayal of the Indians was influenced by the writings of John Gottlieb Ernestus Heckewelder, a Moravian missionary. It was here that he found much information on Indian life and religion. It must be concluded, therefore, that C's. descriptions of the native Americans, for which he has been severely criticized, are probably very close to reality.

881 Stovall, Floyd. AMERICAN IDEALISM. Norman: University of Oklahoma Press, 1943. Pp. 31-34.

C. possessed the ideal situation for an author. He was near enough to the western frontier to know something about it, but far enough removed to be creative in its description.

882 Swann, Charles. "James Fenimore Cooper: Historical Novelist." AMERICAN FICTIONS: NEW READINGS. Edited by Richard Gray. London: Vision, 1983. Pp. 15-37.

C's. views on justice, law, and nature, and his treatment of American history.

883 Swigg, Richard. LAWRENCE, HARDY, AND AMERICAN

LITERATURE. London: Oxford University Press, 1972. Pp. 249-80.
On C's. concern for the creation of order and morality in the frontier society.

884 Terence, Martin. "Surviving on the Frontier: The Doubled Consciousness of Natty Bumppo." SOUTH ATLANTIC QUARTERLY 75 (Autumn 1976):447-59.
Natty Bumppo's relationship with Chingachgook allowed C. to protect Natty's innocence while vindicating it through experience.

885 Tetley-Jones, Ines. SENTIMENTALISM VERSUS ADVENTURE AND SOCIAL ENGAGEMENT: A STUDY OF J. F. COOPER'S 'LEATHER-STOCKING TALES.'" Heildelberg, 1970.
C. began his career writing in the vein of the English sentimental novelists. He soon discovered that he was better suited to the historical romance. This genre allowed him to create more masculine plots that, although never completely free of sentiment, provided a realism that was both new and completely American.

886 Thigpen, Buelah Virginia. "Indians of the 'Leather-stocking Tales': A Study of the Noble and Ignoble Savage." Ph.D. dissertation, East Texas University, 1981.
C. was unable to fully accept the Romantic idea of the noble savage and, therefore, could not portray him as such.

887 Tompkins, Jane P. "No Apologies for the Iroquois: A New Way to Read the Leatherstocking Novels." CRITICISM 23 (Winter 1981):24-41. Also in SENSATIONAL DESIGNS: THE CULTURAL WORK OF AMERICAN FICTION. New York: Oxford University Press, 1985. Pp. 94-121.
The L. S. TALES should not be viewed from the perspective of historical or social realism, but as allegory. This allows the reader/critic to accept those aspects of C's. fiction for which he was most often taken to task, and concentrate on the social and political thought expressed.

888 "Town Marks Grave of 'Natty Bumppo.'" NEW YORK TIMES, July 4, 1937, Sect. II, p. 3.
The grave of Nathaniel Foster, Jr., of Ava, N. Y., the real-life Natty Bumppo according to this article.

889 Vivian, Dorothy Sherman. "The Protagonist in the Works of Sarmiento and Cooper." HISPANIA 48 (December 1965):806-10.
Both C., with Natty Bumppo, and Domingo Faustino Sarmiento, with Facundo Quiroga, attempted to show that man is a product of his

environment. They, however, arrived at different conclusions. According to C., civilization acted to destroy morality, whereas Sarmiento saw its preservation only by increasing the spread of modern society.

890 Vlach, John M. "Fenimore Cooper's Leatherstocking as Folk Hero." NEW YORK FOLKLORE QUARTERLY 27 (December 1971):323-38.

    The widespread popularity of Daniel Boone and Davy Crockett, due to both oral tradition and the written word, led C. to believe that a fictional hero cut out of the same mold would prove equally appealing to a country eager for national heroes.

891 Wade, Beatrice G. "Cooper's 'Leatherstocking Tales': The American Epic." Master of Arts degree, Boston University, 1947.

892 Walker, Warren S. "Buckskin West: Leatherstocking at High Noon." NEW YORK FOLKLORE QUARTERLY 24 (June 1968):88-102.

    The life of the frontiersman, including Natty Bumppo's, possesses elements of myth, melodrama, and morality not common to other types in American history. For this reason, the western hero has become the American folk hero.

893 _____. "The Frontiersman as Recluse and Redeemer." NEW YORK FOLKLORE QUARTERLY 16 (Summer 1960):110-22.

    Presents Natty Bumppo as an individualized symbol of the frontiersman heroic myth.

894 _____. "Natty Bumppo's 'Anan.'" AMERICAN SPEECH 28 (December 1953):309.

    Natty Bumppo's use of the word 'anan,' an archaic form of 'anon,' is illustrative of C's. background as a sailor. As late as 1867 this term was listed as a standard sea term.

895 _____, ed. LEATHERSTOCKING AND THE CRITICS. Chicago: Scott Foresman Co., 1965.

896 Wallace, Paul A. "Cooper's Indians." NEW YORK HISTORY 35 (October 1954):423-46.

    The Indians found in C's. L. S. TALES are not accurately portrayed, either historically or in their day to day life. Much of the blame for this fact must be placed upon John Heckewelder's ACCOUNT OF THE HISTORY, MANNERS, AND CUSTOMS OF THE INDIAN NATIONS. This book mistakenly divided the Indians of the forests into two groups: one good, one bad. C. seized upon this idea when he realized that it could provide him, not only with the source for action and color in his novels, but with moral pronouncements as well.

897 West, E. "James Fenimore Cooper and the Leatherstocking Saga." AMERICAN HISTORY ILLUSTRATED 18 (1983):8-15.
        Not seen.

898 Wheeler, Edward J., ed. "Introduction." THE LEATHERSTOCKING TALES. Uncas edition. New York: Current Literature Publishing Co., 1907.

899 Wheeler, Otis B. "Faulkner's Wilderness." AMERICAN LITERATURE 31 (May 1959):127-36.
        If the forest is God's work, how then does one rationalize its destruction by an advancing civilization?   For C., there would be no satisfactory answer. Emotionally he sided with Natty Bumppo, but intellectually he sided with civilization. Faulkner, on the other hand, possessed of the twentieth century view that does not always ascribe progress to western civilization, had no such inner division.

900 Wieland, Dennis Paul. "The Transformation of the Cooper Mythos in the Writings of Thomas McGuane." Ph.D. dissertation, Indiana University of Pennsylvania, 1989.
        McGuane as C's. heir has transformed eight aspects of the American romance to modern day writing: superiority of the mythical hero, frontier settings, the hero's bond with savages, society as antagonist, failure of the hero to fall in love, the position of women, the frontier as sport, and mythmaking.

901 Winn,   H.   Harbour,   III.   "Malamud's   Uncas."   NOTES   ON CONTEMPORARY LITERATURE 5, pp. 13-14.
        Not seen.   Citation   from   AMERICAN   LITERARY SCHOLARSHIP, 1975, p. 341.

902 Witkowsky, Paul William. "The Idea of Order: Frontier Societies in the Fiction of Cooper, Simms, Hawthorne, and Wister." Ph.D. dissertation, University of North Carolina, 1978.
        Natty Bumppo, in THE PIONEERS, is a sympathetic character who must eventually be ruled by civil, rather than natural, law. Ishmael Bush, in THE PRAIRIE, on the other hand, understands the need for rule by law and so escapes becoming an outlaw.

903 Wood, Ruth Kedzie. "The Leatherstocking Trail." BOOKMAN (New York) 41 (July 1915):513-21.

On the local scenery that C. drew from while creating the L. S. TALES.

904 Wyatt, Bryant N. "Cooper's Leatherstocking: Romance and the Limits of Character." COLLEGE LANGUAGE ASSOCIATION JOURNAL 29 (March 1986):295-308.

The mythic approach to analysis of C's. fiction espoused by D. H. Lawrence works best for the L. S. TALES.

905 Zanger, Jules. "The Frontiersman in Popular Fiction, 1820-60." THE FRONTIER RE-EXAMINED. Edited by John Francis McDermott. Urbana: University of Illinois Press, 1967. Pp. 141-53.

Leatherstocking possesses characteristics common to the real life Daniel Boone and Davy Crockett, but Boone finally dominates C's. creation as the fictional hero becomes more and more alienated from civilization. Leatherstocking was also given attitudes that did not meet the nineteenth century model of the frontiersman: snobbishness, servility, and a sympathetic outlook toward the Indians.

906 Zoellner, Robert H. "Conceptual Ambivalence in Cooper's Leatherstocking." AMERICAN LITERATURE 31 (January 1960):397-420.

Interpretations of Natty Bumppo that ascribe "mythic-heroic or mythic-Adamic" characteristics to him are not convincing, for C. failed to create the asocial hero that is inherent in Adamism. Although he often moved his character toward the mythic-heroic figure others have seen, C's. need to make social statements invariably put Natty back in his place, far from the position of symbolic American hero.

907 Zolla, Elémire. THE WRITER AND THE SHAMAN: A MORPHOLOGY OF THE AMERICAN INDIAN. Translated by Raymond Rosenthal. Harcourt, Brace, Jovanovich, 1973. Pp. 87-94.

C's. portrayal of the Indian was a romantic one that resulted from his contradictory beliefs in social progress, political conservatism, deism, and tolerance.

The Pioneers (1823)

Articles and Reviews Contemporary with Cooper

908 ALBION (New York), April 19, 1823.

Review of a dramatization--looked forward to with high hopes.

909 THE ALBUM 3 (May 1823):155-78.
      THE PIONEERS possesses the descriptions, characters, and spirited dialogue found in THE SPY, but it lacks a story, thus lessening reader interest.

910 "American Literature." MUSEUM OF FOREIGN LITERATURE, SCIENCE AND ART 5 (July 1824):87-106.
      C. is a dramatic writer who shows man's vices, foibles, and distinctions, but Brockden Brown is more passionate and superior as a narrator.

911 Brainard, John G. C. THE POEMS OF JOHN G. C. BRAINARD. Hartford: S. Andrus & Son, 1847. Pp. 94-96.
      A poem on Leatherstocking's removal from the village of Templeton as he set forth for the unexplored West.

912 BRITISH MAGAZINE 1 (April 1823):65.
      Authentic and original.

913 EXAMINER, no. 790 (March 16, 1823):185-86.

914 [Gardiner, W. H.] "Cooper's Novels." NORTH AMERICAN REVIEW 23 (July 1826):150-201.
      While admitting to well drawn characters and descriptions, Gardiner's review is reserved in its praise. Willing to acknowledge C. as America's greatest novelist until someone better was able to take the title from him.

915 LITERARY GAZETTE 7 (October 18, 1823):661-63.
      Rather than a novel, THE PIONEERS resembles a series of sketches devoted to scenery, customs, and people.

916 LITERARY REGISTER, no. 39 (March 29, 1823):197-98.

917 LITERARY WORLD 7 (December 7, 1850):456.
      On the new edition--an exciting book with artistic landscapes. Of great excitement to the reader.

918 MINERVA 1 (February 8, 1823):348-50.
      C's. descriptions are tedious and uninteresting, his characters are mediocre, and the Indian language is poorly presented. The worst feature of the book is its "Preface."

919 MONTHLY LITERARY REGISTER 3 (March 1823):218-20.
　　　　Includes an attack on critics who extol foreign literature at the expense of English.

920 MONTHLY MAGAZINE 4 n.s. (July 1827):84-85.
　　　　Inferior to THE PRAIRIE although some of the descriptive scenes are excellent. The humor is similar to that of Smollett.

921 NEW MONTHLY MAGAZINE 30 (May 1830):198.
　　　　On an adaptation of THE PIONEERS at the Covent Garden Theatre. A book that is unrivalled as fiction, but when placed on the stage is impossible to reproduce from a descriptive viewpoint. Neither have the characters or dialogue been rendered effective for the theater.

922 NEW YORK AMERICAN, January 13, 1824.

923 NEW YORK SPECTATOR, January 17, February 4, 1823.

924 NILES' WEEKLY REGISTER 23 (February 8, 1823):354.
　　　　By noon of the day of its publication THE PIONEERS had sold 3,500 copies.

925 _____ 24 (March 22, 1823):34.
　　　　A book that will be widely read for it possesses excellent characters and descriptions. Includes comments on Indian John and references to Scott.

926 Paulding, James Kirke. KÖNINGSMARKE, THE LONG FINN. Vol. 2. New York: Charles Wiley, 1823. Book VI, Chapt. 1, pp. 67-74.
　　　　A defense of THE PIONEERS against those critics who claim it is "vulgar and commonplace."

927 PORT FOLIO 15, 5th series (March 1823):230-48.
　　　　THE PIONEERS is superior to THE SPY, but will probably not be as widely read for it is far less interesting.

928 _____ 15, 5th series (June 1823):520.
　　　　On the several paintings by American artists that have been inspired by THE PIONEERS.

929 REPOSITORY OF MODERN LITERATURE 1 (1823):177-92.

930 SARTAIN'S UNION MAGAZINE OF LITERATURE AND ART 8

(April 1851):286.
    On the new edition--an "inviting series" with useful prefaces.

931 Smiles, Samuel, ed. MEMOIR AND CORRESPONDENCE OF THE
LATE JOHN MURRAY. Vol. 2. London: John Murray, 1891. Pp. 134-35.
    Letter from C. to Murray dated November 29, 1822, on the pub-
lication of THE PIONEERS.

932 "The 'Wilderness' and 'The Pioneers.'" NEW-YORK MIRROR 1 (August 2, 9, 16, 1823):4-5, 12-13, 20-21.
    The scenery and characters are skillfully done.   The few faults
found are minor.

Articles from Cooper's Death to the Present

933 Anderson, Douglas. "Cooper's Improbable Pictures in 'The Pioneers.'"
STUDIES IN AMERICAN FICTION 14 (Spring 1986):35-48.
    An imaginative writer, vivid descriptions, but not always real life.
One reads THE PIONEERS not for its accuracy, but for the scenes that are
created in the mind's eye.

934 Barton, Robert. "Natty's Trial, or the Triumph of Hiram Doolittle."
CIMARRON REVIEW 36 (July 1976):29-37.
    In the end, both Natty Bumppo (the symbol of male power) and
Judge Temple (the symbol of civilization) find themselves to be powerless.
Their inability to act leaves the way clear for the triumph of Hiram Doolittle
who is unhindered by moral considerations.

935 Bercovitch, Sacvan. "Huckleberry Bumppo: A Comparison of 'Tom Saw-
yer' and 'The Pioneers.'" MARK TWAIN JOURNAL 14 (Summer 1968):1-4.
    Comparisons between Twain's and C's.   characters: the judges
(Thatcher and Temple), Tom and Edwards, Becky and Elizabeth, Huck and
Natty, the Indians (Joe and John), and the blacks (Jim and Aggy).

936 Brenner, Gerry. "Cooper's 'Composite Order': 'The Pioneers' as
Structured Art." STUDIES IN THE NOVEL 2 (Fall 1970):264-75.
    Contrary to many other critics, Brenner finds C's.   fiction to be
"controlled and unified."

937 Butler, Michael D. "Sons of Oliver Edwards: Or, the Other American
Hero." WESTERN AMERICAN LITERATURE 12 (1977):53-66.
    Comparison of other western heroes, in both literature and the
movies, to Oliver Edwards and Natty Bumppo.

938 Clark, Michael. "Benjamin Franklin and Cooper's 'The Pioneers.'" ENGLISH LANGUAGE NOTES 24 (September 1986):73-78.
>Judge Temple is modeled on Franklin (prudence and success).

939 _____. "Biblical Allusion and William Cooper in James Fenimore Cooper's 'The Pioneers.'" UNIVERSITY OF DAYTON REVIEW 18 (Summer 1987):105-11.
>Not seen.

940 _____. "Caves, Houses, and Temples in James Fenimore Cooper's 'The Pioneers.'" MODERN LANGUAGE STUDIES 16 (Summer 1986):227-36.
>Architectural structures as symbol and metaphor.

941 _____. "The Oak in Cooper's 'The Pioneers.'" ENGLISH LANGUAGE NOTES 22 (September 1984):53-55.
>Symbolism of the oak.

942 Cohen, Lester H. "What's in a Name?: The Presence of the Victim in 'The Pioneers.'" MASSACHUSETTS REVIEW 16 (August 1975):688-98.
>Chingachgook, the last of the Mohicans and the final victim of a philosophy that decreed that the extermination of one race is justified if a perfect society results, serves both a moral and psychological purpose. The frontiersmen, unable to come to terms with the living presence of their deeds, attempt to deny them through conversion and the renaming of Chingachgook. He becomes John Mohegan--Indian John--and thus, no longer a reminder of their actions, but a member of the white society.

943 Davie, Donald. THE HEYDAY OF SIR WALTER SCOTT. London: Routledge & Kegan Paul, 1961. Pp. 129-47.
>Sees THE PIONEERS as a civilization/wilderness conflict. Compares his views with those in Smith's VIRGIN LAND (item no. 874).

944 Dekker, George. "Sir Walter Scott, the Angel of Hadley, and American Historical Fiction." JOURNAL OF AMERICAN STUDIES 17 (August 1983):211-27.
>C's. retelling of Scott's Angel of Hadley story was an attempt to challenge the master's literary superiority and to show how fictionalized events from American history should be dealt with.

945 Doubleday, Neal Frank. VARIETY OF ATTEMPT: BRITISH AND AMERICAN FICTION IN THE EARLY NINETEENTH CENTURY. Lincoln & London: University of Nebraska Press, 1976. Pp. 128-46.
>Praises C. for his ability to design a novel that satisfied the needs

of the reader, while allowing the author to indulge in socially relevant commentary.

946 Edinger, Catarina. "Machismo and Androgyny in Mid-nineteenth-century Brazilian and American Novels." COMPARATIVE LITERATURE STUDIES 27 (1990):124-39.
        It is not the Brazilian novelists of the 1800s whose writings must be considered "macho," but C. and other Americans who saw women as inferior and were insensitive to them.

947 Faver, Susan Pauly. "The Narrative Tie that Binds: Women's Friendship as Aesthetic and Political Strategy in Four Nineteenth Century Novels." Ph.D. dissertation, University of Arkansas, 1988.
        Female friendship from an ideological, rather than a psycho/sexual viewpoint.

948 Finkelstein, Sidney. "Six Ways of Looking at Reality." MAINSTREAM 13 (December 1960):31-42.
        Finkelstein, using a quotation from THE PIONEERS, illustrates that the writer who observes reality is often the one who possesses the greatest originality.

949 Francis, Ian. "James Fenimore Cooper's 'The Pioneers': A Criticism of the Development of American Civilization." OCCASIONAL PAPER (Kano) 1 (1975):54-73.

950 Gallagher, Mary Kathleen. "From Natty to Bigger: The Innocent Criminal in American Fiction." Ph.D. dissertation, University of North Carolina at Chapel Hill, 1981.
        Natty Bumppo as an innocent criminal compared to characters from THE MARBLE FAUN, BILLY BUD, "Life in the Iron Mills," AN AMERICAN TRAGEDY, and NATIVE SON.

951 Gladsky, Thomas S. "The Beau Ideal and Cooper's 'The Pioneers.'" STUDIES IN THE NOVEL 20 (Spring 1988):43-54.
        The characters who are meant to be imitated are members of the aristocracy and show leadership qualities and good character.

952 Grossman, James, ed. "Introduction." THE PIONEERS. New York: Washington Square Press, 1962.

953 Hedges, William L. WASHINGTON IRVING: AN AMERICAN STUDY. Goucher College Series. Baltimore: Johns Hopkins Press, 1965.

Pp. 174-79.

Hedges draws parallels between Irving's BRACEBRIDGE HALL and C's. THE PIONEERS.

954 House, Kay Seymour. "James Fenimore Cooper. 'The Pioneers.'" THE AMERICAN NOVEL; FROM JAMES FENIMORE COOPER TO WILLIAM FAULKNER. Edited by Wallace Stegner. New York: Basic Books, 1965. Pp. 1-12.

On C's. portrayal of America in this one novel. He shows a concern for both the progress of civilization and civilization's invasion of the land.

955 Howard, Leon, ed. "Introduction." THE PIONEERS. New York: Holt, Rinehart & Winston, 1959.

956 Jones, David E. "Temple in the Promised Land: Old Testament Parallel in Cooper's 'The Pioneers.'" AMERICAN LITERATURE 57 (March 1985):68-78.

One must view the settling of Cooperstown/Templeton in the context of C's. religious beliefs. He saw the development of the town as a parallel to the Old Testament era of King Solomon, as a New World promised land, and as a means of laying foundations for lasting institutions and justice.

957 Kehler, Joel R. "Architectural Dialecticalism in Cooper's 'The Pioneers.'" TEXAS STUDIES IN LITERATURE AND LANGUAGE 18 (Spring 1976):124-34.

The village of Templeton represents one point in the novel. Natty Bumppo's hunt is a second and opposite one. It is in the space between these two divergent points that C. chooses to reveal truth and present his object lessons.

958 Krieg, Joann Peck. "The Transmogrification of Faerie Land into Prairie Land." JOURNAL OF AMERICAN STUDIES 19 (August 1985):200-23.

C's. use of landscape and sources from Spenser's THE FAERIE QUEEN.

959 Lindberg, Gary H. "Shape Shifting and Self-reliance." THE CONFIDENCE MAN IN LITERATURE. Oxford: Oxford University Press, 1982. Pp. 140-60.

The character Richard Jones is a type not to be trusted. He possesses a slap-dash, boastful manner that, if emulated, could lead society to lose its sense of order and move away from established institutions.

960 Mills, Nicolaus. "Prison and Society in Nineteenth-century American Fiction." WESTERN HUMANITIES REVIEW 24 (Autumn 1970):325-31.

That C. viewed American society as a prison, in the sense that it subordinated personal freedom to property values, is shown by Natty Bumppo's imprisonment for hunting deer out of season.

961 Monteiro, George. "Fenimore Cooper's Yankee Woodsman." MIDWEST FOLKLORE 12 (Winter 1962):209-16.

C. was the first American writer to depict the professional woodsman. His character, Billy Kirby, probably influenced the later development of Paul Bunyan.

962 Nelson, Andrew. "James Cooper and George Croghan." PHILOLOGICAL QUARTERLY 20 (January 1, 1941):69-73.

George Croghan, a Cooperstown resident who was granted a tract of land prior to the Revolutionary War, but who lost it due to Tory sympathies, died a poor man. His heirs' attempts to reclaim this grant were foiled when William Cooper gained title to it in 1786. Fenimore Cooper seized upon this piece of local history when he created the Temple and Effingham families in THE PIONEERS.

963 Okada, Ryoichi. "Irreconcilable Conflicts in 'The Pioneers.'" CHIBA REVIEW 10 (1988):1-18.

Considers wilderness *vs*. civilization and fatherhood.

964 Owens, Jill T. "Humor in James Fenimore Cooper's 'The Pioneers.'" Arkansas Philological Association, PUBLICATIONS 10 (Fall 1984):49-64.

Not seen.

965 Palmer, F. L. "Dialect Words from 'The Pioneers.'" DIALECT NOTES 5 (1922):185-86.

A list of dialect works with their meanings.

966 Paul, Jay S. "Education of Elizabeth Temple." STUDIES IN THE NOVEL 9 (Summer 1977):187-94.

E. Temple's role in the novel--C's. use of her point of view, observations, and understanding.

967 Philbrick, Thomas. "Cooper's 'The Pioneers': Origins and Structure." Modern Language Association of America, PUBLICATIONS 79 (December 1964):579-93.

Contrary to Cowie, Ringe, and Davie (item nos. 374, 586, 943), Philbrick views THE PIONEERS as a "fully integrated work of art."

968 Robinson, E. Arthur. "Conservation in Cooper's 'The Pioneers.'" Modern Language Association of America, PUBLICATIONS 82 (December 1967):564-78.

The characters in THE PIONEERS can be divided into three groups, each representing a different outlook on preservation of the world's resources. The most numerous are those who plundered nature for their own advancement with little concern for the future (Richard Jones, Billy Kirby). The second group, represented by Judge Temple, sought means of preserving raw materials for future use. Lastly, there were those like Natty Bumppo who could accept neither the waste of the settlers nor the demands for conservation that placed limits on man's freedom.

969 Ross, Morton L. "Cooper's 'The Pioneers" and the Ethnographic Impulse." AMERICAN STUDIES 16 (Fall 1975):29-39.

C's. role as recorder of local life and events.

970 Schachterle, Lance. "The Three 1823 editions of James Fenimore Cooper's 'The Pioneers.'" American Antiquarian Society, PROCEEDINGS 84 (April 17, 1974):219-32.

These three editions prove that C. did take pains to revise and correct the prose style for which he has so often been attacked.

971 Schaub, Thomas Hill. "'Cut in Plain Marble': The Language of the Tomb in 'The Pioneers.'" THE GREEN AMERICAN TRADITION: ESSAYS AND POEMS FOR SHERMAN PAUL. Edited by Daniel H. Peck. Baton Rouge: Louisiana State University Press, 1989. Pp. 58-74.

Uses the cemetery scene to illustrate the relationship between the meanings of events and the memories evoked by them. Concludes that if society cannot remember its past, then it is incapable of capturing and retaining that which was its original promise.

972 Scheckter, John. "History, Possibility, and Romance in 'The Pioneers.'" ESSAYS IN LITERATURE 8 (Spring 1981):33-44.

C. used the romance, combining it with a moral stance, to illustrate how one could reconcile values of a modern society (materialism) with those of the wilderness.

973 Shirkey, Evelyn Loyd. "Cooper's 'The Pioneers': Origins, Components, and Meaning." Ph.D. dissertation, University of Wisconsin, 1979.

Includes C's. theory of fiction, other writers as models, publication data, reception of the book, narrative and descriptive techniques, characterization, comedic elements, and the forest/civilization conflict.

974 Spiller, Robert E., ed. "Afterward." THE PIONEERS. New York: New American Library, 1964.

975 Stineback, David C. "'This Comes of Settling a Country!' James Fenimore Cooper's 'The Pioneers.'" SHIFTING WORLD: SOCIAL CHANGE AND NOSTALGIA IN THE AMERICAN NOVEL. Lewisburg, Pa.: Bucknell University Press, 1976. Pp. 23-42.

THE PIONEERS does not possess the qualities of myth that were present in the rest of the L. S. TALES, but instead is a highly realistic novel. As such, C. was unable to provide final answers to questions of social justice and change that formed such a dominant part of the book. Instead, he remained noncommittal about the final outcome, allowing his hero to escape to the West beyond the bounds of a stable social order.

976 Thomas, Brook. "'The Pioneers', or the Sources of American Legal History: A Critical Tale." AMERICAN QUARTERLY 36 (Spring 1984):86-111. Also in CROSS-EXAMINATIONS OF LAW AND LITERATURE; COOPER, HAWTHORNE, STOWE, AND MELVILLE. Cambridge: Cambridge University Press, 1987. Pp. 21-44.

C's. view of the law and legal system as it relates to both his conservative and democratic visions in general, and to Judge Temple and Natty Bumppo in particular.

977 Valenti, Peter. "'The Ordering of God's Providence': Law and Landscape in 'The Pioneers.'" STUDIES IN AMERICAN FICTION 7 (Autumn 1979):191-207.

Landscape acts as a structural device that helps to determine narrative, theme, and language.

978 Van Valen, Nelson. "James Fenimore Cooper and the Conservative Schism." NEW YORK HISTORY 62 (July 1981):289-306.

Claims that the first "conservative schism" (resource exploiters *vs.* preservers) came not after the Civil War, but with C's. PIONEERS in 1823.

979 Winston, Robert Paul. "From Farmer James to Natty Bumppo: The Frontier and the Early American Romance." Ph.D. dissertation, University of Wisconsin, Madison, 1979.

C. and other authors of his age possessed ambivalence toward the developing national identity. This is shown by heroes who operated in both the wilderness and society and whose experiences led to social tension and instability.

The Last of the Mohicans (1826)

Articles and Reviews Contemporary with Cooper

980 LA BELLE ASSEMBLÉE 3, 3d series (1826):218.

981 ESCRITOR 1 (February 11, 1846):21-22.
A genuine talent who has successfully bound realism in the guise of romance.

982 [Gardiner, W. H.] "Cooper's Novels." NORTH AMERICAN REVIEW 23 (July 1826):150-201.
C. goes out of his way to put his characters into impossible situations that do nothing for the plot except clutter it with far too much action.

983 LADY'S MAGAZINE 7 n.s. (April 1826):210-13.
C. possesses little ability in creation of plot or in composition. This results in a novel of no great interest. His scenic and character descriptions, however, illustrate that he can write well.

984 LITERARY CHRONICLE AND WEEKLY REVIEW 8 (July 29, 1826): 469-73.
An interesting, fresh, and well described romance that enhances C's. already considerable fame. His portraits of Indian life and morality are also praised.

985 LITERARY GAZETTE 10 (April 1, 1826):198-200.
If the ability to maintain interest and paint vivid characters and scenery are criterion for talent, then C. has written a highly recommendable novel.

986 LITERARY WORLD 7 (October 19, 1850):312.
On the revised edition--real life scenery created with a faithfully presented narrative.

987 LIVERPOOL REPOSITORY 1 (July, August 1826):384, 448.
Praises C's. use of religion. Believes him to be superior to Scott as an imparter of information.

988 MONTHLY REVIEW 2 new & imp. series (June 1826):122-31.
C. has woven a tale of incredible suspense whose ending need not have culminated in the tragedy it did. His portraits of Indian life and character

are truthfully and accurately done.

989 [Neal, John]. "The Last American Novel." LONDON MAGAZINE 5 n.s. (May 1826):27-31. Reprinted in MUSEUM OF FOREIGN LITERATURE, SCIENCE AND ART 2 n.s. (July 1826):57-59.

The worst of C's. novels--tedious, improbable, unimaginative and redundant.

990 NEW LONDON LITERARY GAZETTE 1 (August 25, 1827):182-83.

991 NEW-YORK REVIEW AND ATHENEUM MAGAZINE 2 (March 1826):285-92.

As an imaginative writer C. exhibits extraordinary power. The female characters (Cora and Alice) are delightful creations that are superior to any of his previous ones. If the author fails at all, it is in his ability to keep his characters' motives consistent with their actions.

992 "North American Indians." UNITED STATES REVIEW AND LITERARY GAZETTE 2 (April 1827):40-53.

Attacks C's. adoption of many of Heckewelder's Indian "absurdities and improbabilities."

993 PANORAMIC MISCELLANY 1 (April 30, 1826):533-34.

The most vivid and truthful portrait of Indians that has yet been written.

994 PHILADELPHIA NATIONAL GAZETTE, February 18, 1826.

Not seen. Citation from Boynton, AMERICAN CONTEMPORARY FICTION, p. 139.

995 UNITED STATES LITERARY GAZETTE 3 (March 15, 1826):469.

Plan to dramatize THE LAST OF THE MOHICANS announced.

996 _____ 4 (May 1, 1826):87-94.

THE LAST OF THE MOHICANS is superior to those of a similar type that have preceded it. It is, however, capable of improvement. The plot is simple and has little variety, for characters are dragged from one improbable event to the other. There is little development of personality or emotions. The delineation of Hawkeye is the most successful characterization, the Indians are well drawn, but Colonel Munro is a failure.

Articles from Cooper's Death to the Present

997 Allen, Dennis W. "'By All the Truth of Signs': James Fenimore Cooper's 'The Last of the Mohicans.'" STUDIES IN AMERICAN FICTION 9 (Autumn 1981):159-79.

Considers THE LAST OF THE MOHICANS from the viewpoint of semiotic differences in Indian and white societies.

998 Beard, James, ed. "Afterward." THE LAST OF THE MOHICANS. New York: New American Library, 1962.

999 Bergmann, Frank. "The Meaning of the Indians and Their Land in Cooper's 'The Last of the Mohicans.'" UPSTATE LITERATURE: ESSAYS IN MEMORY OF THOMAS F. O'DONNELL. Syracuse: University of Syracuse Press, 1985. Pp. 117-27.

C. asked for a more racially tolerant world than he lived in, but his vagueness illustrates that he often considered his readers' opinions.

1000 Birrell, T. A. " Preface to Cooper's "Last of the Mohicans.'" FROM COOPER TO PHILIP ROTH: ESSAYS ON AMERICAN LITERATURE. Edited by J. Bakker and D. R. M. Wilk. Amsterdam: Rodopi, 1980. Pp. 1-19.

C. created a new literary genre with THE LAST OF THE MOHICANS--dramatic poetry as fiction.

1001 Blakemore, Steven. "Strange Tongues: Cooper's Fiction of Language in 'The Last of the Mohicans.'" EARLY AMERICAN LITERATURE 19 (Spring 1984):21-41.

If the reader listens to C's. language it is clear that it is used as a means of telling us as much about itself as about the world in which it functioned. It then no longer becomes verbose, but is essential to the theme.

1002 _____. "Structure, History, Language, and Transformation in James Fenimore Cooper's 'The Last of the Mohicans.'" Ph.D. dissertation, Marquette University, 1981.

Examination of four thematic elements that suggest a reappraisal of C.

1003 Bradley, Viola. "The Contrast of Cooper's 'The Last of the Mohicans' and Simms' 'The Yemassee.'" Master of Arts degree, Auburn University, 1944.

1004 Burgess, Anthony. "Said Mr. Cooper to His Wife: 'You Know, I Could Write Something Better Than That.'" NEW YORK TIMES, "Magazine Section", May 7, 1972, pp. 108, 112+.
   Deals largely with THE LAST OF THE MOHICANS and C's. use of language. Concludes that while C's. writings exhibit many faults, he had no predecessor to serve as his guide.

1005 Butler, Michael D. "Narrative Structure and Historical Process in 'The Last of the Mohicans.'" AMERICAN LITERATURE 48 (May 1976):117-39.
   A novel not only about the last Mohican, but also about the first of the Americans. Uncas and Duncan are used to illustrate the demise of a European civilization and its replacement by a purely American one.

1006 Clark, Robert. "'The Last of the Mohicans': The Last of the Iroquois." HISTORY, IDEOLOGY, AND MYTH IN AMERICAN FICTION, 1823-1852. New York: St. Martins Press, 1984. Pp. 79-95.
   On C. and historical truth, his inversion of it, and his use of Heckewelder's HISTORY.

1007 Cooke, Agnes Spofford, ed. "Introduction." THE LAST OF THE MOHICANS. New York, Boston, etc.: Silver, Burdett & Co., 1901.

1008 "Cooper First Edition Auctioned for $3,200." NEW YORK TIMES, February 28, 1931, p. 39.

1009 Dargan, E. Preston. "Balzac and Cooper: 'Les Chouans.'" MODERN PHILOLOGY 13 (August 1915):193-213.
   A comparison of Balzac's LES CHOUANS and THE LAST OF THE MOHICANS. Dargan concludes that Balzac borrowed descriptions, names, characters, customs, and incidents from C.

1010 Darnell, Donald. "Uncas as Hero: The 'Ubi Sunt' Formula in 'The Last of the Mohicans.'" AMERICAN LITERATURE 37 (November 1965):259-66.
   Uncas, whose importance appears minor at first, eventually moves to a position of dominance in THE LAST OF THE MOHICANS. It is C's. skillful handling of this character that gives tragic, mythic, and epic elements to the book.

1011 Davenport, Basil, ed. "Introduction." THE LAST OF THE MOHICANS. New York: Dodd, Mead, 1951.

1012 Dekker, George. "Lilies That Fester: 'The Last of the Mohicans' and 'The Woman Who Rode Away.'" NEW LEFT REVIEW no. 28 (November-

December 1964):75-84.

Miscegenation in THE LAST OF THE MOHICANS provided the vehicle by which C. was able to investigate the more general problem of race relations.

1013 Donovan, Ellen Renee. "Narrative Authority in Nineteenth-Century American Literature: A Study of Dialogic Structures." Ph.D. dissertation, University of Wisconsin, Madison, 1988.

The narrative function is not solely reserved for the narrator, but is assumed by other character voices as well.

1014 Dunbar, John B., ed. "Introduction." THE LAST OF THE MOHI-CANS. Boston: Ginn & Co., 1898.

C's. backwoodsmen and Indians are drawn with great accuracy and the others, including the women, with much originality.

1015 Foster, Edward Halsey. THE CIVILIZED WILDERNESS: BACK-GROUNDS TO AMERICAN ROMANTIC LITERATURE, 1817-1860. New York: Free Press, a Division of Macmillan Publishing Co., 1975. Pp. 28-29.

Foster suggests that many of the landscapes pictured by C. were sites well known to travellers. A deeper appreciation of their value was the logical result of C's. historical and literary interest in them.

1016 French, David P. "James Fenimore Cooper and Fort William Henry." AMERICAN LITERATURE 32 (March 1960):28-38.

C's. selection of the subject of the Fort Henry massacre was a predictable one, his use of historical fact did not give way to literary effect, and the character of Duncan Heyward can be identified with Lt. Col. John Young of the Royal American regiment.

1017 Haberly, David T. "Women and Indians: 'The Last of the Mohicans' and the Captivity Tradition." AMERICAN QUARTERLY 28 (Fall 1976):431-43.

On the use of women as a means of reconciling the beauties of nature and the benefits of westward migration, with the barbarity of the Indians.

1018 Hale, Edward Everett, ed. "Introduction." THE LAST OF THE MOHICANS. New York: Heritage Press, 1932.

1019 Halleck, Reuben Post, ed. "Introduction." THE LAST OF THE MOHICANS. New York & Boston: Leach, Shewell & Co., 1898.

1020 "'Hawkeye' the Nickname for Iowans." ANNALS OF IOWA: A MAG-
AZINE OF HISTORY 31, 3d series (July 1952):380-81.
    In 1838, twelve years after the publication of THE LAST OF
THE MOHICANS, Iowa, due to the publicity of Judge David Rorer of Bur-
lington, acquired the nickname of the "Hawkeye" state.

1021 Heller, Louis G. "Two Pequot Names in American Literature." AMER-
ICAN SPEECH 36 (February 1961):54-57.
    On the source for the name Uncas.

1022 Holden, James Austin. "'The Last of the Mohicans', Cooper's Historical
Inventions, and His Cave." New York State Historical Association, PRO-
CEEDINGS 16 (1917):212-55.
    A chronology of historical inaccuracy in THE LAST OF THE
MOHICANS.

1023 Inglis, John A. "Colonel George Monro and the Defence of Fort William Henry, 1757." Society of Antiquaries of Scotland, PROCEEDINGS 2,
5th series (1916):267-74.
    C. presented many details about Col. Monro in THE LAST OF
THE MOHICANS, none of which, with the exception of his nationality, was
accurate. He even spelled the Scotsman's name incorrectly.

1024 J., W. H. "'The Last of the Mohicans' and the Cinema." NOTES AND
QUERIES (London) 185 (July 3, 1943):9-10.
    Questions the usefulness of the motion picture industry's insis-
tence on mediocre renderings of great classics such as THE LAST OF THE
MOHICANS.

1025 Jacobs, Edward Croney. "A Possible Debt to Cooper." POE STUDIES
9 (June 1976):23.
    It is probable that Poe borrowed the motto "Nemo me impune la-
cessit", used in THE CASK OF AMONTILLADA, from THE LAST OF THE
MOHICANS.

1026 Jordan, Cynthia S. "Two Sides to Every Story: Cooper's 'The Last of
the Mohicans.'" SECOND STORIES: THE POLITICS OF LANGUAGE,
FORM AND GENDER IN EARLY AMERICAN FICTION.   Chapel Hill:
University of North Carolina Press, 1989. Pp. 110-32.
    Not seen.

1027 Kaufman, Paul. "Literary Centenaries of 1926." BOOKMAN (New
York) 62 (January 1926):572-75.

Praises C. as the first native American writer. As such he can be forgiven for his less than perfect characterizations, plot, and style.

1028 Kingsley, Maud Elma. "Examination Questions for 'Last of the Mohicans.'" EDUCATION 29 (March 1909):462-63.
Twenty-five questions, a few of which are thought provoking.

1029 Kuester, Martin. "American Indians and German Indians: Perspectives of Doom in Cooper and May." WESTERN AMERICAN LITERATURE 23 (November 1988):217-22.
C's. influence on May was great. His third person narrative is much better than May's first person.

1030 Leaf, Munro. "The Last of the Mohicans." AMERICAN MAGAZINE, December 1940, p. 154.
An irreverent and humorous attack upon THE LAST OF THE MOHICANS.

1031 Maness, E. M. "The Indian Figure in James Fenimore Cooper's 'The Last of the Mohicans' and William Gilmore Simms' 'The Yemassee.'" Master of Arts degree, North Texas State University, 1969.

1032 Martin, Terence. "From the Ruins of History: 'The Last of the Mohicans.'" NOVEL, A FORUM ON FICTION 2 (Spring 1969):221-29.
C. moves back and forth between romance and history to present moral and racial issues that still have relevance today.

1033 Milder, Robert. "'The Last of the Mohicans' and the New World Fall." AMERICAN LITERATURE 52 (November 1980):407-29.
THE LAST OF THE MOHICANS is not the least worthy of C's. L. S. TALES as contemporary criticism claims. Rather, it is carefully contrived and devoted to America and her problems as C. saw them. It differs from the others in the series, however, in the literary techniques employed.

1034 Morris, Mowbray, ed. "Introduction." THE LAST OF THE MOHICANS. London: Macmillan Co., 1900.
C's. masterpiece.

1035 Morse, Ruth. "Impossible Dreams: Miscegenation and Building Nations." SOUTHERLY: A REVIEW OF AUSTRALIAN LITERATURE 48 (March 1988):80-96.
C. compared to Prichard, Masters, and Scott in the areas of race and colonialism.

1036 "Novel By Cooper Sells for $3,100." NEW YORK TIMES, November 14, 1935, p. 19.

1037 Okada, Ryoichi. "Another Source of Crane's Metaphor, 'The Red Badge of Courage.'" AMERICAN NOTES & QUERIES 14 (January 1976):73-74.
        Considers C's. use of the phrase "the bloody badge" in THE LAST OF THE MOHICANS, plus other dialogue and descriptive passages, as proof that Crane made use of this novel, both consciously and subconsciously, in creating his metaphor.

1038 Patee, Fred Lewis. "Critical Studies in American Literature. VI. The Historical Romance: Cooper's 'Last of the Mohicans.'" CHAUTAUQUAN 31 (June 1900):287-92.
        While THE LAST OF THE MOHICANS has an historical basis, most of it is a creation of the author that resulted from a vivid imagination and memories of an earlier life. The novel, whose action is not true to life, is a romance through and through.

1039 _____, ed. "Introduction." THE LAST OF THE MOHICANS. New York: Book League of America, 1929.
        A melodramatic romance that possesses only a small basis in fact, but which is C's best novel from the viewpoint of plot and action. Cora and Hawkeye are the best drawn characters.

1040 Philbrick, Thomas. "'The Last of the Mohicans' and the Sounds of Discord." AMERICAN LITERATURE 43 (March 1971):25-41.
        The presence of conflicting interpretations of THE LAST OF THE MOHICANS is largely due to the improper questions that have been asked. To assume that C. was able to levy any sort of conscious control over his material, resulting in an ideological framework, is incorrect.

1041 _____. "The Sources of Cooper's Knowledge of Fort William Henry." AMERICAN LITERATURE 36 (May 1964):209-14.
        THE LAST OF THE MOHICANS was written with the aid of previously published resources, but to assume that C. indulged in prolonged study is fallacious.

1042 Popov, Igor. "The Immortality of the Last Mohicans." SOVIET LITERATURE 1 (1984):138-42.
        C's reception in Russia from 1826-80.

1043 Prouty, James W. "An Analysis of 'The Last of the Mohicans' and 'The Way West' for Their Contribution to the Learning Process in a High School

Classroom." Master of Arts degree, Chico State College, 1958.

1044 Richardson, Charles F., ed. "Introduction." THE LAST OF THE MOHICANS. New York: Longmans, Green & Co., 1897.

1045 Rose, Marilyn Gaddis. "Time Discrepancy in 'The Last of the Mohicans.'" AMERICAN NOTES & QUERIES 8 (January 1970):72-73.
    Although C. remained close to the historical facts, he violated the chronology of events related in THE LAST OF THE MOHICANS.

1046 Seed, David. "Fenimore Cooper's David Gamut: A Source." NOTES AND QUERIES (London) 29 (June 1982):218-20.
    Irving's Ichabod Crane served as a model for Gamut and represents an attempt by C. to use humor.

1047 Spiller, Robert E., ed. "Introduction." THE LAST OF THE MOHICANS. New York: E. P. Dutton, 1951.

1048 Stallman, R. W. "Stephen Crane and Cooper's Uncas." AMERICAN LITERATURE 39 (November 1967):392-96.
    A reprint of Stephen Crane's "The Last of the Mohicans. His Aspect in Fiction Contradicted by His Fame in Folk-lore," which appeared in the NEW YORK TRIBUNE, February 21, 1892, p. 12. Crane claims that the oral history of Sullivan County shows that the real Uncas was not the brave warrior of C's. tale, but a poor, drunken Indian who died in obscurity.

1049 Sundahl, Daniel J. "Details and Defects: Historical Peculiarities in 'The Last of the Mohicans.'" RACKHAM JOURNAL OF THE ARTS AND HUMANITIES (1986):33-46.
    THE LAST OF THE MOHICANS is flawed in historical detail for C. sacrificed fact for literary effect. He seemed to have his greatest problems with maintaining the historical integrity of his characters. Sundahl suggests that the development of Hawkeye detracts from the book's appeal.

1050 Terence, Martin. "Leatherstocking and the Frontier: Cooper's 'The Last of the Mohicans.'" THE FRONTIER IN AMERICAN HISTORY AND LITERATURE: ESSAYS AND INTERPRETATIONS. Edited by Hans Galinsky. Frankfurt: Verlag Moritz Diesterweg, 1962. Pp. 49-64.
    Characterization and action in THE LAST OF THE MOHICANS show that C. could not envision a role for the savage in civilized society, or a role for civilized man in the wilderness. This led him to introduce racial themes as part of his inquiry into the nature and development of the frontier.

1051 "Ticonderoga." MACMILLAN'S MAGAZINE 73 (February 1896):281-90.

        C's. Indians are his weakest characterizations, for he was born too late to observe them first hand. The backwoodsmen, however, still existed and C. was able to portray them in a realistic fashion.

1052 Twain, Mark. "Fenimore Cooper's Further Literary Offenses." Edited by Bernard DeVoto. NEW ENGLAND QUARTERLY 19 (September 1946):291-301. Reprinted in Richardson, Norman et al., eds. HERITAGE OF AMERICAN LITERATURE. Boston: Ginn, 1951. Pp. 86-90.

        Negative comments on C's. style, use of language, and accuracy as an observer. From a previously unpublished manuscript.

1053 Van Nostrand, Albert D., ed. "Introduction." THE LAST OF THE MOHICANS. New York: Washington Square Press, 1961.

1054 Weaver, John V. A. "Fenimore Cooper--Comic." BOOKMAN (New York) 59 (March 1924):13-15.

        C. could not have written such an incredibly bad book and been serious about it. Somewhat tongue in cheek, Weaver claims that C. must have been trying to create the great comic novel of the nineteenth century.

1055 Weidman, Bette S. "White Men, Red Men." MODERN LANGUAGE STUDIES 4 (1974):14-26.

        Concerns the social and cultural costs that resulted from the establishment of a European society in the American wilderness.

1056 Wight, John G., ed. "Introduction." THE LAST OF THE MOHICANS. Boston: D. C. Heath & Co., 1899.

1057 Willy, Todd Gray. "Antipode to Cooper: Rhetoric and Reality in William Joseph Snelling's 'The Boy's Brule.'" STUDIES IN AMERICAN FICTION 8 (Spring 1980):69-79.

        C's. idea of the frontier was idyllic and surreal, whereas Snelling reported on a frontier that he remembered.

1058 Yonge, Charles Duke. THREE CENTURIES OF ENGLISH LITERATURE. New York: D. Appleton & Co., 1881. Pp. 618-22.

        Extols C's. Indian portraits.

The Prairie (1827)

Articles and Reviews Contemporary with Cooper

1059 THE ARIEL 1 (May 5, 1827):5.
Expected to sell widely. Five editions are being simultaneously prepared: one English, two French, one German, and one American.

1060 [Bryant, William Cullen. "Review".] UNITED STATES REVIEW AND LITERARY GAZETTE 2 (July 1827):306-08.
A good story built around very little material. It contains C's. usual powerful narrative and is possessed of a plot unexcelled since the appearance of THE PILOT. THE PRAIRIE, however, is still the wilderness and new situations and events are soon found wanting. Many of the characters are unworthy of C.

1061 "Critical Notes." BOSTON LYCEUM 2 (July 15, 1827):40.
A book of great descriptive power and one bound to hold the reader's interest, but it has an absurd plot and characters.

1062 LITERARY CHRONICLE AND WEEKLY REVIEW 9 (May 12, June 2, 1827):291-92, 345-46.
C. excells at narration and description.

1063 LIVERPOOL GAZETTE 11 (June 2, 1827):340.
Not seen. Citation from Cairns, p. 127 (item no. 5).

1064 MONTHLY MAGAZINE 3 n.s. (June 1827):650-51.
C. has no equal in his own field. His main object, to describe, is successfully fulfilled here. The story itself, while loosely constructed, is nevertheless interesting.

1065 MONTHLY REVIEW 5, new & imp. series (July 1827):426-29. Reprinted in PORT FOLIO 2, Hall's 2d series (August 1827): 157-58.
C's. characters are artificial, physically peculiar, and possess no moral traits. A heavy and detailed novel whose history, scenery, and Indian life are its strong points.

1066 NEW YORK AMERICAN, April 24, September 18, 1827.

1067 NILES' WEEKLY REGISTER 30 (June 3, 1826):234.
Announcement of publication that praises Cary and Lea for their recognition of American literary talent.

1068 SOUTHERN QUARTERLY REVIEW 19 (April 1851):560.
On the Putnam ed.--a commendable and pleasing story.

Articles from Cooper's Death to the Present

1069 Bier, Jesse. "Lapsarians on 'The Prairie': Cooper's Novel." TEXAS STUDIES IN LITERATURE AND LANGUAGE 4 (Spring 1962):49-57.
C's. Christian realism.

1070 Brunet, Francois. "Linguisters on the Prairie." REVUE FRANCAISE D'ETUDES AMERICAINES 13 (July 1988):238-66.
Not seen.

1071 Budick, Emily Miller. FICTION AND HISTORICAL CONSCIOUS-NESS: THE AKEDIAN ROMANCE OF AMERICA. New Haven: Yale University Press, 1989. Pp. 1-17, 55-78.
Not seen.

1072 Byington, Steven T. "More Words from Cooper's Works." AMERICAN SPEECH 21 (February 1946):39-40.
C's. use of language.

1073 Condit, John Hillyer. "The Exploration of Possibility: An Approach for Teaching Three Classic American Romances to High School Students." Ph.D. dissertation, Columbia University, 1983.
Includes some criticism of THE PRAIRIE.

1074 Davenport, Basil, ed. "Introduction." THE PRAIRIE. New York: Dodd, Mead & Co., 1954.

1075 Ellis, Reuben J. "Cooper's Imps: A Way of Talking About Indians." MASSACHUSETTS STUDIES IN ENGLISH 10 (Fall 1986):209-12.
Not seen.

1076 Engel, Leonard W. "Sam Peckinpah's Heroes: Natty Bumppo and the Myth of the Rugged Individual Still Reign." LITERATURE/FILM QUAR-TERLY 16 (1988):22-30.
The individualism of Natty Bumppo compared to Peckinpah's "Ride the High Country" and "Pat Garret and Billy the Kid".

1077 Fackler, Herbert V. "Cooper's Pawnees." AMERICAN NOTES & QUERIES 6 (October 1967):21-22.
C. over-romanticized the Pawnees at times, but he was in keeping

with contemporary non-fiction descriptions of these Indians.

1078 Fitzmaurice, James Earl. "Migration Epics of the Trans-Mississippi West." Ph.D. dissertation, University of Maryland, 1974.

THE PRAIRIE is included as one example of this type of heroic epic.

1079 Flanagan, John T. "Authenticity of Cooper's 'The Prairie.'" MODERN LANGUAGE QUARTERLY 2 (March 1941):99-104.

THE PRAIRIE, while a good story, is far from authentic. Its plot is often ridiculous, the geographical descriptions are inaccurate, and its dialogue is not truly western.

1080 Goetzman, William H. "James Fenimore Cooper: 'The Prairie.'" LANDMARKS OF AMERICAN WRITING. Edited by Hennig Cohen. New York: Basic Books, 1969. Pp. 66-78.

Considers C's. handling of both nature and civilization.

1081 Grossman, James, ed. "Introduction." THE PRAIRIE. New York: Washington Square Press, 1964.

1082 Hansen, Harry, ed. "Introduction." THE PRAIRIE. Menasha, Wis.: Printed for the Members of the Limited Editions Club, 1940.

1083 Hirsch, David. REALITY AND IDEA IN THE EARLY AMERICAN NOVEL. The Hague: Mouton & Co., 1971. Pp. 101-22.

Questions whether C. helped one to understand the ideas he expressed or whether he only contributed to the use of fiction as a means for promoting ideas.

1084 Jones, Grace McEntee. "The American Epic." Ph.D. dissertation, University of Alabama, 1987.

American epics illustrate the country's inability to live up to the national ideal. C's. use of the "low-life" character in THE PRAIRIE is illustrative of this theme.

1085 Leaming, Hugo P. "The Ben Ishmael Tribe: A Fugitive 'Nation' of the Old Northwest." THE ETHNIC FRONTIER: ESSAYS IN THE HISTORY OF GROUP SURVIVAL IN CHICAGO AND THE MIDWEST. Edited by Melvin G. Holli and Peter d'A. Jones. Grand Rapids, Mich.: Eerdmans, 1977. Pp. 97-141.

Identifies the Ishmaelites as an historic people. C's. rendering of them coincides with what is known.

1086 Lewis, Merrill. "Lost and Found--In the Wilderness: The Desert Metaphor in Cooper's 'The Prairie.'" WESTERN AMERICAN LITERATURE 5 (Fall 1970):195-204.

The desert metaphor serves to explore the physical and moral conditions of C's. characters. By associating the external landscape with the inner well being or "Landscape", C. effectively imparts knowledge about each character's psychological makeup.

1087 Mackenzie, Manfred. "Fenimore Cooper and Conrad's 'Suspense.'" NOTES & QUERIES (London) 208 (October 1963): 373-75.

Conrad utilized Natty Bumppo, C's. descriptions, and the mood created in THE PRAIRIE.

1088 Miller, Edwin Haviland. "James Fenimore Cooper's Elegiac Comedy: 'The Prairie.'" MOSAIC 9 (Summer 1976):195-205.

Asks that THE PRAIRIE be read as a comedy. This viewpoint is better able to account for structure, action, and interactions among characters than are those that insist upon mythological and epic considerations.

1089 Mills, Nicolaus. AMERICAN AND ENGLISH FICTION IN THE NINETEENTH CENTURY. Bloomington: Indiana University Press, 1973. Pp. 32-51.

An analysis of the similarities between Scott's ROB ROY and THE PRAIRIE.

1090 Muszynska-Wallace, E. Soteris. "The Sources of 'The Prairie.'" AMERICAN LITERATURE 21 (May 1949):191-200.

A claim that C's. portrayal of the West and its Indians is authentic. Never having visited the places of which he wrote, C. found it necessary to build a background of knowledge from an array of published sources. Lewis and Clarke's HISTORY OF THE EXPEDITION, Charlevoix's JOURNAL OF A VOYAGE TO NORTH AMERICA, Mackenzie's VOYAGES FROM MONTREAL, and Long's EXPEDITION . . . TO THE ROCKY MOUNTAINS, are four accounts from which he drew much material for THE PRAIRIE.

1091 Nelson, Carl. "Cooper's Verbal Faction: The Hierarchy of Rhetoric, Voice, and Silence in 'The Prairie.'" WEST VIRGINIA PHILOLOGICAL PAPERS 24 (November 1977):37-47.

The reader should not become impatient with C's. use of language for it, not plot or action, is the important factor. Through language C. pleads for man to listen to the wisdom of others and to take a higher moral plane.

1092 Overland, Orm H. "James Fenimore Cooper's 'The Prairie': The Making and Meaning of an American Classic." Ph. D. dissertation, Yale University, 1969. Reprinted as THE MAKING AND MEANING OF AN AMERICAN CLASSIC: JAMES FENIMORE COOPER'S "THE PRAIRIE." Oslo: Universitelsforlaget, 1973.

Discusses C's. theories of literature, his use of history, and three editions of the novel. Includes considerable biographical material during the time that he was writing THE PRAIRIE.

1093 Ringe, Donald A. "Man and Nature in Cooper's 'The Prairie.'" NINETEENTH CENTURY FICTION 15 (March 1961):313-23.

The three main characters in THE PRAIRIE represent different ways of viewing the relationships between man and nature. The trapper, who adopts the proper outlook, is a conservationist who would preserve natural resources. Ishmael Bush desires only to exploit what nature has provided and Dr. Bat seeks fame through his scientific discoveries, caring little for what good they might bring mankind. The death of the trapper at the novel's end marks the defeat of his way of life, leaving the West open to despoilment by those who possess the philosophies of Ishmael Bush and Dr. Bat.

1094 Rucker, Mary E. "Natural, Tribal, and Civil Law in Cooper's 'The Prairie.'" WESTERN AMERICAN LITERATURE 12 (November 1977):215-22.

A discussion of C's. concept of justice and a character analysis of Ishmael Bush.

1095 Sharp, Herbert. "Dialect and Colloquialisms in 'The Prairie' by James Fenimore Cooper." Master of Arts degree, University of Kansas, 1928.

1096 Smith, Henry Nash. "The Western Farmer in Imaginative Literature." MISSISSIPPI VALLEY HISTORICAL REVIEW 36 (December 1949):479-90.

C's. idea of a stratified society with an aristocratic ruling class at the top is best exemplified in his treatment of the squatter Ishmael Bush. (p. 483)

1097 _____, ed. "Introduction." THE PRAIRIE. New York: Rinehart, 1950.

THE PRAIRIE presents a set of conflicting values. On the one hand, the westward movement was viewed as evil (a rape of the land), while on the other, the advance of civilization was beneficial (a means of bringing progress to a wild and savage land).

1098 Stein, William Bysshe. "'The Prairie': A Scenario of the Wise Old Man." BUCKNELL REVIEW 19 (Spring 1971):15-36.

C. ordered the life of the trapper in such a way that he acted as the wise old man--the carrier of C's. ideas of morality and religion. His death at the end of the novel without passing his wisdom on to the young is symbolic of youth's failure to learn from experience.

1099 Suderman, Elmer F. "Cooper's Sense of Place in 'The Prairie.'" NORTH DAKOTA QUARTERLY 55 (Winter 1987):159-64.

Application of the theories of David Lowenthal to C's. treatment of the prairie.

1100 Tanner, James E. "A Possible Source for 'The Prairie.'" AMERICAN LITERATURE 47 (March 1975):102-04.

C's. source for the character Paul Hoover was not drawn from anyone he knew in Cooperstown as Henry Nash Smith has claimed. Rather, it originated from a popular song entitled "The Hunters of Kentucky, or Half Horse and Half Alligator."

1101 Thacker, Robert. "Cooper, Bryant and the Writers of the American Renaissance." THE GREAT PRAIRIE FACT AND LITERARY IMAGINATION. Albuquerque: University of New Mexico Press, 1989. Pp. 104-22.

Use of landscape in theme and as symbolism.

1102 Vance, William L. "Man and Beast: The Meaning of Cooper's 'The Prairie.'" Modern Language Association of America, PUBLICATIONS 89 (March 1974):323-31.

Man is viewed as no more than one species of animal in THE PRAIRIE. Consequently, his relationship to the other beasts of the forest is emphasized throughout the book.

1103 Vandiver, Edward P., Jr. "Cooper's 'The Prairie' and Shakespeare." Modern Language Association of America, PUBLICATIONS 69 (December 1954):1302-04.

While Gates (item no. 410) has made the most extensive study of Shakespeare's influence on C., he failed to point out that the dialogue of Dr. Battius is patterned after that of Holofernes in LOVE'S LABOR LOST.

1104 Ward, John William. RED, WHITE, AND BLUE: MEN, BOOKS AND IDEAS IN AMERICAN CULTURE. New York: Oxford University Press, 1969. Pp. 62-72.

Although C. was successful in portraying a Natty Bumppo whose passing was a sorrowful but necessary event, he failed in his attempt to describe a society that was worth replacing him with.

1105 _____, ed. "Afterward." THE PRAIRIE. New York: New American Library, 1964.

1106 Wasserstrom, William. "The Origins of Culture: Cooper and Freud." THE PSYCHOANALYTIC STUDY OF SOCIETY. Vol. 1. Edited by Warner Muensterberger and Sidney Axelrad. New York: International Universities Press, 1960. Pp. 272-83. Reprinted in AMERICAN IMAGO 17 (Winter 1960):423-37 and Malin, Irving, ed. PSYCHOANALYSIS AND AMERICAN FICTION. New York: E. P. Dutton, 1965. Pp. 47-60.

    Similarities between C. and Freud relating to their concepts of the origin of society.

1107 Wherry, George. "Col. Newcome's Death." NOTES & QUERIES (London) 4, 11th series (September 16, 1911):225.

    Wherry points out the similarity between the death scene created by C. in THE PRAIRIE (the old trapper's) and that by Thackeray in THE NEWCOMES (Col. Newcome's).

The Pathfinder (1840)

Articles and Reviews Contemporary with Cooper

1108 ATHENAEUM [13] (February 22, 1840):149-51.

    As with preceding L. S. TALES, this one creates unflagging interest.

1109 Balzac Honoré de. "Literary Notices." KNICKERBOCKER MAGAZINE 17 (January 1841):72-77. Reprinted in THE WORKS OF HONORÉ DE BALZAC. Vol. 20. Translated by Prescott Wormeley. New York: Athenaeum Club [1899?]. Pp. 114-20.

    Translation of a review that first appeared in the REVUE PARISIENNE, August 1840. A "beautiful book" that follows two failures. It suffers, however, from C's. inability to be humorous, from tediousness, and from the ridicule he heaps upon the French.

1110 BURTON'S GENTLEMAN'S MAGAZINE 6 (April 1840):200.

    THE PATHFINDER is equal to anything C. has written and is superior to any of his recent works. While the characters are not strongly delineated, his descriptive passages are excellent.

1111 CASKET 17 (August 1840):96.

1112 EVENING POST (New York), March 14, 26, 1841.

1113 GODEY'S LADY'S BOOK 20 (May 1840):239.

1114 KNICKERBOCKER MAGAZINE 15 (April 1840):344-45.
       A faithful portrayal of both characters and the landscape.

1115 _____ 15 (May 1840):449.
       Admirable, especially the characterizations.

1116 LADIES' COMPANION 12 (April 1840):296.
       The plot is simple and the characters few, but the scenery is vivid-
ly described. THE PATHFINDER is a welcome change from C's. other recent novels.

1117 _____ 13 (May 1840):47.
       As long as C. stays within his element, he will be successful.

1118 LITERARY GAZETTE 24 (February 29, 1840):132-34.
       Largely free of C's. biases. A meager plot with characters that are
revivals of those found in his other works.

1119 "Mr. Cooper's New World." NEW YORKER 9 (March 21, 1840):2-4.
       Readable. Although C. has written better, it is superior to some
his recent work.

1120 MORNING COURIER AND NEW YORK ENQUIRER, May 14, July
2, 10, 1840.

1121 NEW WORLD 1 (July 11, 1840):94.

1122 NEW YORK EVENING SIGNAL, March 19, 1840.
       An unfavorable review.

1123 NEW-YORK MIRROR 17 (March 21, 1840):305-06.
       Perhaps not equal to THE SPY, but it possesses scenes that are
superior to those of any other author.

1124 NEW YORK REVIEW 6 (April 1840):479-80.
       A work of genius. Unmarred by the faults of C's. last two or
three attempts.

1125 NEW YORKER 8 (March 14, 1840):413.

1126 SOUTHERN LITERARY MESSENGER 6 (March 1840):229-30.

Unlike his more recent works, this one is well written, simple, and beautiful.

1127 SPECTATOR (London) 13 (February 29, 1840):210-11.

Although possessed of a well managed plot and realistic characters, THE PATHFINDER is overly long, resembles similar novels, and is filled with extraneous description and opinion.

Articles from Cooper's Death to the Present

1128 Berger, Thomas, ed. "Afterward." THE PATHFINDER. New York: New American Library, 1961.

1129 Blakemore, Steven. "Language and World in 'The Pathfinder.'" MODERN LANGUAGE STUDIES 16 (Summer 1986):237-46.

On C's. use of language to show how a character understands his world and how he moves to other worlds through the use of that world's language.

1130 Bowden, Mary Weatherspoon. "Mabel and Dew-of-June: Female Friendship in 'The Pathfinder.'" THE SOUTH CENTRAL BULLETIN 40 (Winter 1980):136-37.

Not seen.

1131 Bush, Sargent, Jr. "Charles Cap of 'The Pathfinder': A Foil to Cooper's Views on American Character in the 1840s." NINETEENTH CENTURY FICTION 20 (December 1965):267-73.

THE PATHFINDER, while predominantly a romantic novel, is the precursor to C's. later social fiction. While it was not until 1842 that he became outwardly critical of society and its moral standards, it was the creation of Charles Cap in 1840 that foreshadowed what was to come.

1132 Dekker, George. "'The Pathfinder': Leatherstocking in Love." British Association for American Studies, BULLETIN no. 10 n.s. (June 1965):40-47.

The new role assumed by Leatherstocking in THE PATHFINDER is one in which he takes little lead in the action. Consequently, he fails to attain the proportions of a mythic hero as he did in the other novels in the series. This interpretation is, in part, at variance with Smith's VIRGIN LAND, pp. 70-71 (item no. 874).

1133 Klots, Allen, Jr., ed. "Introduction." THE PATHFINDER. New York: Dodd, Mead & Co., 1953.

1134 Owen, William. "In War as in Love: The Significance of Analogous Plots in Cooper's 'The Pathfinder.'" ENGLISH STUDIES IN CANADA 10 (September 1984):289-98.
    The romantic and military plots are closely interrelated in THE PATHFINDER. They possess the same internal structures and serve to carry C's. theme on the dangers to society of internal subversion.

1135 Pearson, Norman Holmes, ed. "Introduction." THE PATHFINDER. New York: Modern Library, 1952.

1136 Pedrini, Laura and Nancy Duilio T. Pedrini. "Similes and Metaphors in Cooper's 'The Pathfinder.'" NEW YORK FOLKLORE QUARTERLY 23 (June 1967):99-108.
    C. allows his characters, many whom have different backgrounds, to use the language typical of their way of life to express their reactions to situations in which they are placed. Thus, the Pathfinder speaks in terms of nature and the forest; Cap and Jasper, two seafarers, interpret happenings in nautical terms; and David Muir, a soldier, approaches each situation as if it was a military problem.

1137 Rosenzweig, Paul. "'The Pathfinder': The Wilderness Initiation of Mabel Dunham." MODERN LANGUAGE QUARTERLY 44 (December 1983):339-58.
    Psychological treatment of the heroine's introduction to the wilderness and marriage.

1138 Spiller, Robert E., ed. "Introduction." THE PATHFINDER. New York. Heritage Press, 1965.

1139 "Washington Irving Upon the Late Fenimore Cooper." KNICKERBOCKER MAGAZINE 55 (January 1860):94-95.
    In praise of THE PATHFINDER.

1140 Winterich, John T. "The Compleat Collector." SATURDAY REVIEW OF LITERATURE 15 (December 26, 1936):19.
    Price and notes on the first edition of THE PATHFINDER.

The Deerslayer (1841)

Articles and Reviews Contemporary with Cooper

1141 ATHENAEUM [14] (September 11, 1841):708-11.
     Favorable review. Largely excerpts from the book.

1142 GODEY'S LADY'S BOOK 23 (October 1841):189.
     A stereotypical book that proves that C's. popularity is increasing
and that he is aware of his recent mistakes as an author. Will be favorably
compared to his earlier works.

1143 GRAHAM'S MAGAZINE 19 (October 1841):191.
     As thrilling as those tales that have preceded it. Except for Natty
Bumppo, however, there are no well conceived characters.

1144 _____ 37 (December 1850):387.
     A review of the reprint edition that claims that the L. S. TALES
were the best of C's. work.

1145 HOLDEN'S DOLLAR MAGAZINE 6 (December 1850):757-58.
     An interesting and exciting tale, but not a classic for it is marred
by too many defects.

1146 KNICKERBOCKER MAGAZINE 18 (October 1841):349-52.
     A book that will have no lack of readers. The nature scenes are
excellent. Deerslayer is one of C's. best creations.

1147 LADIES' COMPANION 15 (October 1841):310.
     This novel will go far toward retrieving C.'s lost popularity.
Admirable characterizations (especially of the women) and descriptions.

1148 LITERARY GAZETTE 25 (September 11, 1841):585-86.
     THE DEERSLAYER is the best of C's. recent fiction.   Its
depiction of early America is thrilling while the characters, especially the
heroine, are aptly drawn.

1149 LITERARY WORLD 7 (October 5, 1850):271.
     On the revised edition--characterization and dialogue are well
done, the action is compelling, and the whole is simply constructed.

1150 MONTHLY REVIEW 3, 4th series (October 1841):192-200.
     Perhaps the best of the series.

1151 MORNING COURIER AND NEW YORK ENQUIRER, September 3, 1841.

The publication of this book is proof that C's. decline is not the result of personality or politics, but is due to his total lack of ability as an author.

1152 NEW-YORK MIRROR 19 (September 11, 1841):295.

The best book that C. has written in several years. It possesses better characterizations than he is generally known for and lacks the defects of his former novels.

1153 NEW YORK REVIEW 9 (October 1841):537-38.

C's. portrayal of Natty Bumppo as a young man is a successful one. His style has become more polished and the scenic descriptions are better than in any of his previous works.

1154 SOUTHERN LITERARY MESSENGER 7 (October 1841):742-43.

A shallow and silly novel that does not deserve to be criticized.

1155 UNITED STATES MAGAZINE AND DEMOCRATIC REVIEW 9 (October 1841):404-05.

C's descriptive and narrative talents keep reader interest in a book without character or plot.

Articles from Cooper's Death to the Present

1156 Anderson Quentin, ed. "Introduction." THE DEERSLAYER. New York: Collier Books, 1962.

1157 Bradsher, Frieda K. "Christian Morality and 'The Deerslayer.'" RENASCENCE 31 (Autumn 1978):15-24.

Natty Bumppo is not a true Christian for he is unable to lead a virtuous life in his actions toward others.

1158 Browning, Barton W. "Cooper's Influence on Stifter: Fact or Scholarly Myth?" MODERN LANGUAGE NOTES 89 (October 1974):821-28.

Using publication dates as his evidence, Browning proves that it was chronologically impossible for THE DEERSLAYER to have influenced Stifter's HOCHWALD.

1159 Clark, Robert. "'The Deerslayer': Scalps and the Myth of Whiteness." HISTORY, IDEOLOGY, AND MYTH IN AMERICAN FICTION, 1823-1852. New York: St. Martins Press, 1984. Pp. 95-109.

C. placed himself in a difficult position when he idealized the Indian and questioned the superiority of white civilization. Since his contemporaries believed Indians were savages and should be conquered by their superiors, C. became defensive about his own beliefs.

1160 Darnell, Donald. "'The Deerslayer': Cooper's Tragedy of Manners." STUDIES IN THE NOVEL 11 (Winter 1979):406-15.
    A main theme of THE DEERSLAYER concerns knowing one's place in society and the tragedy that can befall one who attempts to rise above his or her position.

1161 Grant, Barry Keith. "The World En-masse: Language and Form in American Literature: 1800-1860." Ph.D. dissertation, State University of New York at Buffalo, 1975.
    C's. attempt to establish an individual morality that would serve as the basis for American society was a self-admitted failure, for THE DEER-SLAYER reveals that he eventually came to believe that a virtuous democracy was not possible.

1162 Grossman, James, ed. "Introduction." THE DEERSLAYER. New York: Washington Square Press, 1961.

1163 Kilby, James Allen, Jr. "A Critical Edition of James Fenimore Cooper's 'The Deerslayer' Based on the Printed Texts." Ph.D. dissertation, University of Iowa, 1972.
    An examination and comparison of eight editions, six of which were published during C's. lifetime.

1164 Lawrence, David Herbert. THE SELECTED LETTERS OF D. H. LAWRENCE. Edited by Diana Trilling. New York: Farrar, Strauss & Cudahy, 1958. P. 145.
    Letter to Catherine Carswell dated November 27, 1916. C's. writing is "pure and . . . exquisite, . . . mature and sensitive."

1165 Matthews, Brander, ed. "Introduction." THE DEERSLAYER. New York: T. Y. Crowell & Co., 1896.

1166 Mizener, Arthur. TWELVE GREAT AMERICAN NOVELS. New York: New American Library, 1967. Pp. 1-8.
    C. uses action to create conflicts between the moral stances taken by each of his characters.

1167 Nevins, Allen, ed. "Afterward." THE DEERSLAYER. New York:

New American Library, 1963.

1168 Paine, Gregory, ed. "Introduction." THE DEERSLAYER. American Author Series. New York: Harcourt, Brace & Co., 1927.
        The Indians of THE DEERSLAYER are noticeably more idealized than their predecessors in the L. S. TALES. This can be attributed to Heckewelder's influence. In spite of these statements, it is also true that C's. Indians were realistically portrayed.

1169 Person, Leland S. "Cooper's Queen of the Woods: Judith Hutter in 'The Deerslayer.'" STUDIES IN THE NOVEL 21 (Fall 1989):253-67.
        Hutter is more important and a more sympathetic character than many critics have claimed. She serves as an ethical yardstick who is well characterized in relation to women's true roles on the frontier.

1170 Sandy, Alan F., Jr. "The Voices of Cooper's 'The Deerslayer.'" EMERSON SOCIETY QUARTERLY no. 60 (Summer 1970):5-9.
        C's. imperfect use of language in both dialogue and narration was one of his greatest strengths. He employed flaws to accentuate the imperfections of the character or narrator concerned.

1171 Schachterle, Lance and Kent Ljungquist. "Fenimore Cooper's Literary Defenses: Twain and the Text of 'The Deerslayer.'" STUDIES IN THE AMERICAN RENAISSANCE (1988):401-17.
        Takes Twain to task for his attacks on C's. plot, characterization, and style. While Twain's criticism was often inaccurate and based upon little evidence, his essay was humorous, satirical, and a work of art.

1172 Selley, April. "'I Have Been and Ever Shall Be, Your Friend': 'Star Trek', 'The Deerslayer', and the American Romance." JOURNAL OF POPULAR CULTURE 20 (Summer 1986):89-104.
        On interracial relations between men.

1173 Vanderbeets, Richard. "Cooper and the 'Semblance of Reality': A Source for 'The Deerslayer.'" AMERICAN LITERATURE 42 (January 1971):544-46.
        Much of the Indian lore, characterization, and plot development of THE DEERSLAYER is similar to information relayed in the 1827 Indian captivity narrative entitled A NARRATIVE OF THE INCIDENTS ATTENDING THE CAPTURE, DETENTION, AND RANSOM OF CHARLES JOHNSTON.

1174 Vasile, Peter. "Cooper's 'The Deerslayer': The Apotheosis of Man and

Nature." American Academy of Religion, JOURNAL 43 (September 1975):485-507.

With publication of THE DEERSLAYER C. had come to realize that his idea of society could exist only as myth. This myth then formed the basis for his future attacks on the development of American society.

1175 Weldon, Robert F. "Cooper's 'The Deerslayer' and the Indian myth of Nanabozho." NEW YORK FOLKLORE QUARTERLY 2 (Summer 1976):61-67.

Suggests that a character in Indian myth forms the basis for Tom Hutter.

LITTLEPAGE TRILOGY

Articles from Cooper's Death to the Present

1176 Christman, Henry. TIN HORNS AND CALICO: A DECISIVE EPISODE IN THE EMERGENCE OF DEMOCRACY. New York: Henry Holt & Co., 1945. Pp. 256-57.

The ALBANY FREEHOLDER'S reply to C's. anti-rent novels.

1177 Cosgrove, William E. "Family Lineage and Narrative Pattern in Cooper's Littlepage Trilogy." FORUM (Houston) 12 (Spring 1974):2-8.

C., by emphasizing the importance of the family unit and criticizing anything that led to its breakdown, sought to impress upon Americans the civilizing effect of the patriarchal landed estate that was handed down from generation to generation.

1178 Dryden, Edgar A. "History and Progress: Some Implications of Form in Cooper's Littlepage Novels." NINETEENTH CENTURY FICTION 26 (June 1971):49-64.

Because society operated without the aid of divine will, human needs decreed that the gentleman be created to preserve liberty and promote progress. It was only through his understanding of history that man was able to move beyond the past while maintaining a stable society.

1179 Ellis, David Maldwyn. "The Coopers and New York State Landholding Systems." NEW YORK HISTORY 35 (October 1954):412-22.

C's, ideas of property had their source in his early family relationships. Land, for the Cooper's, was the purest form of property ownership and it was to these owners that society was to look for its leaders. In keeping with Jefferson, C. expounded a brand of democracy that called for

an aristocratic elite to rule.   Writing the Littlepage Trilogy in response to
those who repudiated this concept, C. showed that he had become alienated
from a society that would no longer accept the paternalism of a landed gentry.

1180 _____. LANDLORDS AND FARMERS IN THE HUDSON-
MOHAWK REGION, 1790-1850. Ithaca, N. Y.: Cornell University Press,
1946. Pp. 101-02, 295-96.
        C. was determined to maintain the leasehold system and often
exaggerated events in his novels in order to express this viewpoint.

1181 Franks, Winifred M. "Social Criticism and Literary Artistry in James
Fenimore Cooper's Littlepage Trilogy." Master of Arts degree, University of
New Mexico, 1966.

1182 French, Florence, "Cooper's Use of Proverbs in the Anti-rent Novels."
NEW YORK FOLKLORE QUARTERLY 26 (March 1970):42-49.
        C. uses proverbs in the Littlepage Trilogy to promote his political
(Jeffersonian) and social (morality and proper behavior) thought.

1183 _____. "Cooper the Tinkerer." NEW YORK FOLKLORE
QUARTERLY 26 (September 1970):229-39.
        C. made extensive use of proverbs and folk sayings, often
changing them to suit his purposes.

1184 Hicks, Granville. "Landlord Cooper and the Anti-renters." ANTIOCH
REVIEW 5 (March 1945):95-109.
        C's. ideas on landed gentry, his aloofness from the people of New
York, and his abstract brand of democracy, led him to write of the anit-rent
movement without considering the historical facts of the situation.   This article
may be contrasted with Bristed's opinion in item no. 1209.

1185 Horvath, John, Jr. "Essays on the Controversy in Literature: The
Certain Uncertainty of Literary Texts." Ph.D. dissertation, Florida State
University, 1989.
        An application of linguistic script analysis to three world views:
identity, separateness, and individualized sovereignty.

1186 Knight, Mabel T. "J. F. Cooper and the Anti-rent Controversy." Master
of Arts Degree, University of Oklahoma, 1942.

1187 O'Donnell, Charles O. "Progress and Property: The Later Cooper."
AMERICAN QUARTERLY 13 (Fall 1961):402-09.
        C. was a social conservative who believed in improvement and

change, but he failed to accept man's progress toward a future perfection.

1188 Reiss, John Peter, Jr. "Problems of the Family Novel: Cooper, Hawthorne, and Melville." Ph.D. dissertation, University of Wisconsin, 1969.

Reiss defines the family novel as a type and sketches its importance to American literature. Included is an essay on the relationships between C., Hawthorne, and Melville, and an analysis of the Littlepage Trilogy as a defense of family property.

1189 Ringe, Donald A. "Cooper's Littlepage Novels: Change and Stability in American Society." AMERICAN LITERATURE 32 (November 1960):280-90.

The Littlepage Trilogy possesses a coherent, well planned theme that is maintained throughout the three books. It is only by reading the whole series that one comes to understand the ideas of change represented by the Littlepages and the values that must replace theirs.

1190 Scapin, Maria. "Fenimore Cooper's Littlepage Manuscripts." Master of Arts degree, Ca Foscari (Italy), 1957.

1191 Wei, Zhang. "Social Progress and Ideology in Cooper's Littlepage Trilogy." Ph.D. dissertation, Michigan State University, 1990.

Explores C's. social beliefs in relation to Jacksonian ideas of political and economic progress.

Satanstoe (1845)

Articles and Reviews Contemporary with Cooper

1192 ANGLO-AMERICAN 5 (July 12, 1845):283.

Simply written in a style suitable to the country reader of 75 years ago.

1193 BROADWAY JOURNAL 1 (June 21, 1845):395.

Of little interest except for those who desire the newest C. novel.

1194 HARBINGER 1 (August 2, 1845):122.

Stereotypical, dull, and repetitive.

1195 LITERARY GAZETTE 29 (June 21, 1845):392-93.

A satirical novel. Shows C's. dislike for New Englanders.

1196 SPECTATOR (London) 18 (June 21, 1845):593-94.
          Not one of C's. best novels.   A failure at depicting colonial manners and repetitive of events and characters.

Articles from Cooper's Death to the Present

1197 Bier, Jesse. "The Bisection of Cooper: 'Satanstoe' as Prime example." TEXAS STUDIES IN LITERATURE AND LANGUAGE 9 (Winter 1968):511-21.
          SATANSTOE, due to C's. own divided social and   political loyalties, fails to make a case for a society based upon an aristocratic elite.

1198 Dondore, Dorothy. "The Debt of Two Dyed-in-the-Wool Americans to Mrs. Grant's 'Memoirs': Cooper's 'Satanstoe' and Paulding's 'The Dutchman's Fireside.'" AMERICAN LITERATURE 12 (March 1940):52-58.
          All but nine of SATANSTOE's thirty chapters draw local color and narrative from Mrs. Grant's MEMOIRS OF AN AMERICAN LADY.

1199 Hough, Robert L., ed. "Introduction." SATANSTOE.   Lincoln: University of Nebraska Press, 1962.
          C. failed to combine social ideas (anti-rentism and democracy) with action in SATANSTOE. Consequently, one finds that these ideas remain superficial to the plot.   He did, however, create an excellent picture of eighteenth century New York society.

1200 Pickering, James. "Fenimore Cooper and Pinkster." NEW YORK FOLKLORE QUARTERLY 22 (March 1966):15-19.
          SATANSTOE, which is C's. best example of American historical romance, is notable for its use of Anglo-Dutch folk culture. This is especially true of Chapters IV and V where C. describes the Pinkster festival, undoubtedly a reference to those festivals celebrated in Albany each year.

1201 _____. "'Satanstoe': Cooper's Debt to William Dunlap." AMERICAN LITERATURE 38 (January 1967):468-77.
          It is evident that C. borrowed material for descriptions of New York City, her stage, and the British occupation there from William Dunlap's HISTORY OF THE AMERICAN THEATRE and his HISTORY OF THE NEW NETHERLANDS.

1202 Slater, Joseph. "The Dutch Treat in Cooper's 'Satanstoe.'" AMERICAN SPEECH 26 (May 1951):153-54.
          The origin of the term "Dutch treat" has never been determined, but C's. SATANSTOE throws some light on the matter. It would appear from

an episode here that it was a custom of the time actually practiced by the Dutch of New York.

1203 Spiller, Robert E. and Joseph D. Coppock, eds. "Introduction." SATANSTOE. American Fiction Series. New York: American Book Co., 1937.

SATANSTOE is the most accurate portrayal of eighteenth century American society before Hawthorne. In it, C. was able to successfully combine the elements of romance with that of social criticism. Reviews of this edition are found in AMERICAN LITERATURE 10 (May 1938):232-35 and ANGLIA BEIBLATT 50 (1939):306-08.

The Chainbearer (1845)

Articles and Reviews Contemporary with Cooper

1204 HARBINGER 1 (December 6, 1845):411-12.
Better than SATANSTOE and beyond the average historical work, but certainly not an immortal one.

1205 LITERARY GAZETTE 29 (December 6, 1845):809.
Interesting comments upon American society, many of which are worthy of English attention.

1206 SPECTATOR (London) 18 (December 3, 1845):1192-93.
A personal narrative that does not catch the reader's sympathy. The story is uneven and slow, but is interesting and has good characterizations and dialogue.

1207 YOUNG AMERICA 2 (December 20, 845):unpaged.
The arguments propounded here have been better put in other places. Uninteresting.

Articles from Cooper's Death to the Present

1208 Deane, Paul. "James Fenimore Cooper and 'The Chainbearer': An Examination." REVUE DES LANGUES VIVANTES 34 (1968):261-68.
Deane maintains that THE CHAINBEARER's greatest strength lies in its ideas (social and political) and its characterizations. The plot, which has been severely criticized by others, is of less importance to the novel.

The Redskins (Ravensnest [English Title]) (1846)

Articles and Reviews Contemporary with Cooper

1209 [Bristed, C. A.] "Cooper's 'Indian and Ingin.'" AMERICAN WHIG REVIEW 4 (September 1846):276-81.
An uninteresting book whose plot is subordinate to the author's moral. It is a valuable work, however, for it presents a true picture of the anti-rent controversy.

1210 HARBINGER 3 (August 1, 1846):123.
Tolerable as a moral tract, but repetitive and stupid.

1211 LITERARY GAZETTE 30 (August 1, 1846):681-82.
A "curious" book, but of interest. Evenhanded in its condemnation and just in the statement of facts and the drawing of conclusions.

1212 "Novels and Novel-writing." CHRISTIAN EXAMINER 42 (January 1847):101-18.
Vain and with little wisdom. (pp. 105-06)

1213 SPECTATOR (London) 19 (July 25 1846):711-12.
Inferior to its predecessors in the series and lacking in novelty and adventure, although both descriptions and dialogue are well done. The characters are sometimes overly exaggerated. All in all, the incidents and arguments presented do not support the denunciations provided by the author.

1214 Thackeray, William Makepeace. "Cooper's 'Ravensnest; or the Red Skins.'" CONTRIBUTIONS TO THE "MORNING CHRONICLE." Edited by Gordon Ray. Urbana: University of Illinois Press, 1955. Pp. 167-74. Originally printed in the London MORNING CHRONICLE, August 27, 1846.
Critical of C's. denouncement of the very political institutions for which he claims to be so proud.

1215 UNITED STATES MAGAZINE AND DEMOCRATIC REVIEW 19 (September 1846):237.
An enlightening and amusing volume that accurately reports the relationship between landlord and tenant

Articles from Cooper's Death to the Present

1216 Bliss, Carey S. "Intramuralia: Books and People." HUNTINGTON

LIBRARY QUARTERLY 41 (November 1977):65-77.
About the Huntington Library's acquisition of an 1846 English edition of THE REDSKINS (p. 68). C. was so popular in England that the book was published there before its appearance in the U. S.

1217 Ringe, Donald A. "The Source for an Incident in Cooper's 'The Redskins.'" ENGLISH LANGUAGE NOTES 24 (December 1986):66-68.
Thacher's MILITARY JOURNAL as a source.

MISCELLANEOUS FICTION

The Spy (1821)

Articles and Reviews Contemporary with Cooper

1218 THE ALBUM 1 (July 1822):400-28.
From a review of Irving's BRACEBRIDGE HALL. C's. characters, incidents, and manners are exclusively American and should be inoffensive to a British audience. His sketch of Washington is skillfully done. (p. 403)

1219 AMERICAN WHIG REVIEW 9 (June 1849):648.
Already enjoyed by one generation, THE SPY will continue to delight the next.

1220 ATLAS 6 (May 22, 1831):348.
A great improvement in style with this edition.

1221 Barnum, H. L. THE SPY UNMASKED; OR MEMOIRS OF ENOCH CROSBY, ALIAS HARVEY BIRCH, THE HERO OF MR. COOPER'S TALE OF THE NEUTRAL GROUND. 2d ed. Cincinnati: A. B. Roff, 1831.
There were several real-life secret agents of the Revolutionary War that C. could have drawn from to create Harvey Birch. It is evident, however, that Enoch Crosby is the model he used to form his character. See also the review of the first edition of this book in the New-York Mirror 6, (July 19, 1828):9.

1222 "David Gray." NILES' WEEKLY REGISTER 23 (February 8, 15, 1823):354, 373.
On David Gray, a Revolutionary War spy who had petitioned the Massachusetts legislature for compensation for his services. The claim is made that he was the basis for C's. spy. See also NEW-ENGLAND GALAXY 6

(February 7, 1823):unpaged, for disposition of the petition and a note on Gray's honesty.

1223 Edgeworth, Maria. THE LIFE AND LETTERS OF MARIA EDGEWORTH. Vol. 2. Edited by Augustus J. C. Hare. London: Edward Arnold, 1894. P. 29.

Letter to Mrs. Ruxton dated July 8, 1821, concerning THE SPY. See also PORT FOLIO 16, 5th series (July 1823):86, for a second undated letter on the same subject.

1224 [Gardiner, W. H.]. "The Spy, a Tale of the Neutral Ground." NORTH AMERICAN REVIEW 15 (July 1822):250-82.

THE SPY is blemished (e.g. the character Harper and Captain Wharton's trial and escape), but the characterization of Harvey Birch and the action scenes redeem it as an historical novel. C. is not comparable to Scott.

1225 GAZETTE OF FASHION AND MAGAZINE OF THE FINE ARTS, April 6, 1822, pp. 163-64.

Hastily written, although interesting. It falls short of the Waverly novels. Not seen. Citation from Clavel, p. 30 (item no. 5).

1226 GENERAL WEEKLY REGISTER no. 7 (May 19, 1822):265-69.

1227 GRAHAMS AMERICAN MONTHLY MAGAZINE 35 (August 1849):132.

A revised edition that is enhanced by its introduction and notes. Its popularity is richly deserved.

1228 HOLDEN'S DOLLAR MAGAZINE 4 (June 1849):383-84.

The revised edition. The new preface gives interesting insights into the book.

1229 LADY'S MAGAZINE 4 n.s. (1823):193-98.

1230 LITERARY CHRONICLE AND WEEKLY REVIEW 4 (July 6, 1822):421-23.

Praises THE SPY as national literature while comparing C. favorably with Brockden Brown.

1231 LITERARY WORLD 4 (May 5, 1849):393-94.

Largely concerned with C's. combative nature and the unhappy results of his political and social pronouncements.

1232 MONTHLY CENSOR 1 (June 1822):114.
>A patriotic action novel that attempts to infuse the reader with the principles of honor and morality.

1233 MONTHLY LITERARY REGISTER 1 (June 1822):121-24.
>Excellent characterizations (except for the lack of a distinct hero), fine humor, and a moral tone are marred only by C's, occasional lengthy dialogue.

1234 MONTHLY MAGAZINE 53 (July 1, 1822):549.
>A clever novel with well drawn characters, although somewhat partial.

1235 MONTHLY REVIEW 2, 4th series (June 1831):308.
>Unequal in style and interest.

1236 NEW EDINBURGH REVIEW 3 (October 1822):345-59.
>A patronizing review that comments unfavorably on C's. patriotism and his imitation of Scott.

1237 NEW-ENGLAND GALAXY 5 (January 11, 1822):[2].
>ighly positive in its praise.

1238 NEW YORK AMERICAN, January 3, 1822.

1239 NEW YORK COMMERCIAL ADVERTISER, December 28, 1821.

1240 NEW YORK SPECTATOR, January 1, 1822.
>Grudgingly favorable.

1241 _____, January 29, 1822.
>Highly favorable.

1242 NILES' WEEKLY REGISTER 22 (May 25, 1822):193.
>Superior to Scott.

1243 PORT FOLIO 13, 5th series (February 1822):90-101.
>This volume confirms the opinion that ample subject matter exists for developing an American literature. Both the characters and their dialogue are excellently presented, with the exception of that of George Washington (Mr. Harper). If lapses in literary style do exist, the intense interest created by the story allows them to pass nearly unnoticed.

1244 _____ 15, 5th series (March 1823):226-29.
       Not an overly interesting book, nor possessed of a well constructed plot, but it should stand as a model for future delineations of the American character.

1245 SOUTHERN LITERARY MESSENGER 15 (June 1849):370.
       C's. return to the romance is preferable to his more recent literary attempts.

1246 "The Spy--Harvey Birch. "THE ARIEL 5 (August 20, 1831):141.
       Basically a reprint of a pertinent section of the "Preface" to a republished London edition of THE SPY relating to the original Harvey Birch.

Articles from Cooper's Death to the Present

1247 Blanck, Jacob. "News from the Rare Book Shops." PUBLISHERS' WEEKLY 133 (April 23 1938):1696.
       A short article that denies Enoch Crosby was the model for Harvey Birch.

1248 Boynton, Percy H., ed. "Introduction." THE SPY. New York: Macmillan Co., 1928.

1249 Brenner, C. D. "The Influence of Cooper's 'The Spy' on Hauff's 'Lichtenstein.'" MODERN LANGUAGE NOTES 30 (November 1915):207-10.
       THE SPY (1821) appeared in translation in Germany in 1824 and evidence shows that Hauff was familiar with C's. writings. The character of the Piper of Hardt in LICHTENSTEIN, published in 1826, resembles Harvey Birch too closely in physical make-up, action, and social class not to have been drawn from him.

1250 Bryan, William Alfred. GEORGE WASHINGTON IN AMERICAN LITERATURE, 1775-1865. New York: Columbia University Press, 1952. Pp. 195-200.
       A discussion of C's. handling of the Mr. Harper/Washington character.

1251 Canby, Henry Seidel, ed.   "Introduction." THE SPY. New York: Bowling Green Press, 1929.

1252 "Cooper and 'The Spy.'" NEW-YORK TRIBUNE, June 8, 1902, p. 7.
       On C's. familiarity with Westchester County and John Jay's

supposed influence on THE SPY.

1253 "Cooper Volume Tops Sale." NEW YORK TIMES, May 25, 1932, p. 17.

First edition of THE SPY sold for $750.

1254 Deane, James E. "Enoch Crosby Not a Myth." MAGAZINE OF AMERICAN HISTORY 18 (July 1887):73-75.

Written in response to the May article by Hatfield (item no. 1259) who claimed that Enoch Crosby was not the model for Harvey Birch.

1255 Diemer, James S. "A Model for Harvey Birch." AMERICAN LITERATURE 26 (May 1954):242-47.

Henry Lee's story of Sergeant John Champe in MEMOIRS OF THE WAR IN THE SOUTHERN DEPARTMENT OF THE UNITED STATES provided C. with the model for Harvey Birch.

1256 Edwards, Oliver. "The First Civil War." TIMES (London), August 20, 1964, p. 11.

C's. best novel needs only a few concessions to nineteenth century fictional writing to be enjoyed today.

1257 Fink, Robert A. "Harvey Birch: The Yankee Peddler as an American Hero." NEW YORK FOLKLORE QUARTERLY 30 (June 1974):137-52.

The portrayal of Harvey Birch as a Yankee peddler not only helped to perpetuate the myth surrounding the early American peddler, but it gave C. the opportunity to develop one of the great literary paradoxes--the lowly, money grubbing citizen who illustrates the utmost in unselfishness and altruism.

1258 Haswell, Charles Haynes. REMINESCENCES OF NEW YORK BY AN OCTOGENARIAN. New York: Harper & Bros., 1896. Pp. 129-30.

On Enoch Crosby and his claim to being the original for Harvey Birch.

1259 Hatfield, Guy. "Harvey Birch and the Myth of Enoch Crosby." MAGAZINE OF AMERICAN HISTORY 17 (May 1887):431-33.

Hatfield, basing his conclusions on Susan Cooper's A GLANCE BACKWARD, claims that Enoch Crosby was not the original Harvey Birch. See also item nos. 1254 and 1260.

1260 _____. "Harvey Birch Not Enoch Crosby." MAGAZINE OF AMERICAN HISTORY 18 (October 1887):341.

A reply to Deane (item no. 1254) who had attacked Hatfield's conclusions in an earlier article.

1261 Howe, Herbert Barber. "Written in Westchester County--Cooper's Tale of the Neutral Ground." Westchester County Historical Society, BULLETIN 28 (January):16-21.
　　　　　Not seen.　　Citation from WRITINGS IN AMERICAN HISTORY, 1952, p. 197.

1262 Krzyzanowski, Julian. "James Fenimore Cooper and Adam Mickiewicz: A Stylistic Device from Prison Lore." INTERNATIONAL JOURNAL OF SLAVIC LINGUISTICS AND POETICS no. 4 (1961):75-83.
　　　　　Mickiewicz's poem KONRAD WALLENROD was influenced by THE SPY.

1263 Lodge, Henry Cabot. STUDIES IN HISTORY.　Boston: Houghton, Mifflin & Co., 1884. Pp. 353-54.
　　　　　The success of THE SPY lies in its American origin, the first of its type.　C., driven by an intense patriotism, was able to throw off the colonialism of the past to gain a world-wide reputation.

1264 McBride, John. "Cooper's 'Spy' on the French Stage." TENNESSEE STUDIES IN LITERATURE no. 1 (1956):35-42.
　　　　　French adaptations of THE SPY were generally unsatisfactory, for the complicated plot, lack of interest to Europeans, and the sameness of C's. stories, made dramatization difficult.

1265 McDowell, Tremaine. "The Identity of Harvey Birch." AMERICAN LITERATURE 2 (May 1930):111-20.
　　　　　Harvey Birch is a product of C's. imagination and was not suggested by John Jay, nor patterned after Enoch Crosby.

1266 _____. "James Fenimore Cooper as Self-critic." STUDIES IN PHILOLOGY 27 (July 1930):508-16.
　　　　　McDowell maintains that C's revision of THE SPY was more than nominal. Although he failed to correct all stylistic errors, the changes made were considerable and show that he was a conscientious critic of the book.

1267 _____, ed. "Introduction." THE SPY. New York, Chicago, etc.: C. Scribner's Sons, 1931.

1268 Maurice, Arthur Bartlett. NEW YORK IN FICTION. New York: Dodd, Mead & Co., 1901. Pp. 192-202.

Discusses Harlem Heights and the Jumel mansion (reputedly one of Harvy Birch's places of concealment during the Revolution), the northern end of Manhattan, and Westchester County as they were utilized by C. in THE SPY.

1269 Miller, Harry Edward. "The Spy of the Neutral Ground." NEW ENGLAND MAGAZINE 18 n.s. (May 1898):307-19.
A claim that Enoch Crosby was the original Harvey Birch. Includes an account of Crosby's life.

1270 Morpurgo, J. E., ed. "Introduction." THE SPY. London: Oxford University Press, 1968.

1271 Pennypacker, Morton. GENERAL WASHINGTON'S SPIES ON LONG ISLAND AND IN NEW YORK. Brooklyn: Long Island Historical Society, 1939. Pp. 44, 113.
On Revolutionary War incidents that formed the basis for Chapter 10 and a portion of the last chapter of THE SPY.

1272 Pickering, James H. "Enoch Crosby, Secret Agent of the Neutral Ground: His Own Story." NEW YORK HISTORY 47 (January 1966):61-73.
A reprint of a deposition given by Enoch Crosby in 1832 detailing his Revolutionary War experiences.

1273 _____. "Shube Merrit: Freeboater of the Neutral Ground." NEW YORK FOLKLORE QUARTERLY 21 (March 1965):31-39.
Pickering hypothesizes that C. may have incorporated the personality and deeds of Shube Merrit, a nineteenth century Westchester, N. Y., folk hero, into one or more of the characters in THE SPY.

1274 Pumpelly, J. C. "Enoch Crosby, the Continental Soldier, the Original of Cooper's Harvey Birch, the Patriot Spy." AMERICANA 9 (October 1914):829-38.
Includes information on Crosby's family and early life.

1275 "Record Price Paid for Cooper's 'Spy.'" NEW YORK TIMES, December 7, 1927, p. 32.

1276 St. Armand, Barton Levi. "Harvey Birch as the Wandering Jew: Literary Calvinism in James Fenimore Cooper's 'The Spy.'" AMERICAN LITERATURE 50 (November 1978):348-68.
C. gave Harvey Birch all the characteristics possessed by the Wandering Jew. That the sacrifice, guilt, and suffering he endured were never

forgiven or redeemed, is in keeping with American Calvinism of this period.

1277 Sheperd, James L., III. "Balzac's Debt to Cooper's 'Spy' in 'Les Chouans.'" FRENCH REVIEW 28 (December 1954):145-52.

Balzac, who had decided to become the French C., selected an area in France and an incident in French history that would allow him to create a work of fiction very similar to THE SPY in setting, plot, and characterization.

1278 "Some Classic Novels." NEW-YORK TRIBUNE, April 26, 1896, p. 26.

Magical and imaginative in spite of simplicity and excessive rhetoric. C's. ability to define and lend vitality to the American frontier will continue to captivate.

1279 Starke, Catherine Juanita. BLACK PORTRAITURE IN AMERICAN FICTION: STOCK CHARACTERS, ARCHETYPES AND INDIVIDUALS. New York: Basic Books, 1971. Pp. 30-35.

Contends that C's. characterization of the slave Caesar was meant to create a "ludicrous", less than human, being who would serve to present a contrast to the whole landed class and point up its virtues.

1280 Thomas, Charles Swain, ed. "Introduction." THE SPY. Boston, New York, etc.: Houghton, Mifflin Co., 1911.

1281 Thurber, Samuel, Jr., ed. "Introduction." THE SPY. New York: Macmillan Co., 1909.

1282 Vandiver, Edward P., Jr. "Simms' Porgy and Cooper." MODERN LANGUAGE NOTES 70 (April 1955):272-74.

Simms' Lieutenant Porgy (THE PARTISAN) is based largely upon C's. Captain Lawton of THE SPY.

1283 Walker, Warren S. "The Prototype of Harvey Birch." NEW YORK HISTORY 37 (October 1956):399-413.

Walker claims that it was Samuel Culper, a pseudonym for two Revolutionary War New York spies (Abraham Woodhull and Robert Townsend), and not Enoch Crosby, who was the prototype for Harvey Birch.

1284 _____, ed. "Introduction." THE SPY. New York: Scribners, 1931.

1285 Wilson, Rufus Rockwell and Otilie Erickson Wilson. NEW YORK IN LITERATURE: THE STORY TOLD IN THE LANDMARKS OF TOWN

AND COUNTRY. Elmira, N. Y.: Primavera Press, 1947. Pp. 223-26, 258-60.

Concerns the conditions under which C. came to write THE SPY and the career of Enoch Crosby, C's. model for Harvey Birch.

1286 Winterich, John T. "Romantic Stories of Books: 'The Spy.'" PUBLISHERS' WEEKLY 119 (June 20, 1931):2882-86.

Includes biographical material as well as information on the value of the first edition of THE SPY.

1287 _____, ed. "Introduction." THE SPY. New York: Heritage Press, 1963.

Lionel Lincoln (1825)

Articles and Reviews Contemporary with Cooper

1288 LA BELLE ASSEMBLÉE 1, 3d series (1825):172.

1289 CINCINNATI LITERARY GAZETTE 2 (December 4, 1824):182.
A mention of the book's impending publication.

1290 GENTLEMAN'S MAGAZINE 102 (September 1832):629.
Brief praise for C. in general.

1291 LITERARY GAZETTE 9 (March 5, 1825):149-51. Quoted from and commented on in AMERICAN ATHANAEUM 1 (May 26, 1825):47.

Not a very good novel, but of sufficient merit to amuse a certain class of readers. It suffers from credibility, especially where the characters Job Pray and Ralph are concerned.

1292 MONTHLY CRITICAL GAZETTE 2 (April 1825):358-61.

Bemoans the fact that C. has attempted to imitate a bad example (Scott), that he has misled his readers where historical fact is concerned, and that he has reopened old wounds between America and England.

1293 MUSEUM OF FOREIGN LITERATURE 7 (November 1825):435-41.

A poor book that does not add to C's. reputation. What he wrote that was good in the past was accomplished purely by accident. Others will now surpass him and he will never catch up.

1294 Neal, John. AMERICAN WRITERS: A SERIES OF PAPERS

CONTRIBUTED TO "BLACKWOOD'S MAGAZINE" (1824-1825). Edited by Fred Lewis Pattee. Durham, N. C.: Duke University Press, 1937. Pp. 205-13. Originally in BLACKWOOD'S MAGAZINE 18 (September 1825):323-28. Partially reprinted in UNITED STATES LITERARY GAZETTE 2 (September 15, 1825):467.

C. is a poor novelist and LIONEL LINCOLN is no exception. While he has tried to create a truly American book, he has not been capable of doing so. If he is due any praise, it is for his attempt to avoid writing a British novel and for making those mistakes from which future American writers can profit.

1295 NEPENTHES 1 (March 12, 1825):68.

An overall favorable review that criticizes C. for his less than realistic characters.

1296 NEW-YORK REVIEW AND ATHENEUM MAGAZINE 1 (June 1825):39-50.

The plot is both improbable and inconsistent, the Yankee disposition and dialect is inadequate, and there are several lapses in style and language. Overall, however, the book is highly successful and will be a significant addition to America's national literature.

1297 NEW YORK SPECTATOR, February 17, 1825.

Comments on C's. patriotism.

1298 "Note-Book of a Literary Idler. No. I." BLACKWOOD'S MAGAZINE 17 (June 1825):736-44.

C., although a very fair man, has found it impossible to develop his Revolutionary era characters without the bias expected of an American. (p. 739)

1299 UNITED STATES LITERARY GAZETTE 1 (March 1, 1825):337-40.

Inferior to THE SPY, but superior to THE PIONEERS or THE PILOT. Perhaps of less interest than some of his other novels, but one that is less tedious and offensive to no one.

Articles from Cooper's Death to the Present

1300 Nichols, Betty Elaine. "James Fenimore Cooper's 'Lionel Lincoln': A Source and Literary Study." Ph.D. dissertation, Michigan State University, 1973.

C. journeyed to Boston to view Revolutionary War settings he planned to use in LIONEL LINCLON. He also read widely to give the novel the authenticity he felt was necessary. Many of his most successful scenes are those that depend upon these sources for their existence. Less successful is C's. attempt to integrate the elements of theme and plot, leading one to question the novel's credibility.

1301 Ringe, Donald A. "Cooper's 'Lionel Lincoln': The Problems of Genre." AMERICAN TRANSCENDENTAL QUARTERLY 24 (Fall 1974):24-30.
   Emphasizes C's. shift in point of view in LIONEL LINCOLN occurring toward the end of the book. Up to that time he had operated on a sound basis that successfully took into account both historical and romantic components.

1302 Steinbrink, Jeffrey. "Cooper's Romance of the Revolution: 'Lionel Lincoln' and the Lessons of Failure." EARLY AMERICAN LITERATURE 11 (Winter 1976-77):336-43.
   LIONEL LINCOLN is C's. only piece of historical fiction and it was a failure. It is weighted down by too much historical detail and possesses no integration of historical fact with storytelling.

The Wept of Wish-ton-Wish (The Borderers [English Title]) (1829)

Articles and Reviews Contemporary with Cooper

1303 "Adelphi Theatre." ATHENAEUM [4] (December 3, 1831):788-89.
   Unsuccessful as a drama.

1304 THE ARIEL 3 (October 3, 1829):93.
   A fine example of C's. genius that grabs both the reader's attention and feelings.

1305 _____ 3 (November 28, 1829):125.
   The most interesting Indian story ever written.

1306 _____ 3 (December 26, 1829):141.
   C. is accused of plagiarism from Sedgwick's HOPE LESLIE.

1307 CABINET OF RELIGION 2 (November 28, 1829):662-63.
   For all its carelessness, rambling, lack of originality, and inconsistency, the book possesses great action, description and Indian characters.

1308 EDINGURGH LITERARY JOURNAL no. 49 (October 17, 1829):271-74.

The least successful of C's. novels--tedious, improbable, and repetitious.

1309 LADIES' MUSEUM 2, 4th series (November 1829):290.

As good as any of those novels that have preceded it. Once he leaves the frontier or sea to enter the drawing room of polite society, however, C. fails. Neither is his humor effective.

1310 LADY'S MAGAZINE 10 n.s. (October 1829):512.

Fails to comment specifically on the novel, but claims that C. improves with each new publication.

1311 LITERARY GAZETTE 13 (September 26, 1829):627-29.

Worthy of C's. great reputation, except for the attempts at humor and an occasional bit of dullness.

1312 MONTHLY MAGAZINE 8 n.s. (November 1829):566-68.

A unique novel. As full of history as it is of romance.

1313 NEW MONTHLY MAGAZINE 27 (December 1829):508-09.

C. is the exclusive possessor "of the historico-fictitious literature of the day." He is unsurpassed in his description of Indian life and manners.

1314 NEW YORK COMMERCIAL ADVERTISER, December 9, 1829.

1315 NILES' WEEKLY REGISTER 37 (November 14, 1829):182.

A short positive notice.

1316 PHILADELPHIA ALBUM 4 (January 16, 1830):21.

A failure whose occasional excitement is overshadowed by C's. love of minute detail and a previous exhaustion of Indian subjects.

1317 SOUTHERN REVIEW 5 (February 1830):207-26.

A complete failure. Dull, repetitious, and hastily composed.

1318 Whittier, John Greenleaf. WHITTIER ON WRITERS AND WRITING. Edited by Edwin Harrison Cady and Harry Hayden Clark. Syracuse, N. Y.: Syracuse University Press, 1950. Pp. 26-28. Originally in the ESSEX GAZETTE (Haverhill, Mass.), January 2, 1830.

This narrative lacks the originality of C's. sea stories. The female characters are burdensome to the tale. It does, however, contain descriptive passages that have never been excelled.

Articles from Cooper's Death to the Present

1319 Davis, Richard Beale, ed. "Introduction." THE WEPT OF WISH-TON-WISH. Columbus, Ohio: Charles E. Merrill Publishing Co., 1970.

THE WEPT OF WISH-TON-WISH is not a hostile portrayal of Puritan New England as many critics have claimed. Rather, as C. did in other novels dealing with people far removed from the Calvinistic mode, he made use of evil (destruction of the Indians) to show how a more perfect society (a civilized European one) could result from it.

1320 Orians, G. Harrison. "The Angel of Hadley in Fiction: A Study of the Sources of Hawthorne's 'The Grey Champion.'" AMERICAN LITERATURE 4 (November 1932):257-69.

On C. and other authors who used William Goffe as a character in their fiction.

1321 "The Puritan as Drawn By Two Masters in Fiction." NEW ENGLANDER AND YALE REVIEW 18 n.s. (February 1891):139-50.

Although C. disliked New Englanders he was able to put aside his prejudices and present his readers with true to life characters who reflected both traditional and historical concepts.

Wyandotte (1843)

Articles and Reviews Contemporary with Cooper

1322 ATHENAEUM [16] (September 2, 1843):792-93.

Of no great interest to those who expect continuous action or scenic descriptions.

1323 BROTHER JONATHAN 6 (September 9, 1843):46.

The incidents and time period should appeal to the country's sense of nationalism.

1324 LADIES' COMPANION 19 (October 1843):308.

An indifferent, spiteful, anti-American book that creates, at the least, feelings of indifference, if not dislike.

1325 "A Leash of Novels." MONTHLY REVIEW 3, 4th series (October 1843):224-43.

A true picture of American scenery and life, written in a calm and attractive manner.

1326 LITERARY GAZETTE 27 (September 9, 1843):576-79.
A fast moving tale. Reminiscent of much of C's. early fiction.

1327 METROPOLITAN MAGAZINE 38 (November 1843):72-77.
A combination of C. at home (the wilderness) and C. abroad (the household hearth). That of the hearth is dull.

1328 Poe, Edgar Allan ["Review".] GRAHAM'S MAGAZINE 23 (November 1843):261-64. Reprinted in Banks, Stanley M. AMERICAN ROMANTICISM: A SHAPE FOR FICTION. New York: G. P. Putnam's Sons, 1969. Pp. 181-84; Harrison, James A., ed. THE COMPLETE WORKS OF EDGAR ALLAN POE. Vol. 9. New York: AMS Press, 1965. Pp. 205-20; and Stedman, Edmund Clarence and George Edward Woodberry, eds. THE WORKS OF EDGAR ALLAN POE. Vol. 7. New York: Charles Scribner's Sons, 1914. Pp. 3-22.
Faulty, but absorbing. Well drawn black characters.

1329 SOUTHERN LITERARY MESSENGER 9 (November 1843):700.
Trite, carelessly constructed, and lacking in national pride.

1330 SOUTHERN QUARTERLY REVIEW 4 (October 1843):515-16.
A feeble attempt that is plotless, has poorly drawn characters, too much description, and inadequate action.

1331 SPECTATOR (London) 16 (September 9, 1843):857-58.
Little of C's. social preachments are found here. Minutely told with well developed characters, but sparse action and no striking narrative.

Articles from Cooper's Death to the Present

1332 Barnett, Louise K. "Coopers 'Wyandotte': The Indian as Split Personality." CIMARRON REVIEW 46 (January 1979):25-31.
WYANDOTTE was a more ambitious attempt to characterize the Indian than were previous novels, but less successful than the L. S. TALES.

1333 Hall, Joan N. "Romance as History; Cooper's 'Wyandotte.'" KENTUCKY REVIEW 2 (1968):38-46.

1334 Pickering, James H. "New York in the Revolution: Cooper's 'Wyandotte.'" NEW YORK HISTORY 49 (April 1968):121-41.

C's. failure to maintain historical accuracy is a minor criticism of the book. The freedom afforded the novelist allowed him to present the core of truth at the same time that it released him from the limitations placed upon the historian. The article includes material on Captain William Edmeston, the source for Hugh Willoughby.

Oak Openings (The Bee Hunter [English Title]) (1848)

Articles and Reviews Contemporary with Cooper

1335 ATHENAEUM [21] (September 23, 1848):951-53.
 The novel represents an attempt to recover readers by returning to an old theme. It is a failure, however, for C. has lost his powers, leaving only a slender story of exaggerated escapades and unrealistic dialogue.

1336 GODEY'S LADY'S BOOK 38 (February 1849):152.
 One of C's. best books. Free from the stylistic faults of some of his earlier works.

1337 HOLDEN'S DOLLAR MAGAZINE 2 (December 1848):753-55.
 A valuable work whose interest lies in its descriptions of local events and places. Its characters are uninteresting and the politics no different from what C. has forced upon his readers in the past.

1338 LITERARY GAZETTE 32 (August 26, 1848):562-64.
 While C. proves that he is at home with Indian life and can entertain, this novel lacks the emotion (both in incident and characterization) that makes a great story. As usual, his dislike of anything English is evident.

1339 SPECTATOR (London) 21 (August 26, 1848):831-32.
 Similar to other C. works, but his scenic and societal descriptions give him an advantage over other American novelists. He has, however, become too serious in his recent works.

1340 UNITED STATES MAGAZINE AND DEMOCRATIC REVIEW 23 (November 1848):472-74.
 Inferior to its predecessors. A moral tale of great dullness that is filled with degenerate Indians and scenic descriptions unworthy of C.

Articles from Cooper's Death to the Present

1341 Dawson, Lawrence R., Jr. "James Fenimore Cooper and Michigan: His

Novels, Visits, and Attitude." MICHIGAN HISTORY 59 (Winter 1975):275-92.

 C. did not visit Michigan to gather material for his novel, but to conclude a lawsuit and sell property owned there. Neither can a case be made for the historical accuracy of sites mentioned in THE OAK OPENINGS, or for real life persons as a basis for some of the book's characters. Includes many references to C. in local Michigan newspapers and county histories.

1342 Dunbar, Willis F. KALAMAZOO AND HOW IT GREW. Kalamazoo, Mich., 1959. P. 31.

 A discussion of Ben Boden that concludes that he was a composite of several real people.

1343 Hedges, James S. "'Oak Openings': Fenimore Cooper's Requiem for the American Indian." OLD NORTHWEST: A JOURNAL OF REGIONAL LIFE AND LETTERS 11 (Spring-Summer 1985):25-34.

 Not seen.

1344 Kuiper, Kenneth Wayne. "James Fenimore Cooper's 'The Oak Openings', or 'The Bee Hunter': An Interpretation and Evaluation." Ph.D. dissertation, University of Michigan, 1963.

 THE OAK OPENINGS is a better novel than has generally been claimed. C's. later life as a writer was one of quality and his ideas of national destiny and providence were significant to nineteenth century literature.

1345 Oakley, Kate Russell. "James Fenimore Cooper and 'Oak Openings.'" MICHIGAN HERITAGE 1 (Autumn/Winter 1959):5-8.

1346 Stone, James H. "Bazel Harrison." HISTORY OF KALAMAZOO COUNTY, MICHIGAN. Philadelphia: Everts & Abbott, 1880. Pp. 439-40.

1347 _____. A BIOGRAPHICAL SKETCH OF JUDGE BAZEL HARRISON, THE FIRST WHITE SETTLER IN KALAMAZOO COUNTY. Kalamazoo, Mich., 1874.

 Includes the various claims concerning the real life original of the bee hunter.

1348 Weissert, Charles. "Southwest Michigan." HISTORIC MAGAZINE 3 (1924):152-53.

 Conjecture that C. visited southwestern Michigan during the 1840s.

1349 Williams, J. Gary. "The Post-shift in Cooper's 'The Oak Openings.'"

ENGLISH LANGUAGE NOTES 16 (September 1978):25-32.

C. changed his plan for this novel once he started writing it. The bee hunter was to be the hero, but is not. Rather, the focus is on Scalping Peter and Parson Amen.

1350 Williams, Mentor L. "Cooper, Lyon and the Moore-Hascall Harvesting Machine." MICHIGAN HISTORY 31 (March 1947):26-34.

C. was in Michigan in the summer of 1848, but not to gather material for THE OAK OPENINGS. He had finished the book the previous winter in Cooperstown and was now acting in the capacity of land speculator.

1351 _____. "They Wrote Home About It." MICHIGAN ALUMNUS QUARTERLY REVIEW 51 (July 28, 1945):337-51.

On C's. visit to Michigan in 1848, the writing of THE OAK OPENINGS, and his impressions of the countryside. (pp. 349-50)

5

LITERATURE OF THE SEA

GENERAL STUDIES

1352 Hall, Edwin Malburn. "Cooper and the Navy." Ph.D. dissertation, Pennsylvania State University, 1959.

        Explores C's. connection with the Navy and the influence it had upon his life, his HISTORY OF THE NAVY, and those novels in which naval interest are displayed.

FICTION

ARTICLES AND REVIEWS CONTEMPORARY WITH COOPER

1353 "French Naval Romances." FOREIGN QUARTERLY REVIEW 21 (July 1838).

        Not seen. Citation taken from Clavel, p. 239 (item no. 5). It is C., not Smollett, who must be considered as the originator of the sea novel.

1354 GRAHAMS AMERICAN MONTHLY MAGAZINE 39 (July 1851):64.

        On reprints of TWO ADMIRALS and THE WATER WITCH. Both are realistic, well characterized, and possessed of an excellent narrative.

1355 MONTHLY MAGAZINE 9 n.s. (May 1830):561-69.

        From a review of Marryat's KING'S OWN. Claims that C. was only a purser and must have had someone knowledgeable about sea life at his side as he wrote.

1356 "Naval Sketch-book." BLACKWOOD'S MAGAZINE 19 (March 1826):353-74.

  While C. has exaggerated his naval characters somewhat, his descriptions are excellent and he refuses to be unjust to the British Navy in his stories. (p. 354)

ARTICLES FROM COOPER'S DEATH TO THE PRESENT

1357 Anderson, Charles. "Cooper's Sea Novels Spurned in the Maintop." MODERN LANGUAGE NOTES 66 (June 1951):388-91.

  On the authenticity of C's. characters and language. Evidence shows that the novel reading public of his day readily accepted him as a realistic writer. This viewpoint was not shared by the non-reader who often had the first-hand knowledge necessary for a critical appraisal of the sea novels.

1358 Bird, Christine M. "Melville's Debt to Cooper's Sea Novels." Ph.D. dissertation, Tulane University, 1972.

  Bird claims that Melville, like C., moved from romance, to realism, to metaphysics, in his sea novels. Unlike C. though, he was able to produce the great sea novel (MOBY DICK). Part of the reason for his success, however, must be attributed to what he learned from his predecessor. Parallels Philbrick's thesis (item no. 1376).

1359 Bonner, William H. "Cooper and Captain Kidd." MODERN LANGUAGE NOTES 61 (January 1946):21-27.

  Using several of C's. sea stories, Bonner shows that the author was familiar with the Kidd legends.

1360 Borowsky, Anton G. "Social Content in Cooper's Sea Novels." Master of Arts degree, University of North Carolina, 1964.

1361 Brownlee, Carole G. "James Fenimore Cooper and Herman Melville: Voyagers on the Same Sea?" Master of Arts degree, University of Maryland, 1968.

1362 Chapman, Edward Mortimer. ENGLISH LITERATURE IN ACCOUNT WITH RELIGION. Boston: Houghton Mifflin Co., 1910. Pp. 258-60.

  C. would, at times, support theological or ecclesiastical tenets of special interest to him. He was both orthodox for his day and a man with little humor.

1363 Clagett, John H. "The Maritime Works of James Fenimore Cooper as Sources for Sea Lore, Sea Legend, and Sea Idiom." SOUTHERN FOLKLORE QUARTERLY 30 (December 1966):323-31.

C's. extensive knowledge of the sea and sailing allowed him to impart little known details of sea lore, create authentic dialogue, and recreate characters that were natural and believable.

1364 Connolly, J. B. "Cooper and Stories of the Sea." FICTION AND ITS MAKERS. Edited by F. X. Talbot. New York, 1928. Pp. 171-78.

1365 Conrad, Joseph. NOTES ON LIFE AND LETTERS. Garden City, N. Y.: Doubleday, Page & Co., 1921. Pp. 55-57. Originally in OUTLOOK, June 1898. Reprinted in MODERN ENGLISH ESSAYS. Vol. 4. Edited by E. Rhys. New York: E. P. Dutton, 1922. Pp. 44-45.

Conrad saw C's. renderings of sea life as realistic.

1366 Cooksey, Philip Neil. "A Thematic Study of James Fenimore Cooper's Nautical Fiction." Ph.D. dissertation, Louisiana State University and Agricultural and Mechanical College, 1977.

An examination of C's. progression from romancer, to symbolist, to allegorist.

1367 DUBLIN UNIVERSITY MAGAZINE 47 (March 1856):294-308. Also in "James Fenimore Cooper." ECLECTIC MAGAZINE 37 (March 1856):313-16.

From a review of Marryat's sea fiction. C. was the superior of the two writers when dealing with descriptions of ships and the ocean. This is true even of HOMEWARD BOUND and AFLOAT AND ASHORE, two of his poorer novels. (pp. 299-300)

1368 Egan, Hugh McKeever. "Gentleman-Sailors: The First Person Narratives of Dana, Cooper, and Melville." Ph.D. dissertation, University of Iowa, 1983.

C. made use of the vernacular in his first person novels, a technique not found in his other fiction.   Includes comments on NED MYERS, MILES WALLINGFORD, and AFLOAT AND ASHORE.

1369 Hannay, James. "Sea Novels--Captain Marryat." CORNHILL MAGAZINE 27 (February 1873):170-90.

C. was superior as a delineator of sea scenery, but he lacked the comedy and easy style of Marryat. (pp. 176-78)

1370 Hoyt, George L. "Religious Aspects of Cooper's Sea Stories." Master of

Arts degree, University of Iowa, 1965.

1371 Miller, Paul A. "James Fenimore Cooper and the South Seas." Master of Arts degree, University of North Dakota, 1930.

1372 Neeser, R. W. "Cooper's Sea Tales." New York State Historical Association, PROCEEDINGS 16 (1917):63-68.
        Includes the circumstances under which C. came to write his first sea tale, the identification of some real life people who were models for his characters, a discussion of his realism, and criticism of his narrative style.

1373 Nelson, Paul David. "James Fenimore Cooper's Maritime Nationalism, 1820-1850." MILITARY AFFAIRS 41 (1977):129-32.
        C., alone among the literary men of his age, agitated for greater support of American naval interests. It was on the sea, not along the frontier that he saw America carrying out her policy of manifest destiny. He underestimated the force exerted by westward movement, however, at a time when the politics of the country would not support his call for increased naval power.

1374 Parry, Elsie A. "When Literature Went to Sea: Taken By Those Immortal Mariners, Cooper, Dana, Melville." BOOKMAN (New York) 75 (July 1932):243-48.
        Disregarding both technique and proper English, C. used action to weave highly popular tales of the sea.

1375 Peck, H. Daniel. "A Repossession of America: The Revolution in Cooper's Trilogy of Nautical Romances." STUDIES IN ROMANTICISM 15 (Fall 1976):589-605.
        Although C. considered the Revolutionary War to be a necessary development, he consistently expressed concern over the social upheaval it had caused and over the implications these new forces had for America's future.

1376 Philbrick, Thomas. JAMES FENIMORE COOPER AND THE DEVELOPMENT OF AMERICAN SEA FICTION. Cambridge, Mass.: Harvard University Press, 1961.
        C. as the originator of the sea novel. Philbrick attempts to discover why so much sea fiction was written during this period, why readers were so interested in it, what changes where experienced over time in its writing, and how these changes related to the United States as a nation.

1377 Ross, Ernest C. "The Development of the English Sea Novel From Defoe to Conrad." Ph.D. dissertation, University of Virginia (mimeographed and printed at Edwards Bros., Ann Arbor, Mich.), [1926]. Pp. 16-27.

        Covers C's. use of the Byronic hero, his turn to social criticism, his style, the characterization of his seamen, his idealized women, and his adaptation of history to fiction.

1378 "A Trio of American-Sailor Authors." DUBLIN UNIVERSITY MAGAZINE 47 (January 1856):47-54. Reprinted in ECLECTIC MAG-AZINE 37 (March 1856):313-16 and LITTEL'S LIVING AGE 48 (March 1, 1856):560-66.

        C's. genius as a novelist was most evident in his early works, although those that were written later in his career are still worthy of praise. His greatest attributes include his descriptive abilities and his characterizations.

1379 Walker, Warren S. "Ames *vs.* Cooper: The Case Re-opened." MODERN LANGUAGE NOTES 70 (January 1955):27-32.

        C's. poor choice of dialogue in his sea fiction made it unrealistic according to Nathaniel Ames, a contemporary critic. Walker contends that Ames was not being objective in his analysis, for the diction employed, while exaggerated, was accurate. See Ames's A MARINER'S SKETCHES (1830), NAUTICAL REMINISCENCES (1832), and AN OLD SAILOR'S YARNS (1835) for his attacks.

1380 Zoellner, Robert H. "James Fenimore Cooper's Sea Novels: His Social Theories as Expressed Symbolically Through the Gentleman-leader of the Microcosmic Ship on the Sea-frontier." Ph.D. dissertation, University of Wisconsin, 1962.

        Only with the sea novels was C. able to fully develop his political and social theories of the gentleman-leader. This was be cause the sea had a permanency of social structure not found on the frontier.

THE PILOT (1823)

Articles and Reviews Contemporary with Cooper

1381 ATLAS 6 (March 20, 1831):188.

1382 LA BELLE ASSEMBLÉE 29 n.s. (March 1824):123-24.
        Improbable, but humorous, fresh, and original.

1383 Brainard, John G. C. THE POEMS OF JOHN G. C. BRAINARD. Hartford: S. Andrus & Son, 1847. Pp. 112-13.
        A poem about Long Tom.

1384 CHRISTIAN SPECTATOR 7 (February 1825):87-88.
A carefully written novel that has interesting narrative and a skillfully constructed plot. Superior to those books that would seek to compete with it.

1385 CINCINNATI LITERARY GAZETTE 1 (February 14, 1824):49-51.
A faithful representation of sea life with excellent descriptions. The story is less absorbing than the descriptions.

1386 GENTLEMAN'S MAGAZINE 101 (June 1831):609-10.
Comments favorably on C's. seamen, their humor, and the novel's continuous action.

1387 GRAHAMS AMERICAN MONTHLY MAGAZINE 36 (February 1850):168.
Should continue to be popular and maintain a position among other similar novels of its day.

1388 Hazlitt, William. THE COLLECTED WORKS OF WILLIAM HAZLITT. Vol. 6. Edited by A. R. Waller and Arnold Glover. London: J. M. Dent, 1903. Pp. 385-86.
C. was best when dealing with the sea. THE PILOT's picture of American character and manners is a prime example.

1389 HOLDEN'S DOLLAR MAGAZINE 4 (December 1849):764.
A classic. As the inventor of the sea novel C. has many imitators, but none are his equal.

1390 [Hunt, Leigh. "A Review of Cooper's 'The Pilot' and Godwin's 'Caleb Williams.'"] TATLER 2 (April 7, 1831):737. Reprinted in Houtchens, Lawrence Huston and Carolyn Washburn Houtchens, eds. LEIGH HUNT'S LITERARY CRITICISM. New York: Columbia University Press, 1956. Pp. 372-75.
Original and truthful. Sure to become a standard of American sea literature. It, however, is deficient in its female characterizations and is often too detailed.

1391 LADIES' MONTHLY MUSEUM 19 imp. series (March 1824): 158-59.
Original. Compares C. favorably to Smollett.

1392 LITERARY GAZETTE 8 (January 31, 1824):77.
As Smollett, C. has used much of his own seafaring knowledge in THE PILOT.

1393 _____ 8 (February 7, 1824):82-84.
          The story is improbable for it is too idealized and the author is overly patriotic. Most of the characters are admirably drawn and the book is original enough that it should prove to be popular.

1394 LITERARY MUSEUM 3 (January 31, 1824):61-63.
          The near equal of Scott--less powerful than Smollett.

1395 MONTHLY REVIEW 103 n.s. (March 1824):330-31.
          The character of John Paul Jones is skillfully presented   and, although the nautical aspects of the story will be acceptable to the seaman, the general novel reader will not appreciate them.

1396 _____ 2, 4th series (May 1831):145-46.
          An unreadable novel.

1397 MUSEUM OF FOREIGN LITERATURE 4 (May 1824):428.
          This novel adds to C's. reputation. All the characters are well drawn except for the pilot. C. is compared to Smollett.

1398 "Naval Novels." METROPOLITAN MAGAZINE 1 (August 1831): 370-76.
          C. must be credited with having written the first genuine naval romance. (p. 376)

1399 NEW MONTHLY MAGAZINE 12 (March 1824):123-24. Reprinted in LADY'S MAGAZINE 5 n.s. (August 1824):445.
          While the sea fiction of Smollett is humorous, that of C. possesses a romantic quality.

1400 NEW YORK AMERICAN, January 13, July 15, 1824, April 12, 1825.

1401 NEW-YORK MIRROR 1 (April 17, 1824):301.
          With the exception of an occasional lapse, THE PILOT is written plainly and with imagination. The pictures that C. draws of the sea are unsurpassed.

1402 _____ 2 (December 4, 1824):151. Reprinted from the EDINBURGH SCOTSMAN.
          Superior to Smollett for C. is a realist who has an intimate knowledge of the sea. While his patriotism is evident in the skill shown by the Americans, he does not underrate the knowledge and bravery of the English seaman.

1403 NEW YORK SPECTATOR, October 7, 1823, January 23, 1824.
        Praised for its accuracy of observation.

1404 NEWCASTLE MAGAZINE 4 n.s. (February 1827):68-70.
        THE PILOT is superior to either THE SPY or THE PIONEERS
and more polished and professional than Smollett's RODERICK RANDOM.

1405 NILES' WEEKLY REGISTER 25 (February 7, 1824):357.
        First edition of 3,000 copies sold out within a few days.

1406 [Phillips, W.] "'The Pilot', a Tale of the Sea: By the Author of 'The
Pioneers.'" NORTH AMERICAN REVIEW 18 (April 1824):314-29.
        An important work of nation literature that makes much use of
American history and manners. If the book has one fault, it is the author's
predilection toward too much detail, leaving nothing to the reader's
imagination.

1407 PORT FOLIO 17, 5th series (February 1824):132-46.
        An adventuresome book as long as it remains on land.   The
author's nautical descriptions are related in a dialogue that is comprehensible
only to the seaman. C. is not a rival to Smollett.

1408 SARTAIN'S UNION MAGAZINE OF LITERATURE AND ART 6
(February 1850):174.
        Comments on the public service aspect of the new Putnam edition.

1409 Scott, Walter. MEMOIRS OF SIR WALTER SCOTT. Vol. 4. Edited
by J. G. Lockhart. London: Macmillan, 1900. P. 164.
        Reference to THE PILOT which Scott considers "very clever."

1410 SOMERSET HOUSE GAZETTE 1 (1824):283-85.

1411 SOUTHERN LITERARY MESSENGER 15 (December 1849):763.
        New edition--much worthier that other romances available to the
reader.

1412 UNITED STATES LITERARY GAZETTE 1 (April 1, 1824):6.
        Superior to either THE SPY or THE PIONEERS for it has humor,
pathos, and eloquence.   The language is well selected, the characters are
adequately sketched, and the reader's interest is maintained from beginning to
end. C's. greatest failure is his portrayal of John Paul Jones. Neither do his
female characters offer anything new.

1413 UNIVERSAL REVIEW 1 (May 1824):382.

       The sea is C's. element. Often approaches Smollett in ability.

Articles from Cooper's Death to the Present

1414 Greene, G. W. ["The Pilot."] NEW YORK QUARTERLY (June 1852):225.

       C. is superior to Marryat in his ability to describe and to create such characters as Tom Coffin.

1415 Kligerman, Jack. "Notes on Cooper's Debt to John Jay." AMERICAN LITERATURE 41 (November 1969):415-19.

       A 1781 letter from John Jay to Colonel John Laurens concerning the proposed capture of British statesmen during the Revolutionary War bears a remarkable similarity to a like scheme in THE PILOT. C's. knowledge of this plan could have come only from Jay.

1416 McDowell, Tremaine. "Scott on Cooper and Brockden Brown." MODERN LANGUAGE NOTES 45 (January 1930):18-20.

       Scott praised THE PILOT as a "clever" novel that drew its strength from its depiction of adventure and sea life. See item no. 1409.

1417 Walker, Warren S. "A 'Scottish Cooper' for an 'American Scott.'" AMERICAN LITERATURE 40 (January 1969):536-37.

       Walker comments upon an anonymous 1826 pamphlet that confused Scott's THE PIRATE with C's. THE PILOT. The result was that John Paul Jones (a C. character) was endowed with the characteristics of Clement Cleveland/John Gow (a Scott character).

1418 Williams, Marvin. "A Concealed Impression in the First English Edition of James Fenimore Cooper's 'The Pilot.'" THE DIRECTION LINE 9 (1979):7-8.

1419 Winterich, John T., ed. "Introduction." THE PILOT. New York: Heritage Press, 1968.

THE RED ROVER (1827)

Articles and Reviews Contemporary with Cooper

1420 THE ARIEL 1 (January 26, 1828):157.

Equal, if not superior, to anything C. has done previously.

1421 EVENING POST (New York), January 25, 1828.

1422 GRAHAMS AMERICAN MONTHLY MAGAZINE 36 (May 1850):348.
        This new edition deserves the popularity enjoyed by the original one.

1423 HOLDEN'S DOLLAR MAGAZINE 5 (April 1850):252.
        Second only to THE PILOT in interest and popularity as a sea story.

1424 LADY'S MAGAZINE 9 n.s. (January 1828):13.
        A favorable review.

1425 LITERARY CHRONICLE AND WEEKLY REVIEW 9 (December 8, 1827):770-73.
        THE RED ROVER will enhance C's. reputation as a tale of the land could not. On land he losses much of his power, for his characters are weak here, especially the women.

1426 LITERARY GAZETTE 11 (December 8, 1827):787.
        Superior to THE PILOT and valuable for its historical accuracy, although somewhat melodramatic and disappointing in its conclusion.

1427 LONDON MAGAZINE 10 n.s. (January 1828):101-20.
        The ship is the heroine of a story in which the characters are merely accessories to it. Nevertheless, the characterizations of the sailors are masterfully done. As long as C. stays at sea he is a powerful writer despite much tedious dialogue and description.

1428 LONDON WEEKLY REVIEW 1 (December 8, 1827):419.
        An American story that has thrown off the prejudices of Europe and addressed itself to the Yankee mind.

1429 [Mellen, G.] "The Red Rover." NORTH AMERICAN REVIEW 27 (July 1828):139-54.
        The sea is C's. favorite element and he is praised for returning to it.

1430 [Melville, Herman.] "A Thought on Book-binding." LITERARY WORLD 6 (March 16, 1850):276. Reprinted in Birss, John Howard, ed. "A

Book Review by Herman Melville." NEW ENGLAND QUARTERLY 5 (April 1932):346-48.

        Concerns the binding of a revised Putnam edition of THE RED ROVER.

1431 MONTHLY MAGAZINE 5 n.s. (February 1828):187-88.

        As a delineator of the American character, especially as it relates to naval scenes and subjects, C. has no equal, not even Scott.

1432 MUSEUM OF FOREIGN LITERATURE, SCIENCE AND ART 13 (May 1828):91-92.

        Inferior to those C. novels that have preceded it. The plot lacks originality, the characters are poorly drawn, and technical descriptions are overdone.

1433 NEW LONDON LITERARY GAZETTE 1 (December 8, 1827):417.

        Not equal to THE PILOT.

1434 NEW MONTHLY MAGAZINE 22 (January 1828):69-76. Reprinted in MUSEUM OF FOREIGN LITERATURE, SCIENCE AND ART 12 (February 1828):362-69.

        The best C. novel yet--realistic, graphically portrayed, and action filled. It is marred only by the author's anti-English bias.

1435 NEW-YORK MIRROR 5 (May 10, 1828):351.

        The dramatization of THE RED ROVER is skillfully done and should enjoy a long run.

1436 _____ 5 (May 31, 1828):375.

        A strong cast and beautiful scenery characterize the dramatization of THE RED ROVER at Lafayette Theatre.

1437 NEW YORK SPECTATOR, January 18, 1828.

1438 PHILADELPHIA ALBUM 2 (January 9, 1829):252-53.

        C's. greatest merits are his ability to describe and to design truly original characters. This volume, which has much good writing and an ingenious plot, is no exception. Brief comparisons are made to Brockden Brown, Byron, and Scott.

1439 PORT FOLIO 2, Hall's 2d series (October 1827):324-33.

        Inferior to C's. previous works, but exciting, imaginative, and well written.

1440 SARTAIN'S UNION MAGAZINE OF LITERATURE AND ART 6 (April 1850):309.

      On the new edition--"admirable."

1441 UNITED STATE MAGAZINE AND DEMOCRATIC REVIEW 26 (March 1850):282.

      Brilliant and enduring.

1442 WESTERN MONTHLY REVIEW 1 (February 1828):603-08.

      If C. would lose his fear of the critics he would undoubtedly write a novel more faulty, but of greater interest and merit than this one. His descriptions do not equal those of the master, Lord Byron, although there are some powerful scenes. The book's greatest defect is its probability; a defect, along with others, that C. has copied from Scott.

Articles from Cooper's Death to the Present

1443 Adams, Charles H. "Cooper's Sea Fiction and 'The Red Rover.'" STUDIES IN AMERICAN FICTION 16 (Autumn 1988):155-68.

      Like most sea fiction THE RED ROVER takes place mostly on the neutral ground between shore and the deep sea, not unlike a second neutral ground of conflict--that between authority and identity.

1444 Gordon, John D. "'The Red Rover' Takes the Boards." AMERICAN LITERATURE 10 (March 1938):66-75.

      Gordon seeks to prove, using stage productions of THE RED ROVER and four of the adaptations that were still in-print in 1938, that C's. sea fiction was popular with more than just the reading public.

1445 Walker, Warren S., ed. "Introduction." THE RED ROVER. Lincoln: University of Nebraska Press, 1963.

THE WATER-WITCH (1831)

Articles and Reviews Contemporary with Cooper

1446 "American Life and Manners" NEW MONTHLY MAGAZINE 31 (January 1831):42-50.

      C. is the master of the sea novel even though the similarity of his works justify accusations of a "poverty of invention." THE WEPT OF WISH-TON-WISH is also discussed. (pp. 47-49)

1447 THE ARIEL 4 (November 27, 1830):126.
    Equal to anything C. has done previously.

1448 _____ 4 (December 11, 1830):134.
    To be dramatized before the book is published. Expects this may
cut into sales.

1449 _____ 4 (December 25, 1830):142.
    Equal to C's. best.

1450 _____ 4 (February 5, 1831):161-62.
    Original, admirable, and well written.

1451 ATHENAEUM [3] (October 23, 1830):658-59.
    Characterized by a few incidents that arouse excitement. Exces-
sive dialogue.

1452 ATLAS 5 (November 14, 1830):747.
    Although C's. sea novels are all similar, this one possesses a clev-
er plot and fascinating descriptions of sea life that will be irresistible to the
reader.

1453 EDINBURGH LITERARY JOURNAL no. 104 (November 6,
1830):290-92.
    Skillfully conceived characters and powerfully described ocean
scenes, but the plot is contrived and lacks originality.

1454 EVENING POST (New York), December 14, 30, 1830.

1455 FAMILY MAGAZINE 2 (1831):281.
    An anti-English novel, but one that has an interesting plot, well
drawn characters, and "spirit-stirring" scenery.

1456 "French Notions of the American Novelist." NEW-YORK MIRROR 8
(April 16, 1831):323.
    An exciting story whose descriptions, action, and sympathies are
far superior to those novels with a social theme. Translated from the REVUE
ENCYCLOPÉDIQUE.

1457 GENTLEMAN'S MAGAZINE 101 (August 1831):152-53.
    The patriotic tone of this review seems to indicate that it was writ-
ten by someone who was unaware of the book's American authorship.

1458 LADIES' MAGAZINE 4 (January 1831):44-47.
Merely a log book whose characters are dull and disagreeable, and whose dialogue is unnatural. The author's love for America and its institutions is ever present.

1459 LADIES' MUSEUM 2, 5th series (December 1830):335-36.
One of C's. less successful novels, lacking his usual power and excitement.

1460 LITERARY GAZETTE 14 (October 23, 1830):685-86.
A false and malicious attack upon England, but an exciting novel.

1461 _____ 14 (November 20, 1830):756.
A stage adaptation. Successful, although not especially suited to the theater.

1462 MONTHLY MAGAZINE 10 n.s. (December 1830):699-700.
Not a good novel as C's. never are. Lacks originality, being much like THE RED ROVER, but an extremely readable tale nevertheless.

1463 NEW YORK AMERICAN, November 10, 29, 1830.

1464 NEW-YORK MIRROR 8 (December 18, 1830):190-91.
C. has repeated all the faults found in his previous novels--poor characterization, awkward dialogue, and stylistic errors. The book does have, however, the action and description necessary to maintain reader interest.

1465 [Peabody, O. W. B.] "The Water-Witch." NORTH AMERICAN RE-VIEW 32 (April 1831):508-23.
THE WATER-WITCH is too similar to other C. novels that deal with the sea. His powers of description are unsurpassed though, and he is assured a prominent place in American literature.

1466 PHILADELPHIA NATIONAL GAZETTE
Not seen. Cited in CORRESPONDENCE OF JAMES FENI-MORE COOPER. Vol. 1, p. 195 (item no. 56).

1467 SOUTHERN QUARTERLY REVIEW 4 n.s. (July 1851):270-71.
On the reprint edition--one of C's. most ambitious, but least successful novels.

1468 Whittier, John Greenleaf. WHITTIER ON WRITERS AND WRITING. Edited by Edwin Harrison Cady and Harry Hayden Clark. Syracuse, N. Y.:

Syracuse University Press, 1950. P. 69.

C. has failed again in the portrayal of his heroine, but his descriptions of action scenes are "engrossing."

Articles from Cooper's Death to the Present

1469 Baym, Max I. and Percy Matenko. "The Odyssey of 'The Water Witch' and a Susan Fenimore Cooper Letter." NEW YORK HISTORY 51 (January 1970):33-41.

The Coopers' stay in Europe and the writing and publication of THE WATER-WITCH. Includes a letter from Susan Cooper dated October 4, 1886, relating to a leaf from the original manuscript of the book.

1470 Bunce, O. B. "Fenimore Cooper and Last Week's Storm." CRITIC 15 (September 21, 1889):140.

Claims that an inlet described in THE WATER-WITCH did actually exist at Shrewsbury River and the Atlantic Ocean. A storm uncovered it after it had been closed by sand for years.

1471 Davie, Donald. THE HEYDAY OF SIR WALTER SCOTT. London: Routledge & Kegan Paul, 1961. Pp. 148-65.

Favorable comparison with Scott who failed to equal C. in originality or imaginative power.

1472 "An Early American Novelist on the Re-education of Subjugated Peoples." SCHOOL AND SOCIETY 62 (October 6, 1945):213.

On C's. desire that man become a meditative, independent being.

1473 Philbrick, Thomas. "Language and Meaning in Cooper's 'Water-Witch.'" EMERSON SOCIETY QUARTERLY no. 60 (Summer 1970):10-16.

Comments on the use of rhetoric.

1474 Szladits, Lola L. "New in the Berg Collection." New York Public Library, BULLETIN 73 (April 1969):227-52.

A Dresden, 1830, copy of THE WATER-WITCH.

MERCEDES OF CASTILE (1840)

Articles and Reviews Contemporary with Cooper

1475 ARCTURUS 1 (January 1841):90-92.   Partially reprinted in NEW-

YORKER 10 (January 2, 1841):253.

Inadequate characterizations (especially the females), a clumsy style, and too much free advice. C. is, however, one of the great American novelists.

1476 ATHENAEUM [13] (December 19, 1840):1005.

C's. worst book with the exception of THE HEIDENMAUER. "Hackneyed characters, few adventures or episodes."

1477 EVENING POST (New York), November 25, 1840.

1478 GODEY'S LADY'S BOOK 22 (January 1841):47.

One of C's. best novels. The characterizations and simple plot are well managed.

1479 THE IRIS 1 (December 1840):96.

The most interesting of the romances.

1480 _____ 1 (January 1841):137.

There is nothing here to remind one that MERCEDES OF CAS-TILE was written by the same genius who produced THE PATHFINDER. The story fails to hold reader interest, the characters are shallow, and although the descriptions are well done, they cannot compensate for the novel's many weaknesses.

1481 KNICKERBOCKER MAGAZINE 16 (December 1840):536.

A skillful depiction of the voyages of Columbus. Exciting.

1482 LADIES' COMPANION 14 (January 1841):148.

C's. worst novel. It lacks both plot and characterization.

1483 LITERARY GAZETTE 24 (December 19, 1840):815.

A well told story, but of little interest to the reader.

1484 MONTHLY REVIEW 1, 4th series (February 1841):185-86.

Unreal and contrived. The only interest is with the historical characters and events of which there is nothing new provided by C.

1485 MORNING COURIER AND NEW YORK ENQUIRER, November 27, 1840.

The worst of C's. novels.

1486 NEW YORK AMERICAN, December 1, 1840.

1487 NEW-YORK MIRROR 18 (December 5, 1840):191.
    Vigorous and powerful but, best of all, devoid of C's. penchant for fault finding.

1488 NEW YORK REVIEW 8 (January 1841):271.
    That portion of the book dealing with historical events is well done and interesting, but C's. romantic embellishments are artificial and inadequate. He has written nothing comparable, from a stylistic viewpoint, in many years.

1489 NEW-YORKER 10 (December 28, 1840):173.
    C. has once again failed in his attempt to portray the life of a great man as he had failed to do in THE SPY. This book will do little to rescue his earlier reputation, for he has shown himself unable to describe the etiquette and ceremonies of the Spanish court.

1490 [Poe, Edgar Allan.] "Mercedes of Castile." GRAHAM'S MAGAZINE 18 (January 1841):47-48. Reprinted in Harrison, James A., ed. THE COMPLETE WORKS OF EDGAR ALLAN POE. Vol. 10. New York: AMS Press, 1965. Pp. 96-99.
    A very good book as history, but as a work of fiction it is nearly worthless.

1491 SPECTATOR (London) 13 (December 26, 1840):1236-37.
    The romantic episodes, while well done, form a minor portion of this novel. The historical and nautical sections, which comprise the major part of the tale, are uninteresting and more suited to a chronicle than a novel.

1492 TIMES (London), December 24, 1840, p. 3.
    Tedious, lacking quality dialogue and description, repetitive, and written in a "log-book" style.

Articles from Cooper's Death to the Present

1493 Goodfellow, Donald M. "The Sources of 'Mercedes of Castile,'" AMERICAN LITERATURE 12 (November 1940):318-28.
    There are few fictitious episodes in MERCEDES OF CASTILE for C. drew most of his material from Prescott's FERDINAND AND ISABELLA and Irving's CONQUEST OF GRANADA.

THE TWO ADMIRALS (1842)

Articles and Reviews Contemporary with Cooper

1494 ATHENAEUM [15] (March 19, 1842):248-49.

THE TWO ADMIRALS lacks the power C. showed in his earlier days, but it is far superior to THE HEIDENMAUER or EVE EFFINGHAM (HOME AS FOUND).

1495 "Cooper's New Novel." ARMY AND NAVY CHRONICLE 13 (April 16, 1842):190-91.

The marine characters best. The ending is not hackneyed as is often the case with C.

1496 GODEY'S LADY'S BOOK 24 (June 1842):344.

The opening chapter is tedious, but thereafter the rewards are worth the reader's effort.

1497 GRAHAM'S MAGAZINE 20 (June 1842):356.

The equal of anything that C. has written. The scenery and action are excellent, the plot and characterizations are weak.

1498 KNICKERBOCKER MAGAZINE 19 (June 1842):586-87.

Recommended as a simple, but powerful story.

1499 LADIES' COMPANION 17 (May 1842):67.

This excellent tale is proof that C. has benefited from the recent ordeal through which he has been put as a result of his "Home" novels.

1500 LITERARY GAZETTE 26 (April 2, 1842):229.

Written in a different style. Although C. exhibits a great knowledge of sailing and produces many fine descriptions, he often becomes too involved with the facts of naval history. His continuous deprecation of the English Navy is unjust.

1501 MONTHLY REVIEW 2, 4th series (May 1842):82-85.

Good, but it does not rank with THE WATER-WITCH or THE PILOT.

1502 NEW WORLD 4 (April 30, 1842):288.

A delightful book written by a genius. Superior to C's. other sea fiction.

1503 SARTAIN'S UNION MAGAZINE OF LITERATURE AND ART 9 (September 1851):239.
> On the new edition--the best yet, no library should be without it.

1504 SOUTHERN LITERARY MESSENGER 8 (May 1842):361-62.
> One of C's. best sea stories.

1505 _____ 17 (June 1851):392.
> A very long and drawn out story, but a "graphic and stirring" one.

Articles from Cooper's Death to the Present

1506 Ballinger, Richard H. "Origins of James Fenimore Cooper's 'The Two Admirals.'" AMERICAN LITERATURE 20 (March 1948):20-30.
> Ballinger first draws several parallels between C's. HISTORY OF THE NAVY and THE TWO ADMIRALS. He then presents similarities in battles and characters between these two books and Lord Collingwood's CORRESPONDENCE and Southey's THE LIFE OF NELSON.

THE WING AND WING (THE JACK O'LANTERN [ENGLISH TITLE]) (1842)

Articles and Reviews Contemporary with Cooper

1507 ATHENAEUM [15] (December 3, 1842):1038.
> Unequal to C's. previous sea fiction in action, characterization, and descriptive qualities.

1508 BROTHER JONATHAN 3 (November 26, 1842):375.
> Monotonous and feeble with poorly drawn female characters, but still a favorite author of the reviewer.

1509 GODEY'S LADY'S BOOK 26 (January 1843):59.
> C's. return to his favorite setting shows that he has lost none of his inventiveness, nor ability to amuse and interest.

1510 GRAHAM'S MAGAZINE 21 (December 1842):342.
> Equal to any of C's. previous sea novels.

1511 LADIES' COMPANION 18 (January 1843):153.
> Graphic and life-like as historical fiction.

1512 LITERARY GAZETTE 26 (November 26, 1842):804-06.
 The chases are too technical to be of interest to anyone but naval experts, Lord Nelson is but a caricature, while Ithuel Bolt is one of C's. most original characters.

1513 METROPOLITAN MAGAZINE 36 (January 1843):11-14.
 C. is a skillful and exciting genius who maintains a proper perspective toward the English.

1514 MONTHLY REVIEW 1, 4th series (January 1843):132-35.
 One of C's. best novels. It possesses realism, fine character-izations, and proper dialogue.

1515 SPECTATOR (London) 15 (December 3, 1842):1166-68.
 Although tedious, the characters are natural, the dialogue is excellent, the scenes appear real, and C's. philosophical principles are well presented.

1516 UNITED STATE MAGAZINE AND DEMOCRATIC REVIEW 11 (December 1842):665-66.
 An excellent story that takes its novelty from the fact that C. placed the action on oceans and shores heretofore unvisited by him.

1517 _____ 28 (May 1851):477.
 One of the best, if not the best, of C's. novels.

Articles from Cooper's Death to the Present

1518 Madison, Robert D. "Cooper's 'The Wing-and-Wing' and the Concept of Byronic Pirate." LITERATURE AND LORE OF THE SEA. Edited by Patricia Ann Carlson. Amsterdam: Rodopi, 1986
 Not seen.

NED MYERS (1843)

Articles and Reviews Contemporary with Cooper

1519 ATHENAEUM [16] (November 25, 1843):1039-40.
 Interesting as a tale of adventure, but not as one of character for the reader cares little for Ned Myers the man.

1520 GRAHAM'S MAGAZINE 24 (January 1844):46.
            Its greatest charm is the description of sea life. Undoubtedly the
book will become the most popular one of the season.

1521 LADIES' COMPANION 20 (January 1844):155
            Common place and unworthy of attention.

1522 LITERARY GAZETTE 27 (November 11, 1843):732.
            Entertaining, but its biographical nature makes it of less interest
than if C. had invented a tale of his own.

1523 METROPOLITAN MAGAZINE 39 (January 1844):9-10.
            A mistake. A tedious and dull book. Ned Myers is of no interest
as a person.

1524 MONTHLY REVIEW 3 n.s. (December 1843):550-54.
            Whatever interest there is in the book is not with the character, but
with his experiences which are little more than sea yarns into which C. has
been unable to invest his usual inventive powers.

1525 NEW WORLD 7 (November 25, 1843):722-23.
            NED MYERS is a disappointment. Too detailed, but it is the most
readable of C's. sea tales.

1526 SOUTHERN LITERARY MESSENGER 9 (December 1843):757-58.
            A very slight story that has nothing to offer other than occasional
moral pronouncements.

1527 SPECTATOR (London) 16 (November 18, 1843):1094-95.
            The adventures presented here are well worth preserving.

Articles from Cooper's Death to the Present

1528 DIAL 29 (October 1, 1900):237.

1529 Keese, G. Pomeroy. "A Bit of Forgotten History By Fenimore Cooper."
BOOKMAN (New York) 7 (July 1898):393-98.
            Concerning Ned Myers the person and the way in which C.
eventually came to write of him.

1530 _____, ed. "Introduction." NED MYERS. New York: Putnam,
[1899?].

1531 Sawyer, Edith A. "A Year of Cooper's Youth." NEW ENGLAND MAGAZINE 37 n.s. (December 1907):498-504.

   C's. experiences as a sailor aboard the *Stirling*, his acquaintance with the real Ned Myers, and how these events were use in the novel.

AFLOAT AND ASHORE and MILES WALLINGFORD (LUCY HARDINGE [ENGLISH TITLE]) (1844)

Articles and Reviews Contemporary with Cooper

1532 ARTHUR'S MAGAZINE 2 (December 1844):285-86.

   A plot that is over-long and far from new or fresh. It, however, possesses good moral principles and exhibits. Contains unprejudiced views of America's position in regard to other nations.

1533 GRAHAM'S MAGAZINE 25 (October 1844):192.

   One of C's. best works. Minutely detailed, realistic, and suspenseful, but marred by the author's political prejudices.

1534 KNICKERBOCKER MAGAZINE 24 (August 1844):174-76.

   Entertaining, truthful, instructive, and amusing.

1535 _____ 24 (December 1844):571-72.

   None of C's. recent works can compare with MILES WALLINGFORD, nor will it suffer in comparison with any of his previous sea or frontier fiction.

Articles from Cooper's Death to the Present

1536 Bird, Christine M. "'Redburn' and 'Afloat and Ashore.'" THE NASSAU REVIEW 3 (1979):5-16.

   Not seen.

1537 Gordan, John D. "Novels in Manuscript: An Exhibition From the Berg Collection: Part I." New York Public Library, BULLETIN 69 (May 1965):317-29.

   AFLOAT AND ASHORE, pp. 319-20.

1538 Klots, Allen, Jr., ed. "Introduction." AFLOAT AND ASHORE. New York: Dodd, Mead & Co., 1956.

   The description of shipboard life has a genuineness that is

unequalled by C's. frontier fiction.

1539 Ringe, Donald A. "The Moral Geography of Cooper's 'Miles Wallingford' Novels." HUDSON VALLEY REGIONAL REVIEW 21 (September 1985):52-68.
     Treatment of space, symbolism, and values with an analysis of Wallingford as a character.

JACK TIER (CAPTAIN SPIKE [ENGLISH TITLE]) (1848)

Articles and Reviews Contemporary with Cooper

1540 GODEY'S LADY'S BOOK 36 (June 1848):366.
     Not one of C's. best. Improbable and unnatural.

1541 LITERARY WORLD 3 (April 8, 1848):189.
     The novel's appeal lies in its narrative and descriptive aspects rather than in delineation of character.

1542 SPECTATOR (London) 21 (March 25, 1848):302.
     Imitative of others and repetitive of himself--mechanical, tedious, technical, and uninteresting.

THE SEA LIONS (1849)

Articles and Reviews Contemporary with Cooper

1543 ATHENAEUM [22] (April 14, 1849):374-75.
     Although not completely worthy of being disregarded, this tale is often tedious and rambling.

1544 BROWNSON'S QUARTERLY REVIEW 3 n.s. (July 1849):397-408.
     The best of C's. novels. It possesses the same power and interest as his popular works, but contains a religious theme that his other books lack. Includes a discussion of C's. politics and an explanation of America's failure to understand him.

1545 HOLDEN'S DOLLAR MAGAZINE 3 (June 1849):369-70.
     C. should separate his preaching from his fiction. He might be better suited to saving men's souls than hopelessly harping on the radical politics that he perceives to be taking over the country.

1546 LITERARY GAZETTE 33 (April 14, 1849):275-76.
        A simple and well told tale that is marred by C's. political lectures.

1547 [Melville, Herman.] "Cooper's New Novel." LITERARY WORLD 4 (April 28, 1849):370.
        One of C's. best novels. Should be approved of even by his detractors. Superb descriptions.

1548 SOUTHERN QUARTERLY REVIEW 16 (October 1849):263.
        There is no story here for the average reader. It is of interest only to those who seek descriptions of little known areas of the world.

1549 SPECTATOR (London) 22 (April 14, 1849):349-50.
        The subject matter and C's. plan for it are remarkable. Its execution and the incidents created, however, are carried out with considerably less skill.

Articles from Cooper's Death to the Present

1550 Black, Ronald James. "The Paradoxical Structure of the Sea Quest in Dana, Poe, Cooper, Melville, London, and Hemingway." Ph.D. dissertation, Wayne State University, 1979.
        Considers inabilities to reconcile moral ambiguities in THE SEA LIONS.

1551 Gates, W. B. "Cooper's 'The Sea Lions' And Wilkes' 'Narrative.'" Modern Language Association of America, PUBLICATIONS 65 (December 1950):1069-75.
        On the debt owed by C. to Charles Wilkes' NARRATIVE OF THE UNITED STATES EXPLORING EXPEDITION DURING THE YEARS 1838-1842 for Antarctic details and incidents found in THE SEA LIONS.

1552 Stein, Allen F. "Conrad's Debt to Cooper: 'The Sea Lions' and 'The Secret Sharer.'" CONRADIANA 8 (1976):247-52.
        The success of THE SECRET SHARER is due largely to Conrad's character Leggatt, whose similarity to Daggett in THE SEA LIONS is unmistakable.

1553 Walker, Warren S., ed. "Introduction" THE SEA LIONS. Lincoln: University of Nebraska Press, 1965.

NONFICTION

HISTORY OF THE NAVY OF THE UNITED STATES OF AMERICA (1839)

Articles and Reviews Contemporary with Cooper

1554 "American Naval History" SOUTHERN REVIEW 2 (November 1828):349-83.
    His first-hand experience with nautical affairs, his ability to de - scribe events and delineate character, and his excellent style of writing, make C. the perfect author for a naval history. (pp. 350-51)

1555 ARMY AND NAVY CHRONICLE 8 (June 6, 1839):361.
    An impartial account devoid of C's. jaundiced views and overblown language.

1556 ATHENAEUM [12] (June 22, 1839):461-63.
    A successful history in which C. has attempted to keep his prejudices from the book, but has not always been able to do so.

1557 BALTIMORE LITERARY MONUMENT 2 (June 1839):89.
    Creditable and dependable.

1558 BRITISH AND FOREIGN REVIEW 15 (1843):440-79.
    Deficient as a history. It is merely a litany of naval actions that is anti-English and filled with an exaggerated sense of nationalism and vanity. It does have, however, many observations and opinions to recommend it.

1559 BURTON'S GENTLEMAN'S MAGAZINE 5 (July 1839):56-58.
    A proper history that shows that C. has regained his common sense. The statements on marine policy are comprehensive and knowledgeable.

1560 "Commodores Perry and Elliott." NILES' WEEKLY REGISTER 69 (December 20, 1845):247-48.
    Concerns a medal in honor of C. sent to the Rhode Island Historical Society by Jesse D. Elliott in acknowledgment of C's. literary efforts in support of Commodore Elliott, and the Society's refusal of it in light of C's. negative opinions of Oliver H. Perry.

1561 [Cooper, James Fenimore.] "Autograph Letter." Massachusetts Historical Society, PROCEEDINGS 60 (October 1926):34-35.

From C. to George H. Preble, dated January 27, 1843. On C's. biography of Commodore Preble and his HISTORY OF THE NAVY.

1562 "Cooper's 'History of the Navy.'" ARMY AND NAVY CHRONICLE 12 (November 18, 1841):363.
　　　Review of the abridged edition. Style, narrative quality, and descriptions make it suitable as a school book.

1563 THE CORSAIR 1 (May 25, 1839):168-69.
　　　A fair and truthful volume whose language and descriptions are excellent. The most valuable book written by an American author since Irving's LIFE OF COLUMBUS.

1564 THE CRUISE OF THE SOMERS: ILLUSTRATIVE OF THE DESPOTISM OF THE QUARTER DECK; AND OF THE UNMANLY CONDUCT OF COMMANDER MACKENZIE . . . New York: J. Winchester, 1844.
　　　An attack upon MacKenzie that has been attributed to C.

1565 [Duer, William A.] NEW YORK COMMERCIAL ADVERTISER, June 8, 9, 1839.
　　　Questions C's. integrity as a writer of history.

1566 EDINBURGH REVIEW 71 (April 1840):120-70.
　　　Not an intentionally biased history, but one that fails to take British opinion into account in controversial areas.

1567 "'Edinburgh Review' on James's 'Naval Occurrences', and Cooper's Naval History." UNITED STATES MAGAZINE AND DEMOCRATIC REVIEW 10 (May, June 1842):411-35, 515-41.
　　　A critique of the EDINBURGH REVIEW's comments on C's. HISTORY OF THE NAVY (see above) that had relied heavily upon James's NAVAL OCCURRENCES to discredit the New York author. These articles were probably written by C.

1568 EVENING POST (New York), May 16, 1839, October 28, 1841.
　　　A fair and accurate history.

1569 EXPOSITOR 1 (June 1, 1839):277-79.
　　　One would have to be filled with bigotry and a dislike for C. not to agree that the book is a classic.

1570 _____ 1 (June 15, 1839):304-05.

A second review written in response to attacks from other sources.

1571 "History of the United States." THE ALBION 1, 3d series (July 13, 1839):223.
Impartial, except for a few introductory remarks concerning British seamen of aristocratic background.

1572 JOURNAL OF BELLES LETTRES 13 (May 28, 1839):no. 22.
Interestingly and ably done.

1573 _____ 13 (June 5, 1839):no. 23.
Written with little sympathy. The Revolutionary War is largely overlooked and needs to be pursued by a competent naval historian.

1574 _____ 13 (June 18, 1839):no. 25.
A reply to the June 5 review above.

1575 KNICKERBOCKER MAGAZINE 13 (June 1839):538.
An excellent history. Complete, detailed, and with able description.

1576 LADIES' COMPANION 11 (June 1839):97.
An impartial and clear account.

1577 [Mackenzie, A. S.] "Cooper's 'Naval History.'" NORTH AMERICAN REVIEW 49 (October 1839):432-67.
A diligently researched, detailed, and clearly written account of the country's early naval history. It is marred only by the author's false account of the Battle of Lake Erie. See the EVENING POST (New York), March 29, 1841, for C's answer.

1578 "Mr. Cooper in England." THE CORSAIR 1 (July 27, 1839):316.
On English acceptance of THE HISTORY OF THE NAVY.

1579 MONTHLY REVIEW 2, 4th series (August 1839):524-35. Reprinted in "Cooper's History of the American Navy." MUSEUM OF FOREIGN LITERATURE, SCIENCE AND ART 37 (September 1839):74-79.
Not completely free from bias. A more knowledgeable history still needs to be written. Compared unfavorably with Marryat's A DIARY IN AMERICA.

1580 MORNING COURIER AND NEW YORK ENQUIRER, January 26, 1839.

Should be met with contempt for it exhibits C's. usual low standard for truthfulness.

1581 _____, November 26, 1840.
From a review of Mackenzie's LIFE OF PERRY. This account was accepted by C's. detractors as the real story of the Battle of Lake Erie. See also the EVENING POST (New York), March 31, 1841, for an account by C's. supporters that points out what they perceived as Mackenzie's inaccuracies.

1582 NEW WORLD 3 (October 30, 1841):286.
Admits to the popularity of HISTORY OF THE NAVY. The first time that C. is mentioned in other than disparaging terms in this publication.

1583 NEW YORKER 7 (May 18, 1839):141.
Creditable.

1584 NILES' WEEKLY REGISTER 57 (December 28, 1839):277.
Comments on the UNITED SERVICES JOURNAL review (not seen).

1585 "Remarks on Fenimore Cooper's 'Naval History of the United States.'" ARMY AND NAVY CHRONICLE 11 (July 23, 1840):56-58.
Attacks the UNITED SERVICES JOURNAL review (not seen).

1586 "Remarks on the Naval History of the United States." MUSEUM OF FOREIGN LITERATURE, SCIENCE AND ART 37, 38 (December 1839, January 1840):449-55, 52-62.
An error-filled, hurried work.

1587 SPECTATOR (London) 12 (June 15, 1839):563-64.
An overly long book about a country that never fought a real sea battle. Of use only to those with a national or professional interest.

1588 "The Tale of the Wasp, Sloop-of-War." SOUTHERN QUARTERLY REVIEW 15 (July 1849):449-60.
Excellent, but deficient in some of the biographies.

Articles from Cooper's Death to the Present

1589 Gordon, John D. "An Anniversary Exhibition: The Henry W. and Albert A. Berg Collection, 1940-1965. Part III, Conclusion." New York Public

Library, BULLETIN 69 (December 1965):665-77.
> A holograph of THE HISTORY OF THE NAVY, p. 667.

1590 KNICKERBOCKER MAGAZINE 43 (February 1854):189.
> A one volume reprint. Readable and accurate.

1591 Madison, Robert D. "Materials for an Edition of James Fenimore Cooper's 'History of the Navy of the United States' (1841)." Ph.D. dissertation, Northwestern University, 1981.
> Comparison of the one and two volume editions and a review of C's. naval writings.

1592 _____. "Melville's Edition of Cooper's 'History of the Navy.'" MELVILLE SOCIETY ABSTRACTS 47 (1981):9-10.
> Not seen.

1593 SOUTHERN QUARTERLY REVIEW 22 (January 1854):264-65.
> A book of great value, written by an authority.

1594 Weissbuch, Ted N. "A James Fenimore Cooper Medal: The Real Battle of Lake Erie." NUMISMATIC SCRAPBOOK MAGAZINE 26 (February 1960):289-98.
> Concerns the criticism of C.'s handling of the Battle of Lake Erie in his HISTORY OF THE NAVY, C's. libel suit against William A. Duer for his libelous review (see item no. 1551), and the C. medal that Captain Jesse Duncan Elliott had struck in his honor.

1595 Whitehill, Walter Muir. "Cooper as a Naval Historian." NEW YORK HISTORY 35 (October 1954):468-79.
> C. was eminently suited by experience and personal friendship to write his HISTORY OF THE NAVY. He made use of all the available sources to produce a detached and impartial account that still has value today.

THE BATTLE OF LAKE ERIE (1843)

Articles and Reviews Contemporary with Cooper

1596 SOUTHERN QUARTERLY REVIEW 4 (October 1843):511-12.
> C. provides both the history and logic needed to totally disprove the claims of those who oppose his view.

1597 UNITED STATES MAGAZINE AND DEMOCRATIC REVIEW 13

(September 1843):330-31.
    This book only proves that C's. original interpretation was the accurate one.

Articles from Cooper's Death to the Present

1598 Parsons, Usher. BATTLE OF LAKE ERIE. A DISCOURSE, DELIVERED BEFORE THE RHODE ISLAND HISTORICAL SOCIETY . . . FEBRUARY 16, 1852. Providence: Benjamin T. Albro, 1853.
    An attempt to discredit C's. interpretation.

LIVES OF DISTINGUISHED NAVAL OFFICERS (1846)

Articles and Reviews Contemporary with Cooper

1599 AMERICAN REVIEW: A WHIG JOURNAL 3 (June 1846):673-74.
    Typical of C's. narrative style and effectively shows an aspect of American history.

1600 GRAHAM'S MAGAZINE 28 (May 1846):240.
    Informative, vivid, direct, and forceful.

1601 SOUTHERN LITERARY MESSENGER 12 (March 1846):190.
    Attractive to those who would not consider a more elaborate work.

1602 _____ 12 (July 1846):453.
    Better able than any other person to deal with the subject.

6

SOCIAL AND POLITICAL WRITINGS

GENERAL STUDIES

ARTICLES FROM COOPER'S DEATH TO THE PRESENT

1603 Becker, George J. "James Fenimore Cooper and American Democracy."
COLLEGE ENGLISH 17 (March 1956):325-34.
        As a social critic C. possessed no idea of social progress, for he
believed that the Union had been created perfect. While the possibility of
decay and destruction abounded, he failed to see that the greatness of America
resided in the ability of her institutions to change and adapt to meet new cir-
cumstances.

1604 Blanck, Jacob. "The Bibliography of American Literature: James Fenimore Cooper." PUBLISHERS' WEEKLY 151 (February 1, 1947):1383-84.
        Collation of an 1832 Carey and Lea edition of THE HEIDEN-
MAUER and of an 1838 Lea and Blanchard edition of HOME AS FOUND.

1605 Conboy, Lawrence J. "Social Criticism in the Writings of James Fenimore Cooper." Master of Arts degree, Brooklyn College of City University of
New York, 1942.

1606 Davis, Elizabeth A. "The Spirit of the Letter: Richardson and the Early
American Novel. A Study in the Evolution of Form." Ph.D. dissertation, Yale
University, 1973.
        Cooper's use of the letter as a stylistic device served as a means of
pointing out the social and moral standards of his characters.

1607 Lasky, Melvin J. "America and Europe." ENCOUNTER 18 (January 1962):66-78.

NOTIONS OF THE AMERICANS sought to explain America to the Europeans in an intelligent and unbiased manner. It succeeded to the extent that it was no propaganda tract and formed one of the more important examples of dialogue between the two people. It, however, was not accepted by either America or Europe. HOME AS FOUND, which followed ten years later, possessed an entirely different theme, for it was intent on pointing out America's inferiority rather than her superiority.

1608 Owens, Sarah C. "A Study of Three of Cooper's Controversial Novels: 'The Monikins', 'Homeward Bound', and 'Home as Found.'" Master of Arts degree, University of Kentucky, 1936.

1609 Ringe, Donald A. "Go East, Young Man, and Discover Your Country." THE KENTUCKY REVIEW 10 (Spring 1990):3-20

C's. European experiences allowed him to view America's failings from a fresh viewpoint at a time when many changes were occurring in the country. His inherent dislike of change, especially of levelling influences he perceived, led him to social and political statements that were widely criticized by his contemporaries. Mention of NOTIONS OF THE AMERICANS and THE BRAVO is made.

1610 Spiller, Robert E. THE AMERICAN IN ENGLAND DURING THE FIRST HALF CENTURY OF INDEPENDENCE. New York: Henry Holt & Co., 1926. Pp. 318-45. Originally a Ph.D. dissertation, University of Pennsylvania, 1924. Reprinted in Spiller's OBLIQUE LIGHT: STUDIES IN LITERARY HISTORY AND BIOGRAPHY. New York: Macmillan Co., 1968. Pp. 49-70.

C., an extremely patriotic man, sought to define a strictly American national culture that would avoid the evils that he believed were invading the country.

1611 Tuttleton, James W. "The New England Character in Cooper's Social Novels." New York Public Library, BULLETIN 70 (May 1966):305-17.

Although C. occasionally tried to draw portraits of New Englanders that were not unattractive, he carried an innate dislike for them that proved to be nearly impossible to control.

1612 _____. THE NOVEL OF MANNERS IN AMERICA. Chapel Hill: University of North Carolina Press, 1972. Pp. 28-47.

C's. social and political novels present a true picture of early eighteenth century times and manners.

FICTION

THE EUROPEAN TRILOGY

Articles from Cooper's Death to the Present

1613 Denne, Constance Ayers. "Setting as Meaning in Cooper's European Trilogy." Ph.D. dissertation, University of Pittsburgh, 1968.
    Setting, which is artistic rather than socio-political in nature, is the key element to an understanding of C's. European trilogy.

1614 Diemer, James S. "The European Novels of James Fenimore Cooper: A Study in the Evolution of Cooper's Social Criticism, 1820-1832." Ph.D. dissertation, Northwestern University, 1949.
    C's. stay in Europe did not change his political and social thought, although he did become increasingly aware of American problems after 1833. The European novels should be viewed as essential to his development as a social critic and, in this way, are important to an understanding of C. as a novelist.

1615 Kirk, Russell. "Cooper and the European Puzzle." COLLEGE ENGLISH 7 (January 1946):198-207.
    Praises C. as the first American author to use political and social criticism in his fiction. His European trilogy attacked tyranny as he saw it, but had little influence on his fellow Americans.

1616 McCarthy, Harold T. THE EXPATRIATE PERSPECTIVE: AMERICAN NOVELISTS AND THE IDEA OF AMERICA. Cranbury, N. J.: Associated University Presses, 1974. Pp. 25-46.
    C's. European novels show little concern for historical accuracy. Events and facts are often shifted to better enable him to comment upon the widening gulf between his view of what American society should be and the realities of nineteenth century life. Includes C's. views on slavery.

1617 Redekop, Ernest Henry. "Real 'Versus' Imagined History: Cooper's European Novels." MOSAIC 22 (Fall 1989):81-97.
    On C's. use of history in the European trilogy and WING-AND-WING. Concludes that the relationship between fact and fiction differs from book to book and depends upon the author's purpose.

1618 Wehmeyer, William Anthony. "The European Novels of James Fenimore Cooper: A Critical Study." Ph.D. dissertation, University of Notre Dame, 1962.

An attempt to show that three of C's. neglected novels deserve critical reassessment as works of art. Emphasizes theme, action, characterization, and scene.

1619 Whitfield, Marguerite Lipscomb. "J. Fenimore Cooper and Sir Walter Scott: American Liberal and British Tory." Master's thesis, The American University, 1969.

Uses two of C's. European novels (THE HEIDENMAUER and THE HEADSMAN) and two of Scott's novels to compare and contrast C's. liberal, democratic attitudes with the political opinions of Scott.

The Bravo (1831)

Articles and Reviews Contemporary with Cooper

1620 AMERICAN MONTHLY REVIEW 1 (February 1832):147-53.

The novel succeeds as a political piece with its excellent characterizations and descriptions.

1621 THE ARIEL 5 (December 10, 1831):268.

A riveting novel, with "great power," and large sales.

1622 ATHENAEUM [4] (October 22, 29, 1831):688-91, 702-03. Excerpted in MUSEUM OF FOREIGN LITERATURE, SCIENCE AND ART 20 (January 1832):38-39.

Although possessing considerable merit, THE BRAVO is inferior to each of C's. previous works. It is an improbable novel that suffers from a lack of imagination.

1623 CHRISTIAN EXAMINER AND GENERAL REVIEW 12 (March 1832):78-80.

Graphic descriptions that often lack the finer distinctions of life, manners, and character. While imaginative, C. has little versatility or inventiveness.

1624 EDINBURGH LITERARY JOURNAL no. 155 (October 29, 1831):251-53.

1625 [Hunt, Leigh.] TATLER 3 (October 21, 1831):385-86.

C's. most exciting novel in which much of his criticism of Italian society and politics could also be applied to England. Includes a comparison of C. and Scott in which C. is considered superior in holding the reader's interest and in drawing female characters and heroes.

1626 LADIES' MAGAZINE 5 (January 1832):42-46.
   A great success as a political novel. It does suffer from C's. stylistic failures though, especially that of dialogue.

1627 LITERARY GAZETTE 15 (October 15, 1831):657.
   Original, exciting, and real. A comparison is made between C's. and Byron's responses to Venice.

1628 LITERARY GUARDIAN 1 (October 22, 1831):51-53.
   Recommended, although with reservations.

1629 MONTHLY MAGAZINE 12 n.s. (November 1831):561.
   C. is too somber here, although he effectively uses the past to teach his fellow man the folly of crime.

1630 MORNING COURIER AND NEW YORK ENQUIRER, August 31, 1832.

1631 _____, November 30, 1831.
   The book's republicanism, action, and descriptive passages will make it popular in England.

1632 NATIONAL OMNIBUS 1 (October 21, 1831):137.
   Perhaps the best C. novel yet.

1633 NEW-ENGLAND MAGAZINE 2 (January 1832):83-85.
   As a picture of an ancient social system it is accurate, but as romantic fiction it is a failure. C. provides no real story, nor a hero to fill it.

1634 NEW MONTHLY MAGAZINE 33 (November 1831):485-86. Reprinted in the NEW YORK SPECTATOR, December 30, 1831.
   Imaginative, vividly described, and finely portrayed.

1635 NEW YORK AMERICAN, December 3, 1831.
   C's. attempt to foster understanding of America in Europe should increase his popularity with his countrymen. Other comments on the book are found in the June 7, 9, 1832 and June 24, December 3, 7, 1833 issues.

1636 NEW-YORK MIRROR, editors. "Mr. Cooper the Novelist." NEW-YORK MIRROR 10 (February 16, 1833):262.
   Written in response to a letter (reprinted here) that had praised

THE BRAVO and called for C. to pursue his moral and political fiction.

1637 NEW-YORK TRIBUNE, January 17, 1902, p. 8.
    Letter from C. to his publishers concerning the anticipated reception of THE BRAVO.

1638 PHILADELPHIA ALBUM 5 (December 10, 1831):396.
    Equal, if not superior, to any of C's. previous works.

1639 SOUTHERN REVIEW 8 (February 1832):382-99.
    A novel that has readable passages, poorly drawn female characters, and glowing descriptions. It continues long after the climax has been reached.

1640 WESTMINSTER REVIEW 16 (January 1832):180-92.
    A book that will take its place beside C's. great frontier and sea novels. It is marred somewhat by trivial and tedious dialogue, and by the author's selection of adjectives in many of his descriptions.

Articles from Cooper's Death to the Present

1641 Churchill, Kenneth. "The American Novelists in Italy: James Fenimore Cooper." ITALY AND ENGLISH LITERATURE, 1764-1930. London: Macmillan Press, 1980. Pp. 147-48.
    C. was the first American to treat Italy in fiction at any length. He wrote for an American audience, hoping to use a corrupt, oppressive Europe as an example of what the young republic should not become.

1642 Goggio, Emilio. "Cooper's 'Bravo' In Italy." ROMANTIC REVIEW 20 (July-September 1929):222-30.
    THE BRAVO received a great deal of bitter criticism in Italy, much of it unjustified. This criticism, however, did not prevent the book from being widely read, or from C. maintaining his considerable fame there.

1643 Levine, Robert S. CONSPIRACY AND ROMANCE: STUDIES IN BROCKDEN BROWN, COOPER, HAWTHORNE, AND MELVILLE. "'Soulless Corporation': Oligarchy and the Countersubversive Presence in James Fenimore Cooper's 'The Bravo.'" Cambridge, etc.: Cambridge University Press, 1989. Pp. 58-103.
    C. saw a conspiracy of international aristocrats intent on subverting all republics and concluded that they would win the struggle.

1644 Loveland, Anne C. "James Fenimore Cooper and the American

Mission." AMERICAN QUARTERLY 21 (Summer 1969):244-58.
    American attacks on C's. involvement in the French finance controversy of 1831-32 and on his European novels led him to believe that the country was experiencing a decline in republicanism.

1645 Ringe, Donald A., ed. "Introduction." THE BRAVO. New Haven, Conn.: College & University Press, 1963.

1646 Tuten, Frederic J. "James Fenimore Cooper's 'The Bravo': A Critical and Textual Study." Ph.D. dissertation, New York University, 1971.
    THE BRAVO, long held to be a mere "political tract," is described here as a complicated and successfully written work of art. Included is an investigation of the changes made in the revised 1834 British edition.

1647 Wallace, David H. "The Princess and 'The Bravo': A Pleasant Passage in Anglo-American Relations." New York Historical Society, QUARTERLY 37 (October 1953):317-25.
    Concerns Princess Victoria's request for C's. autograph and his response that included a manuscript chapter of THE BRAVO.

The Heidenmauer (1832)

Articles and Reviews Contemporary with Cooper

1648 AMERICAN MONTHLY REVIEW 2 (November 1832):411-15.
    Pleasant, but not one of C's. best. It is lacking in descriptive ability and reader interest while being too detailed and too concerned with social comment.

1649 ATHENAEUM [5] (July 28, 1832):485.
    C. has ability as a writer, but it is limited. The HEIDENMAUER is a prime example that his power quickly dissipates when he leaves the ocean or wilderness.

1650 BOSTON DAILY ADVERTISER, October 16, 1832.
    Not comparable to Scott's Reformation era novels.

1651 Burch, Francis F. "Cooper: An Unpublished Letter and Ms Excerpt from 'The Heidenmauer.'" AMERICAN NOTES & QUERIES 12 (May-June 1974):134-35.
    Letter to Mary E. Carr dated March 20, 1832, with a handwritten excerpt from THE HEIDENMAUER.

1652 [Dunlop, W.] EVENING POST (New York), October 4, 1832.
   The only favorable American review of substance.

1653 LADIES' MAGAZINE 5 (October 1832):475-77.
   C. has shown his genius in the creation of the female character, while illustrating his extensive knowledge of human nature in a book that admirably fulfills his stated objective.

1654 LITERARY GAZETTE 16 (July 14, 1832):435-36. Paraphrased in the LADIES' MAGAZINE 5 (September 1832):428.
   Spirited.

1655 _____ 16 (July 21, 1832):457.
   This novel only further proves C's. versatility. The Burgomaster, Hurich, is perfectly drawn.

1656 LITERARY GUARDIAN 2 (August 4, 1832):250.
   C. is less successful in Europe than he is in America or on the sea.

1657 METROPOLITAN MAGAZINE 18 (January 1837):9.

1658 MORNING COURIER AND NEW YORK ENQUIRER, September 26, 1832.
   A polite advance notice.

1659 NATIONAL OMNIBUS 2 (July 20, 1832):226.

1660 NEW-ENGLAND MAGAZINE 3 (November 1832):423-24.
   A lesser book than THE BRAVO with only ordinary characterizations and a barren plot. There is far too much dialogue by characters who all sound alike. Some original thoughts, however, are expressed by the author.

1661 NEW YORK AMERICAN, September 29, November 10, 1832.

1662 NEW YORK COMMERCIAL ADVERTISER, February 1, July 17, 1833.

1663 NEW-YORK MIRROR 10 (October 6, 1832):107.
   The novel possesses nothing to hold the reader's attention and, with the exception of PRECAUTION, it is the worst that C. has written.

1664 "Novel Reading--and the Novels of 1832." AMERICAN MONTHLY

MAGAZINE 1 (March 1833):96-104.
        A feeble story that has no hero and displays a deficiency in both style and grammar. (pp. 102-03)

1665 TAIT'S EDINBURGH MAGAZINE 1 (September 1832):660-65.
        C's. worst novel. Discusses characterization, plot, and nationalism as they relate to C. in general and this novel in particular.

Articles from Cooper's Death to the Present

1666 Williams, J. Gary. "Cooper and European Catholicism: A Reading of 'The Heidenmauer.'" ESQ: A JOURNAL OF THE AMERICAN RENAISSANCE 22 (3d Quarter 1976):149-58.
        THE HEIDENMAUER, long considered a political novel, was probably written by C. as a means of pointing out the differences between Protestantism and Catholicism.

The Headsman (1833)

Articles and Reviews Contemporary with Cooper

1667 AMERICAN MONTHLY MAGAZINE 2 (November 1833):194-200.
        An utter failure, especially as a political novel. There are a few passages whose beauty is reminiscent of C's. former writings, but they are overshadowed by the inferiority of his characters and language.

1668 ATHENAEUM [6] (September 7, 1833):593-95.
        The story is amusing and keeps the reader's speculation alive, although the mystery toward which the author builds is never properly unraveled.

1669 EVENING POST (New York), October 22, 1833.
        The only favorable American review of substance.

1670 "Festival of Vine Dressers." NILES' WEEKLY REGISTER 45 (October 19, 1833):117.
        A description of this ancient festival with the comment that C. attended it in 1832 and then incorporated it into THE HEADSMAN.

1671 LADIES' MAGAZINE 6 (November 1833):520-24.
        Most of the characters have been drawn to illustrate how they suffer or are uneasy in their position in society. This is unfortunate, for it will

detract from the book's popularity even though it teaches excellent political and moral lessons. The female characters are the most skillfully done.

1672 LITERARY GAZETTE 17 (September 7, 1833):561-63.
> The two greatest faults of this novel are the characters' propensity toward excess dialogue and toward espousing platitudes not in keeping with their time or station.

1673 _____ 18 (January 1, 1834):84-85.
> A stage adaptation. Successful, but requires that the plot be compressed and the ending altered.

1674 LITERARY JOURNAL 1 (December 28, 1833):237-38.
> Worthy of attention. More perfect as a novel than are the romances.

1675 METROPOLITAN MAGAZINE 8 (October 1833):36-37.
> The book degenerates from the exciting and suspenseful to the boring before attaining its earlier excellence. The humor is poorly done and C. ultimately fails Americans as a social critic.

1676 MONTHLY REVIEW 3, 4th series (December 1833):530-35.
> Powerfully written scenes.

1677 MORNING COURIER AND NEW YORK ENQUIRER, December 9, 1833.
> As a result of this novel, C. will never regain his former position in the literary world.

1678 NEW-ENGLAND MAGAZINE 6 (January 1834):88-89.
> The novel is marred by awkward phraseology, the use of pet words, the failure to draw a proper female character, contradictions in the Headsman's character, and by the author's attempt to interject political biases where they do not belong.

1679 NEW MONTHLY MAGAZINE 39 (October 1833):229-30.
> Better than THE HEIDENMAUER and equal to THE PILOT and THE PRAIRIE.

1680 NEW YORK COMMERCIAL ADVERTISER, October 21, 1833.

1681 NEW-YORK MIRROR 11 (November 2, 1833):143.
> The works by C. based upon a European theme are far inferior to

his writings about the American scene.

1682 NEW-YORK MIRROR 11 (December 7, 1833):183.
        A satirical attack upon C. as an author and upon THE HEADSMAN.

1683 NILES' WEEKLY REGISTER 45 (October 19, 1833):118.
        The 1,000 guineas received from his English publisher and the $5,000 received from his American one for THE HEADSMAN, is about equal to what C. has realized from earlier novels.

1684 NORTH AMERICAN QUARTERLY MAGAZINE 3 (November 1833):70-71.
        A satirical critique in which the reviewer marvels that the publisher would pay $5,000 for the privilege of inflicting on the public one of the worst books ever written.

Articles from Cooper's Death to the Present

1685 Denne, Constance Ayers. "Cooper's Artistry in 'The Headsman.'" NINETEENTH CENTURY FICTION 29 (June 1974):77-92.
        Denne critiques THE HEADSMAN, not as social and political literature, but as a literary work that tells much about its author's artistic and creative abilities.

1686 Palfrey, Thomas R. "Cooper and Balzac: 'The Headsman.'" MODERN PHILOLOGY 29 (February 1932):335-41.
        Although C. and Balzac never met, C. was familiar with the latter's work.   Internal evidence suggests that he borrowed from Balzac's JÉSUS-CHRIST EN FLANERS when writing THE HEADSMAN.

THE HOME NOVELS

Articles and Reviews Contemporary with Cooper

1687 Benjamin, Park "Fenimore Cooper's Libels on America and Americans." NEW WORLD 1 (August 29, September 5, 1840):193-95, 210-15.
        Reviews of HOWEWARD BOUND and HOME AS FOUND. Conclude that C's. novels only prove that he is a "vain, weak, self-inflated, and silly" person and, therefore, it cannot be libelous to say so.   Rather, it is C. who has libelled America, her institutions, and everything American.

1688 DUBLIN REVIEW 6 (May 1839):490-529.

HOMEWARD BOUND is praised for its suspense and the ingenuity of its author. HOME AS FOUND, on the other hand, is described as a "heavy and tedious" book of no interest. C's. social comments are passed off as attempts to indulge his own prejudices. As proof, the reviewer points out that C. has been unnecessarily caustic (the mark of a vengeful man) and has failed to discuss the inhuman treatment of blacks and Indians.

Articles from Cooper's Death to the Present

1689 Kligerman, Jack. "Style and Form in James Fenimore Cooper's 'Homeward Bound' and 'Home as Found.'" JOURNAL OF NARRATIVE TECHNIQUE 4 (January 1974):45-61.

C's. style (use of abstractions in this instance) controlled to a large extent what he was able to bring to the reader regarding America's social ills.

1690 Lawrence, David Herbert. "Studies in Classic American Literature (IV): Fenimore Cooper's Anglo-American Novels." ENGLISH REVIEW 28 (February 1919):88-99. Reprinted in Arnold, Armin, ed. THE SYMBOLIC MEANING: THE UNCOLLLECTED VERSIONS OF "STUDIES IN CLASSICAL AMERICAN LITERATURE." London: Centaur Press, 1962. Pp. 74-87; STUDIES IN CLASSICAL LITERATURE. New York: Thomas Seltzer, 1923. Pp. 50-66; and Wilson, Edmund, ed. SHOCK OF RECOGNITION: THE DEVELOPMENT OF LITERATURE IN THE UNITED STATES, RECORDED BY THE MEN WHO MADE IT. Garden City, N. Y.: Doubleday, Doran & Co., 1943. Pp. 938-49.

Essentially an essay giving Lawrence's thought on democracy. The Effingham's of C's. novels are used by Lawrence to show that aristocracy is normal, whereas democracy is artificial.

1691 O'Donnell, Charles. "The Moral Basis of Civilization: Cooper's Home Novels." NINETEENTH CENTURY FICTION 17 (December 1962):265-73.

HOMEWARD BOUND and HOME AS FOUND should be read as one novel. The first, which takes place upon the sea and is concerned with a closed society, investigates man and his relation to the forces of nature. HOME AS FOUND, on the other hand, describes an open society and the political and social issues important to it. Only by reading HOMEWARD BOUND is a proper frame of reference created through which the corruption in the second novel can be viewed.

Homeward Bound (1838)

Articles and Reviews Contemporary with Cooper

1692 THE ALBION 6 n.s. (August 18, 1838):263.
         A readable story in which the characterization suffers from occasional exaggeration.

1693 ARMY AND NAVY CHRONICLE 6 (March 8, 1838):154.
         Publication announcement.

1694 ATHENAEUM [11] (June 9, 1838):404-05.
         HOMEWARD BOUND is both lively and exciting and one of C's. best.

1695 [Bowen, F.] "Cooper's 'Homeward Bound.'" NORTH AMERICAN REVIEW 47 (October 1838):488-89.
         A tiresome, absurd, and stupid novel, with poorly drawn characters, no plot, and a boring dialogue.

1696 BURTON'S GENTLEMAN'S MAGAZINE 3 (September 1838):216-18.
         Hastily constructed and filled with technical jargon, but one of the best novels of its day. The characters are not only well drawn, but Captain Truck has been made amusing when necessary.

1697 JOURNAL OF BELLES LETTRES 12 (August 14, 1838):no. 7.
         Although it includes many of C's. former errors, HOMEWARD BOUND is a good sea novel. Unfortunately the author insists on disparaging his countrymen, continues to fail as a humorist, and cannot create female characters.

1698 KNICKERBOCKER MAGAZINE 12 (September 1838):263-67.
         Regretfully, this novel is a vehicle for the author's own prejudices and has little merit beyond some of the descriptions (the sea) and characterizations (Captain Truck, Eve Effingham).

1699 LADIES' COMPANION 9 (September 1838):250.
         Wordy at the outset, but the story develops to become one of C's. best and most interesting.

1700 LITERARY GAZETTE 22 (May 19, 1838):308-11.
         Spirited and interesting, but discussions of national questions and

characteristics do not belong here.

1701 MONTHLY REVIEW 2, 4th series (July 1838):417-27.
    One of C's. best sea novels.

1702 MORNING COURIER AND NEW YORK ENQUIRER, August 7,
1838.
    C., a poor politician, should not attempt political tracts.

1703 NEW YORK AMERICAN, October 27, 1838.

1704 NEW-YORK MIRROR 16 (August 18, 1838):63.
    A worthy addition to C's. other sea stories. Little plot or action,
but it hold one's interest by means of strong characters and excellent nautical
descriptions.

1705 SOUTHERN LITERARY JOURNAL 3 (October 1838):307-11.
    Poorly drawn females and gentleman. C. has cheated his public
by giving them an outpouring of wrongs done to him, rather than the expected
romance.

1706 SOUTHERN LITERARY MESSENGER 4 (November 1838):724-34.
    Includes two reviews. 1. A very good book when limited to de-
scriptions of incidents at sea. It suffers from unnatural dialogue and characters
who are caricatures of the originals. 2. An interesting book, but a failure at
depicting genteel society.

1707 "The 'Southern Literary Messenger.'" NEW-YORKER 6 (October 27,
1838):94.
    An advance notice referring to the two reviews immediately
above. Suggests that the press should ignore C. as the proper means of showing their contempt for his writings.

1708 SPECTATOR (London) 11 (May 19, 1838):468-70. Reprinted in
JOURNAL OF BELLES LETTRES 11 (June 26, 1838):no. 26 and MUSEUM
OF FOREIGN LITERATURE, SCIENCE AND ART 33 (July 1838): 374-76.
    An uninteresting novel that, even with lifelike characters, has too
few incidents to sustain it.

    Articles from Cooper's Death to the Present

1709 "Cooper as Critic of His Countrymen." CHAUTAUQUAN 50 (March
1908):134-38.

Largely comments of Steadfast Dodge that reflect C's. criticism of nineteenth century America.

1710 Lease, Benjamin. "'Homeward Bound': The Two Voices of Fenimore Cooper." ANGLO-AMERICAN ENCOUNTERS; ENGLAND AND THE RISE OF AMERICAN LITERATURE. Cambridge: Cambridge University Press, 1982. Pp. 36-50.
Not seen.

1711 Martien, Norman Gerald. "I. An Essay and Materials Toward an Edition of Fenimore Cooper; II. 'Mansfield Park' and Jane Austen's Heroine; III. A Reading of Marvell's 'Upon Appleton House.'" Ph.D. dissertation, Rutgers University, 1969.
Investigates C's. editing techniques and concludes that, although he must be considered a poor writer, he did attempt to make corrections in his work.

1712 Ross, Morton L. "Captain Truck and Captain Boomer." AMERICAN LITERATURE 37 (November 1965):316.
Melville copied a portion of the character of Captain Boomer (MOBY DICK) from C's. Captain Truck.

1713 Scudder, Harold H. "Cooper and the Barbary Coast." Modern Language Association of America, PUBLICATIONS 62 (September 1947):784-92.
The story upon which HOMEWARD BOUND is based was learned by C. from Captain James Riley's A NARRATIVE OF THE SHIPWRECK OF THE SHIP OSWEGO ON THE COAST OF SOUTH BARBARY . . . . (1818).

1714 Wright, Nathalia. "The Confidence Men of Melville and Cooper: An American Indictment." AMERICAN QUARTERLY 4 (Fall 1952):266-68.
Both C's. Steadfast Dodge and Melville's Frank Goodman are used to attack the concept that the majority should rule in a democracy, and that the majority is always correct in its decisions.

Home as Found (Eve Effingham [English Title]) (1838)

Articles and Reviews Contemporary with Cooper

1715 ATHENAEUM [11] (December 15, 1838): 894. Reprinted in NEW-YORKER 6 (February 23, 1839):356.
Not equal to HOMEWARD BOUND. As a novel of manners it is

tedious, slow, and possessed of much national vanity.

1716 BURTON'S GENTLEMAN'S MAGAZINE 4 (January 1839):64-66.
Inane. C. Finds fault with everything and everyone except himself.

1717 KNICKERBOCKER MAGAZINE 12 (December 1838):539.
The worst book yet to come from C's. pen. A plotless, arrogant, and vain caricature.

1718 LADIES' COMPANION 10 (January 1839):147.
A book that will be read with "curiosity."

1719 NEW-YORK MIRROR 16 (December 8, 1838):192.
No plot, of no interest, and it deserves to be censored.

1720 NEW YORK REVIEW 4 (January 1839):209-21. Reprinted in the NEW-YORKER 6 (January 5, 1839):244.
More malicious than its predecessors. C's. moral offenses are so serious that his literary ones need not even be mentioned.

1721 NEW-YORKER 6 (December 1, 1838):173.
Duller even than HOMEWARD BOUND. Once C. discovered that his readers would not purchase the GLEANINGS books, he returned to novel writing to abuse the public.

1722 _____ 6 (February 9, 1839):323-24.
A monomaniac when he leaves the sea or frontier. C. no longer considers what the world is or thinks, but how the world treats him.

1723 SOUTHERN LITERARY MESSENGER 5 (March 1839):169-78.
A complete failure that does nothing to redeem C's. reputation. It is dull, ungrammatical, poorly constructed, and possessed of characters who have degenerated since they were introduced in HOMEWARD BOUND.

1724 [Webb, James Watson.] MORNING COURIER AND NEW YORK ENQUIRER, November 22, 1838.
C. has written HOME AS FOUND only as a means of making a profit in England. As such, he is a traitor to his country and should leave it.

1725 [Weed, Thurlow.] ALBANY EVENING JOURNAL, November 2, 1838.
Acknowledges that C. is an eminent author, but believes that the

book was written to attack those who had offended him.

Articles from Cooper's Death to the Present

1726 Gates, W. B. "A Neglected Satire on James Fenimore Cooper's 'Home as Found.'" AMERICAN LITERATURE 35 (March 1963):13-21.
 The unfavorable picture of American life that C. created in HOME AS FOUND was attacked by many Whig authors. Among them was Frederick Jackson in THE EFFINGHAM'S, OR HOME AS I FOUND IT (1841).

1727 Grossman, James. "Cooper and the Responsibility of the Press." NEW YORK HISTORY 35 (October 1954):512-21.
 Concerns the newspaper attacks generated by the publication of HOME AS FOUND and the resulting libel case brought by C. against Webb, the editor of the MORNING COURIER AND NEW YORK ENQUIRER (see item nos. 183-85). C., who believed that the press had outlived its usefulness, maintained that free discussion and inquiry had allowed public opinion to become the prisoner of the nation's newspaper editors.

1728 Kay, Donald. "Major Character Types in 'Home as Found': Cooper's Search for American Principles and Dignity." CLA JOURNAL 14 (June 1971):432-39.
 Describes four classes of characters in HOME AS FOUND. Each type is seen in relation to its search for a set of principles based upon national self-respect.

1729 Leary, Lewis. SOUNDINGS: SOME EARLY AMERICAN WRITERS. Athens: University of Georgia Press, 1975. Pp. 271-91.
 If one does not consider the romance, HOME AS FOUND is the first American novel. It was in this book that C. presented a pattern that later writers would adopt and improve upon.

1730 Meyers, Marvin. THE JACKSONIAN PERSUASION: POLITICS AND BELIEF. Stanford: Stanford University Press, 1960. Pp. 57-100. Reprinted in part as "The Great Descent: Cooper's 'Home as Found.'" INTELLECTUAL HISTORY IN AMERICA. Vol. 1. Edited by Cushing Strout. New York: Harper & Row, 1968. Pp. 160-78.
 C's. fiction lies somewhere between the Jacksonian ideal and reality. His support of the social changes of the 1830s has to be understood in the context of his desire for a greater transformation at the same time that he mourned the loss of much of the past.

1731 Person, Leland S. "'Home as Found' and the Leatherstocking Series."

ESQ; A JOURNAL OF THE AMERICAN RENAISSANCE 27 (3rd quarter 1981):170-80.

> The relationship of HOME AS FOUND to the L. S. TALES.

1732 Schmitz, Neil. "Telling the Truth: Richard Nixon and American Political Fiction." AMERICAN STUDIES 18 (Spring 1977):5-21.

> An analysis of Steadfast Dodge that emphasizes his function as the representative of a perverted form of Jeffersonian democracy.

1733 Sundquist, Eric J. HOME AS FOUND: AUTHORITY AND GENEALOGY IN NINETEENTH-CENTURY AMERICAN LITERATURE. Baltimore: Johns Hopkins University Press, 1979. Originally as "'Home as Found': Authority and Genealogy in Cooper, Thoreau, Hawthorne, and Melville." Ph.D. dissertation, Johns Hopkins University, 1978.

> How C's. treatment of incest, family scenes, parody, and use of biographical events illustrate his interest in tradition, authority, and paternity.

1734 _____. "Incest and Imitation in Cooper's 'Home as Found.'" NINETEENTH CENTURY FICTION 32 (December 1977):261-84.

THE MONIKINS (1835)

Articles and Reviews Contemporary with Cooper

1735 AMERICAN MONTHLY MAGAZINE 5 (August 1835):487.

> A complete waste of time and effort. Vain and prejudiced.

1736 JOURNAL OF BELLES LETTRES 6 (July 21, 1835):no. 3.

> A caricature that tried and failed as satire. Rubbish that is beneath even C's. small reputation. See also July 14, 1835, no. 2, for a short notice of similar sentiments.

1737 KNICKERBOCKER MAGAZINE 5 (April 1835):362.

> A satirical piece with numerous characters and frequent dialogue. It remains to be seen if the book will improve C's. reputation.

1738 _____ 6 (August 1835):152-53.

> A complete failure. No plot and poorly executed. C. is a writer of romance, not of politics. One is based upon unreality, the other on reality, and the two can never successfully come together in a work of fiction.

1739 LITERARY GAZETTE 19 (July 11, 1835):435-37. Partially reprinted in MUSEUM OF FOREIGN LITERATURE, SCIENCE AND ART 27 (October 1835):343.

Able and written with some ingenuity, but it falls short of Jonathan Swift in humor and interest.

1740 MONTHLY REVIEW 2, 4th series (August 1835):541-44.

The reading of a few passages of this book will fatigue the reader and convince him that it should never have been written.

1741 MORNING COURIER AND NEW YORK ENQUIRER, September 3, 22, 1835.

1742 NEW-ENGLAND MAGAZINE 9 (August 1835):136-37.

THE MONIKINS is even worse than C's. LETTER TO HIS COUNTRYMEN and will surely destroy what little reputation he now enjoys.

1743 NEW MONTHLY MAGAZINE 45 (October 1835):240-41.

If this had been C's. first literary experiment one might have been amused by its scenes and characters.

1744 NEW YORK COMMERCIAL ADVERTISER, August 21, 1835.

1745 PORTLAND MAGAZINE 1 (August 1, 1835):352.

Articles from Cooper's Death to the Present

1746 Clees, James Cameron. "James Fenimore Cooper's 'The Monikins': Social Criticism, Satire, and Allegory." Ph.D. dissertation, Columbia University, 1965.

THE MONIKINS, C's. finest attempt at social criticism, fails as a novel. It does contain, however, examples of excellent humor and satire.

1747 Faulkner, Forrest W. "James Fenimore Cooper's 'The Monikins' Edited by Forrest Wilford Faulkner." Master of Arts degree, University of Texas, 1965.

THE CRATER (MARK'S REEF [ENGLISH TITLE]) (1847)

Articles and Reviews Contemporary with Cooper

1748 ATHENAEUM [20] (October 9, 1847):1047-48.

C. would have breathed life into this novel in his heyday, but he is growing feeble as a writer and his faults are prominently displayed here.

1749 GENTLEMAN'S MAGAZINE 184 (March 1848):289.
    Skillful and ingenious.

1750 GODEY'S LADY'S BOOK 36 (January 1848):69.
    Graphic. One of C's. best novels.

1751 LITERARY GAZETTE 31 (October 9, 1847):713-15.
    A minutely detailed novel woven from extraordinary circumstances. Many of C's. observations will more readily be appreciated by an American, than an English, audience.

1752 SPECTATOR (London) 20 (October 23, 1847):1025-26.
    Repetitive of himself and others (Defoe and Marryat) in both plot and political speculations. An artificially contrived plot that takes the reader, very slowly, to just where the author wants to lead him. Unreal.

1753 UNITED STATES MAGAZINE AND DEMOCRATIC REVIEW 21 (November 1847):438-47.
    A slight tale in which C. forces his opinions upon the reader, rather than developing the characters in such a way that they naturally communicate his views to the public.

Articles from Cooper's Death to the Present

1754 "American Dreamer." TIMES (London), "Literary Supplement," March 29, 1963, p. 216.
    Review of a twentieth century edition of THE CRATER. Includes comments on many of C's. sea novels.

1755 Gates, W. B. "Cooper's 'The Crater' and Two Explorers." AMERICAN LITERATURE 23 (May 1951):243-46.
    Discusses C's. use of THE VOYAGES OF CAPTAIN COOK and Lieutenant Charles Wilkes's NARRATIVE OF THE UNITED STATES EXPLORING EXPEDITION as sources for THE CRATER.

1756 _____. "A Defense of the Ending of Cooper's 'The Crater.'" MODERN LANGUAGE NOTES 70 (May 1955):347-49.
    The destruction of the colony at the end of THE CRATER is not ridiculous if one accepts the premise that C. was attempting to show the results

of failure to adhere to democracy's ideals.

1757 _____. "A Note on Cooper and 'Robinson Crusoe.'" MODERN LANGUAGE NOTES 67 (June 1952):421-22.

        C. took several incidents from ROBINSON CRUSOE and transferred them to THE CRATER. Having followed Defoe's narrative closely, he lost track of his own characters, causing them to react in a manner that was not consistent with their nature.

1758 McCloskey, John C. "Cooper's Political Views in 'The Crater.'" MODERN PHILOLOGY 53 (November 1955):113-16.

        C's. change from a liberal to a conservative between 1835 and 1847 was only a temporary one, but one that resulted from a feeling that the spirit of the 1840s posed a threat to true democracy.

1759 McWilliams, John P. "'The Crater' and the Constitution." TEXAS STUDIES IN LITERATURE AND LANGUAGE 12 (Winter 1971):631-45.

        The violent ending of THE CRATER proves that, by 1847, C. believed in the inevitability of the destruction of democracy by party demagogues who would take advantage of the changeability of constitutional law.

1760 Marder, Daniel. "Cooper's Second Cycle." SOUTH CENTRAL RE-VIEW 21 (1985):23-37.

        The second cycle mentioned in the title relates to man's exile from society and closely parallels C's. life in his later years.

1761 Parrington, Vernon Louis, Jr. AMERICAN DREAMS: A STUDY OF AMERICAN UTOPIAS. 2d ed. Brown University Studies, vol. 11. American Series, no. 2. New York: Russell & Russell, 1964. Pp. 22-26.

        C. destroyed his utopian community in THE CRATER in an attempt to show that democracy's downfall could be accomplished by only a few dishonest people. Once the real issues were obscured and confusion set in, it was not long before the minority was able to rule.

1762 Rennick, Robert M. "James Fenimore Cooper: Onomastician." NAMES 30 (March 1982):55.

        C's. use of names.

1763 Ringe, Donald A. "Cooper's 'The Crater' and the Moral Basis of Society." Michigan Academy of Science, Arts, and Letters, PAPERS 44 (1959):371-80.

        To ignore the first half of THE CRATER is to misunderstand C's. theme. From these pages it is clear that the author viewed man as dependent upon God, for it was from Him that the laws by which one lived were received. The prosperity of society for C. then, was equal to the degree to which man allowed his life to be guided by a supreme being. Unfortunately, man often ignored God's teachings, experienced moral decay, and was destroyed.

1764 Scudder, Harold H. "Cooper's 'The Crater.'" AMERICAN LITERATURE 19 (May 1947):109-26.

        C's. seemingly absurd plot may have had some basis in fact. It also appears that THE CRATER was used as a means of offering a defense of the economic views espoused by Henry C. Carey, C's. former publisher.

1765 Wood, James Playsted, ed. ONE HUNDRED YEARS AGO: AMERICAN WRITING OF 1847. Centenary Series in American Literature. New York: Funk & Wagnalls Co., 1947. Pp. 439-41.

        While composed of scenes of little credibility and ill-used supernaturalism, THE CRATER has both "dignity and simplicity" that go far toward rescuing one of America's first utopian novels.

WAYS OF THE HOUR (1850)

Articles and Reviews Contemporary with Cooper

1766 "The Administration of the Law. 'The Ways of the Hour; a Tale'. By J. Fenimore Cooper, 1850." WESTERN LAW JOURNAL 8 (October 1850):1-22.

        C. so distorted the evils of the legal system that the picture he painted of it was both a caricature and a libel.

1767 ATHENAEUM [23] (April 27, 1850):443.

        An improbable novel that has resulted in the spoiling of a good novelist without creating a social reformer.

1768 [Bowen, F.] "The Ways of the Hour. A Tale." NORTH AMERICAN REVIEW 71 (July 1850):121-35.

        C., as a writer, is only a ghost of his former self. All his faults are exhibited in this lame caricature.

1769 BROWNSON'S QUARTERLY REVIEW 5 n.s. (July 1851):273-97.

        A hastily written and exaggerated book, but possessed of an ingeniously devised plot that has much to offer concerning the administration of justice in America.

1770 GRAHAMS AMERICAN MONTHLY MAGAZINE 36 (June 1850):416.

Although C. is a perceptive writer, he allows his dislikes to creep into his fiction. This novel is no exception, but it is still an interesting one.

1771 LITERARY GAZETTE 34 (April 20, 1850):273-74.

Reader interest and curiosity is maintained in a novel that is drawn out in length, repetitious, and somewhat exaggerated.

1772 LITERARY WORLD 6 (April 13, 1850):368-70.

This work has the possibility of being extremely successful, although C. paints a picture of a world far more evil than it actually is. As a novel of American justice it proves nothing.

1773 _____ 6 (May 18, 1850):498-99.

Had this book been written by someone other than C. it would be considered a libel. As it is, it is difficult for the reviewer to know what to make of it.

1774 SARTAIN'S UNION MAGAZINE OF LITERATURE AND ART 7 (August 1850):126-27.

The attempt to meld politics and fiction does not work. C. should stick to one or the other.

1775 UNITED STATES MAGAZINE AND DEMOCRATIC REVIEW 26 (May 1850):479.

Of great interest. Characters equal to C's. best.

Articles from Cooper's Death to the Present

1776 Bardes, Barbara Ann and Suzanne Gossett. "Cooper and the 'Cup and Saucer' Law: A New Reading of 'The Ways of the Hour.'" AMERICAN QUARTERLY 32 (Winter 1980):499-518.

C's. primary reason for writing WAYS OF THE HOUR was to attack the Married Women's Property Act that he feared would upset the existing social order.

1777 Steele, Timothy. "Matter and Mystery: Neglected Works and Background Materials of Detective Fiction." MODERN FICTION STUDIES 29 (Autumn 1983):435-50.

The influence of C. and Balzac on detective fiction.

NONFICTION

ARTICLES FROM COOPER'S DEATH TO THE PRESENT

1778 Ewart, Mike. "Cooper and the American Revolution: The Non-fiction."
JOURNAL OF AMERICAN STUDIES 11 (April 1977):61-79.
     C. viewed the Revolutionary War as a threat to the aristocracy,
whereas other writers have seen it as a triumph of the people over special interest groups.

THE EUROPEAN TRAVELOGUES

1779 Wiley, Marydale Stewart. "Rhetorical Strategies and Narrative Design
in James Fenimore Cooper's Travel Books." Ph.D. dissertation, Northern Illinois University, 1987.
     On C's. use of narrative technique, imagery, metaphor, simile,
and speech.

**Sketches of Switzerland (Excursions in Switzerland [English
Title]). Sketches of Switzerland; Part II (A Residence in France .
. . and a Second Visit to Switzerland [English Title]) (1836)**

Articles and Reviews Contemporary with Cooper

1780 AMERICAN QUARTERLY REVIEW 20 (September 1836):228-44.
     The book is merely a lightheaded description of certain localities
and scenery in Switzerland. It does, however, contain many of C's. extreme
opinions. SWITZERLAND can do little to add to his literary reputation.

1781 ATHENAEUM [9] (June 18, 1836):429-30.
     As a travelogue the book is excellent. As social and political
commentary it has much to offer the reader in both England and America.

1782 _____ [9] (September 24, 1836):686-87.
     It is sad that C. could not display "fewer traces of a sore spirit."

1783 EVENING POST (New York), June 25, 1836.
     A defense of C.

1784 JOURNAL OF BELLES LETTRES 7 (May 31, 1836):no. 22.
     A dull book. Merely a diary. Compared to travelogues of more

accomplished writers, it is a useless production.

1785 KNICKERBOCKER MAGAZINE 7 (June 1836):647.
Should do a great deal to revive C's. literary reputation that was destroyed by THE MONIKINS.

1786 _____ 8 (July 1836):102-03.
An agreeable book that should help to overshadow the unfavorable reception received by some of his recent endeavors.

1787 LITERARY GAZETTE 20 (September 17, 24, October 1, 1836):596-97, 615-16, 627-28.
Pleasant descriptions interspersed with observations whose importance derives from a less prejudicial viewpoint and a more mature attitude than some of his previous works.

1788 MONTHLY MAGAZINE 22 n.s. (September 1836):282-83.
Disappointing.

1789 MONTHLY REVIEW 2, 4th series (August 1836):491-502.
The theme which C. pursues is a worn out one, but the descriptions are so well done and his opinions and judgments are valuable enough, that the book does possess both interest and merit.

1790 MUSEUM OF FOREIGN LITERATURE, SCIENCE AND ART 29 (September 1836):461-63.
As one intimately familiar with Europe, C's. descriptions are much more learned than those of any ordinary traveller. He also imparts a political philosophy that, while not always instructive, is at least amusing.

1791 _____ 30 (December 1836):448-51.
An honest work that has sound opinions.

1792 MORNING COURIER AND NEW YORK ENQUIRER, October 19, 1836.
A boring volume.

1793 NEW MONTHLY MAGAZINE 48 (November 1836):369-70.
C. is no less a patriot for pointing out his country's faults, but his readers will probably fail to agree.

1794 NEW YORK AMERICAN, May 28, 1836.
A positive reaction. Agrees with C's. assessment of the press.

1795 NEW-YORK MIRROR 13 (June 11, 1836):399.
>   Entertaining light reading. The volumes possess factual errors and do not exhibit any of the imagination of which C. is capable.

1796 _____ 14 (November 14, 1836):151.
>   Delightful descriptions of government and human nature.

1797 [Palfrey, John Gorham.] "Sketches of Switzerland." NORTH AMERI-CAN REVIEW 43 (July 1836):280.
>   Excellent descriptions of nature. Marred by its politics.

1798 SOUTHERN LITERARY MESSENGER 2 (May 1836):401-03.
>   Written with "ill-humor," but probably correct in its assessments.

1799 _____ 2 (October 1836):720-21.
>   Fresh and observant.

1800 TIMES (London), June 29, 1836, p. 7.
>   Entertaining and honest descriptions of Swiss scenery and politics.

1801 WESTMINSTER REVIEW 26 (October 1836):84-94.
>   Compared to other writers C. is far superior. The book as a whole, however, falls short of the descriptive writing of which he is capable.

Articles from Cooper's Death to the Present

1802 Gruninger, Hans-Werner. "James Fenimore Cooper in Switzerland." Master of Arts degree, Southern Illinois University, 1955.

1803 Ludeke, Henry. "James Fenimore Cooper and the Democracy of Swit-zerland." ENGLISH STUDIES 27 (1946):33-44. Reprinted in Ludeke. THE "DEMOCRACY" OF HENRY ADAMS, AND OTHER ESSAYS. Swiss Stud- ies in English, vol. 4. Bern: A. Francke, 1950. Pp. 7-22.
>   SWITZERLAND represents the cornerstone of C's. political thought--American democracy imbued with the Swiss sense of social values.

Gleanings in Europe (Recollections of Europe [English Title]) (1837)

Articles and Reviews Contemporary with Cooper

1804 AMERICAN MONTHLY MAGAZINE 3 n.s. (April 1837):401-05.

A useful book with a flowing style that makes interesting reading. The author is perceptive and his habit of comparing European matters to America's adds to the book's utility.

1805 AMERICAN QUARTERLY REVIEW 21 (June 1837):522-23.
C's. political opinions combine in this volume with his extreme egotism to result in a work that is well below his abilities and unworthy of such a famous novelist.

1806 ATHENAEUM [10] (January 28, 1837):57-58.
A pleasant book, although somewhat speculative. It will not be admired in either America or England.

1807 [Bowen, F.] "Cooper's Novels and Travels." NORTH AMERICAN REVIEW 46 (January 1838):1-19.
The book offers a few glimpses of society, life, and fashion, but does not sustain interest. Its greatest peculiarity is the ease with which C's. republican ire is roused; a reaction that must have created negative feelings toward him in French society.

1808 KNICKERBOCKER MAGAZINE 9 (April 1837):421-22.
Written by an unprejudiced patriot who is both just and accurate in his observations.

1809 LADIES' COMPANION 9 (July 1838):149.
Ignores the routine of every day life for that which is interesting to the American reader. A rich and brilliant volume.

1810 LITERARY GAZETTE 21 (January 28, 1837):52-54.
Of both interest and amusement.

1811 MONTHLY REVIEW 1, 4th series (March 1837):321-30.
As descriptions and reflections from the pen of one who is observant, this book is of greater value than the preceding ones in the series.

1812 NEW-YORK MIRROR 14 (March 4, 1837):285.
A favorable work that is free of objections that have marred C's. more recent writings.

1813 QUARTERLY REVIEW (London) 58 (April 1837):497-523.

1814 SOUTHERN LITERARY MESSENGER 3 (April 1837):272.
Never should have been published.

1815 "The World We Live In. No. V." BLACKWOOD'S MAGAZINE 41 (March 1837):325-41.

        On C's. meeting of Scott in Paris. Little in the way of criticism. (pp. 334-36)

Articles from Cooper's Death to the Present

1816 Halligan, John J., Jr. "A Critical Edition of Volume I of James Fenimore Cooper's 'Gleanings in Europe. By an American' [France] (1837)." Ph.D. dissertation, University of Pittsburgh, 1972.

        A comparison of three 1837 editions. Includes information on textual allusions, translations, a biographical sketch, historical background, and a summary of early 1800 travel literature.

1817 Philbrick, Thomas. "Cooper's Naval Friend in Paris." AMERICAN LITERATURE 52 (January 1981):634-38.

        Claims that C's. naval friend mentioned in GLEANINGS IN EUROPE was not Captain Woolsey, but Captain Ichabod Walcott Chauncey.

1818 Spiller, Robert E., ed. "Introduction." GLEANINGS IN EUROPE: FRANCE. London: Oxford University Press, 1928. Reprinted, New York: Kraus Reprint Co.

        A general introduction to C's. social philosophy. Reviews of this edition are found in the following sources: AMERICAN LITERATURE 1 (May 1, 1929):222-24; ANGLIA BEILBLATT 43 (November 1932):347-52; MODERN LANGUAGE NOTES 95 (January 1930):41-43; PENNSYLVANIA MAGAZINE OF HISTORY AND BIOGRAPHY 53 (April 1929):191; REVIEW OF ANGLO-AMERICAINE 6 (August 1929):532-36; SATURDAY REVIEW OF LITERATURE 5 (June 15, 1929):1107-08; TIMES (London) "Literary Supplement," February 14, 1929, p. 114; and University of California, CHRONICLES 31 (January 1929):110-11.

Gleanings in Europe: England (England: with Sketches of Society in the Metropolis [English Title]) (1837)

Articles and Reviews Contemporary with Cooper

1819 AMERICAN MONTHLY MAGAZINE 4 n.s. (October 1837):391-93.

        ENGLAND catalogs the woes of an egotist and is useful only as a form of penance for the sins of the reader.

1820 "Ancient Days--No. I." NEW MONTHLY MAGAZINE 53 (May

1838):82-91.
        Satirical remarks on C's. ability to describe London life after only a short acquaintance with it. (p. 89)

1821 ATHENAEUM [10] (June 10, 1837):412-13.
        A dull, prejudiced work that is hardly superior to what might be expected from any traveler who had spent a month in England.

1822 BURTON'S GENTLEMAN'S MAGAZINE 1 (October 1837):290-91.
        A book of questionable merit.

1823 _____ 2 (February 1838):131.
        Notice of the QUARTERLY REVIEW article below that agrees with its assessment.

1824 FRASER'S MAGAZINE 16 (August 1837):233-41.
        With the publication of this book, no one in England will desire to see C. leave America.

1825 KNICKERBOCKER MAGAZINE 10 (October 1837):350-52.
        This reviewer supports C's. comments on both English and American society, but questions his extreme prejudice against the English, his dislike for the public press, and his antipathy toward New England.

1826 "Mr. Cooper and the British Quarterly." NEW-YORK MIRROR 15 (January 20, 1838):239.
        An attack upon the QUARTERLY REVIEW article above.

1827 "Mr. Cooper and the London 'Quarterly.'" KNICKERBOCKER MAGAZINE 11 (February 1838):184-85.
        Paraphrase of the QUARTERLY REVIEW article found above. Although the two reviewers are in general agreement, this author regrets that C's. ability as a novelist was unjustly slurred by the English periodical.

1828 MONTHLY REVIEW 2, 4th series (July 1837):347-57.
        An irritable book, but one that is observant.

1829 MORNING COURIER AND NEW YORK ENQUIRER, September 8, 1837.

1830 NEW YORKER 3 (October 17, 24, 1837):462-63, 476-77.

1831 OASIS 1 (October 1837):46.

Stylistically and descriptively it is a fine work, but there is much that will anger readers.

1832 QUARTERLY REVIEW (London) 59 (October 1837):327-61. Reprinted in JOURNAL OF BELLES LETTRES (Waldies) Part I (February 6, 18, 1838):nos. 6-7 and MUSEUM OF FOREIGN LITERATURE, SCIENCE AND ART 32 (February 1838):180-95.

Nearly unworthy of being reviewed. A contemptuous book. Trivial, frivolous, confused, ignorant, and malicious. Dekker and McWilliams (item no. 6) claim this review was written by J. G. Lockhart. Brightfield (item no. 1837) attributes it to John Wilson Croker.

1833 SPECTATOR (London) 10 (May 27, 1837):493-94.

Searching and thoughtful while largely lacking in C's. usual Anglophobia.

1834 TIMES (London), July 3, 1837, p. 3.

This book is the product of the disaffection of a man whose success is far less than his self-conceit.

1835 "The World We Live In. No. X." BLACKWOOD'S MAGAZINE 42 (August 1837):195-208.

C., a vulgar man, is not the genius be believes himself to be. His lack of manners and his small reputation will continue to be unacceptable to the English nobility. (p. 199)

1836 "The World We Live In. No. XI." BLACKWOOD'S MAGAZINE 42 (September 1837):309-30.

On C's. description of American and English women. (p. 328)

Articles from Cooper's Death to the Present

1837 Brightfield, Myron F. JOHN WILSON CROKER. Berkeley: University of California Press, 1940. Pp. 390.

Partial republication of a letter from Lockhart to Crocker dated June 8, 1837, concerning C's. disagreeable manners and ideas while in London. Brightfield claims that this letter was written by Lockhart after coming into contact with ENGLAND. Lockhart's views were then reflected in Crocker's review of ENGLAND in the QUARTERLY REVIEW (item no. 1832).

1838 Mowat, R. B. AMERICANS IN ENGLAND. New York: Houghton Mifflin Co., 1935. Pp. 115-21.

Disappointed with America, C. left for Europe, but soon found himself disillusioned with what he found there. He returned home, not a bitter and frustrated man, but one with a renewed belief in America's future.

1839 Spiller, Robert E., ed. "Introduction." GLEANINGS IN EUROPE: ENGLAND. London: Oxford University Press, 1930. Reprinted, New York: Kraus Reprint Co.

C. believed that America must attain both mental and political independence from England before she could develop her own national character. Never a tactful man, he therefore described an England that often enraged others, but which was eminently truthful. Reviews of this edition are found in the following journals: AMERICAN LITERATURE 3 (March 1931):104-07; ANGLIA BEILBLATT 43 (November 1932):347-52; JOURNAL OF MODERN HISTORY 3 (March 1931):127-28; MODERN LANGUAGE NOTES 46 (November 1931):487-88; NATION 133 (December 30, 1931):728; REVUE ANGLO-AMERICAINE 8 (August 1931):538-42; SATURDAY REVIEW OF LITERATURE 7 (February 7, 1931):585; University of California, CHRONICLES 32 (October 1930):515-16.

1840 Staggs, Kenneth Walton. "Cooper's 'Gleanings in Europe: England': A Problem in Copy-text." Center for Editions of American Authors, NEWSLETTER 3, pp. 14-15.

Not seen.   Citation from Modern Language Association, BIBLIOGRAPHY, 1970. p. 105.

1841 _____. "A Facsimile Edition of James Fenimore Cooper's 'Gleanings in Europe: England', Historically annotated, Including Substantive Variants in the English and French Editions of 1837." Ph.D. dissertation, University of Texas, 1968.

Gleanings in Europe: Italy (Excursions in Italy [English Title]) (1838)

Articles and Reviews Contemporary with Cooper

1842 AMERICAN MONTHLY MAGAZINE 6 n.s. (July 1838):75-84.

Less egotistical and ill-natured than other books in the series. C's. views on Catholicism are the volume's only redeeming passages.   Includes comments on C's. review of Lockhart's LIFE OF SCOTT.

1843 ARMY AND NAVY CHRONICLE 7 (August 2, 1838):67-68.

The book possesses good descriptions and valuable ideas, but the reviewer cannot subscribe to all the thoughts expressed.

1844 ATHENAEUM [11] (February 17, 1838):124.

The reader, drawn by C's. name, pays his money and receives nothing in return.

1845 BURTON'S GENTLEMAN'S MAGAZINE 3 (July 1838):65-66.

The best of the series, but it adds nothing new. A trifling book by a man whose deductions are too general and whose observations are too prejudiced.

1846 "Cooper's Excursions in Italy." MUSEUM OF FOREIGN LITERA-TURE, SCIENCE AND ART 33 (May 1838):77-79.

C. is skillful and sees Europe from a fresh viewpoint--that of the American.

1847 EVENING POST (New York), August 18, 1838.

1848 HESPERIAN 1 (July 1838):250-55.

An accurate account of the manners, customs, and character of the Italian people, interspersed with some of C's. best physical descriptions. His anti-English bias continues to show.

1849 JOURNAL OF BELLES LETTRES (Waldies) Part I (June 5, 1838):no. 23.

Pleasant reading, but nothing new.

1850 KNICKERBOCKER MAGAZINE 11 (June 1838):560.

Agreeable. Lacks C's. usual political and personal attacks.

1851   LITERARY GAZETTE 22 (February 17, 1838):100-02.

A pleasing description, but not much that is new.

1852 MORNING COURIER AND NEW YORK ENQUIRER, May 30, 1838.

1853 NEW YORK AMERICAN, June 2, 1838.

1854 NEW-YORK MIRROR 15 (June 16, 1838):407.

Enjoyable, although anti-English throughout.

1855 NEW-YORKER 5 (June 2, 1838):173.

Entertaining and instructive for what C. saw, but often ludicrous when he expresses his feelings.

1856 SPECTATOR (London) 11 (February 17, 1838):161.

1857 TIMES (London), April 19, 1838, p. 5.
     Little that is illuminating or new is found here. The book is sometimes amusing, but often dull. Although less egotistical than his former volumes, it has the same national prejudices.

1858 "Travels and Journals." MONTHLY REVIEW 1, 4th series (March 1838):438-55.
     A disgraceful book of personal irritabilities.

Articles from Cooper's Death to the Present

1859 Neri, Algerina. "James Fenimore Cooper's Gleanings of Italy." REVISTA DI STUDI ANGLO-AMER 3 (1984-85):103-13.
     Not seen.

NOTIONS OF THE AMERICANS (1828)

Articles and Reviews Contemporary with Cooper

1860 ATHENAEUM 9, 2nd series (September 1, 1828):446-47.
     The best book written on the subject, but still full of imperfections (conceit, arrogance, stylistic flaws, false humor). Not as bad, however, as the LITERARY GAZETTE claims it to be (item no. 1867).

1861 BAPTIST MAGAZINE 22 (January 1830):23.
     A favorable review.

1862 CHRISTIAN REVIEW AND CLERICAL MAGAZINE 2 (October 1828):450.
     The reviewer, unaware of the author's identity, states that the book is pleasurable, but not to be taken as a guide to America and her concerns.

1863 "Cooper and Irving." PHILADELPHIA ALBUM 3 (September 24, 1828):134-35.
     NOTIONS lacks both taste and accuracy and will do little to enhance C's. name.

1864 ECLECTIC REVIEW 2, 3d series (November 1829):365-98. Reprinted in MUSEUM OF FOREIGN LITERATURE, SCIENCE AND ART 16

(March 1830):233-48.

  While possessing some drawbacks, the book does contain valuable information.

1865 EDINBURGH REVIEW 49 (June 1829):473-525. Reprinted in MUSEUM OF FOREIGN LITERATURE, SCIENCE AND ART 15 (December 1829):510-33.

  Although not completely unfriendly toward C., this reviewer was annoyed by his boastfulness.

1866 LADIES' MAGAZINE 1 (September 1828):431.

  Entertaining and informative, especially the portion on women. Its fictitious origin, however, creates a degree of mistrust that would not have been present had the information been presented in a different manner.

1867 LITERARY GAZETTE 12 (June 21, 1828):385-87.

  C. should stick with novels and romance lest he become laughable as an author.

1868 LITERARY REGISTER 1 (September 1, 1828):219.

  Well drawn scenery.

1869 LONDON WEEKLY REVIEW 2 (June 28, 1828):404.

  A flawed book, but one that is amusing and informative. The author attacks the review found in the LITERARY GAZETTE (item no. 1867).

1870 MONTHLY MAGAZINE 6 n.s. (July 1828):81-84.

  A superior book by one who has the knowledge lacking by those who have gone before him. It will go far toward removing the impressions of American inequality, coarseness, and vulgarity created by earlier writers.

1871 MONTHLY REVIEW 8 new & imp. series (August 1828):465-80.

  Informative, but exaggerated. C. places the United States under a magnifying glass, thus making her deficiencies seem much larger than they are in reality.

1872 NEW MONTHLY MAGAZINE 23 (August 1828):164-73.

  C. neither overly praises his country, nor acts toward England with excessive prejudice. The volumes hold many truths and should be read by all Englishmen.

1873 NEW YORK AMERICAN, September 5, November 4, 5, 1829.

1874 NEW-YORK MIRROR 6 (August 23, 1828):55.
	A favorable notice that contrasts with the LITERARY GAZETTE review (item no. 1867).

1875 _____ 6 (September 13, 1828):77-78.
	Of no value as a political tract. Duller than THE RED ROVER as entertainment.

1876 PHILADELPHIA ALBUM 3 (October 29, 1828):173.
	A book filled with error that will eventually give its author great embarrassment.

1877 [Sparks, Jared.] "Pitkin's 'History of the United States.'" NORTH AMERICAN REVIEW 30 (January 1830):1-25.
	On C's. false statements concerning American peace negotiations at the end of the Revolutionary War. (pp. 15-17)

1878 WESTMINSTER REVIEW 10 (January 1829):51-71.
	Stylistically poor and often intemperate in language, but containing valuable information about the United States.

Articles from Cooper's Death to the Present

1879 Arndt, Karl J. "The Cooper-Sealsfield Exchange of Criticism." AMERICAN LITERATURE 15 (March 1943):16-24.
	NOTIONS OF THE AMERICANS was influenced by Sealsfield's anonymous publication, THE UNITED STATES OF NORTH AMERICA, which had pictured a crude and corrupt America. C's. aristocratic ideas caused him to depict an America that was far more civilized than Sealsfield would admit to.

1880 Frisch, Morton J. "Cooper's 'Notions of the Americans': A Commentary on Democracy." ETHICS, AN INTERNATIONAL JOURNAL OF SOCIAL, POLITICAL, AND LEGAL PHILOSOPHY 71 (October 1960):114-20.
	C's. ability to consider democracy in light of its aristocratic foundations enabled him to develop a theory of politics and society that showed both knowledge and understanding.

1881 Spiller, Robert E., ed. "Introduction." NOTIONS OF THE AMERICANS. New York: Unger, 1963.

1882 Taft, Kendall B. "The Nationality of Cooper's 'Travelling Bachelor.'" AMERICAN LITERATURE 28 (November 1956):368-70.

It was C's. intention not to ascribe any nationality to his "Travelling Bachelor," but to merely make him a European traveler.

1883 Wasserman, Renata R. Mautner. "The Reception of Cooper's Work and the Image of America." ESQ: A JOURNAL OF THE AMERICAN RENAISSANCE 32 (3d quarter 1986):183-200.

NOTIONS OF THE AMERICANS was not well received, but is informative because it illustrates the boundaries of acceptance C's. readers set for his works.

A LETTER TO HIS COUNTRYMEN (1834)

Articles and Reviews Contemporary with Cooper

1884 ATHENAEUM [7] (August 2, 1834):569.

C., who cannot tolerate the aristocratic English, has discovered that he also despises his republican countrymen for failing to be republican enough.

1885 BOSTON DAILY ADVERTISER AND PATRIOT, August 1, June 16, 1834.

Decries C's. decision to enmesh his writings in the politics of the day.

1886 "Cooper Coopered." NEW WORLD 1 (July 18, 1840):97-100.

A ludicrous, vain book written by a man who has very limited powers.

1887 EVENING POST (New York), June 13-June 18, 1834.

Reviews and comments interspersed throughout these issues.

1888 KNICKERBOCKER MAGAZINE 4 (July 1834):75-76.

C's. LETTER TO HIS COUNTRYMEN shows him to be overly sensitive to criticism. The book embodies all the unfavorable traits of his character.

1889 LITERARY GAZETTE 18 (August 2, 1834):527.

Of no great interest to either Englishmen or New Yorkers.

1890 NEW-ENGLAND MAGAZINE 7 (August 1834):154-57.

An absurd book of hallucinations by a man who is losing his wits. Unfortunately, those few portions that are good tell the reader nothing new.

1891 NEW YORK AMERICAN, June 21, 1834.
A satirical attack upon C.

1892 NEW YORK COMMERCIAL ADVERTISER, June 20, 23, 1834.

1893 NEW-YORK MIRROR 12 (July 5, 1834):7.

1894 NILES' WEEKLY REGISTER 46 (June 21, August 23, 1834):292, 428.

1895 "A Reply to the 'Letter' of J. Fenimore Cooper. By One of His Countrymen." NEW ENGLAND JOURNAL 7 (October 1834):333-36.
An attempt to show that C. was wrong in his statement that the people have more to fear from the legislative, than the executive, branch of government.

1896 SOUTHERN LITERARY MAGAZINE 11 (August 1834):18.
Regrets that C. has fallen prey to party politics and hopes for a return to his former works.

THE AMERICAN DEMOCRAT (1838)

Articles and Reviews Contemporary with Cooper

1897 [Brownson, Orestes.] BOSTON QUARTERLY REVIEW 1 (July 1838):360+.
An able book written in a clear style, but one that will do little to correct the faults pointed out by the author.

1898 KNICKERBOCKER MAGAZINE 11 (April 1838):392.
Notice of publication.

1899 _____ 11 (May 1838):461-63.
A non-critical review.

1900 MORNING COURIER AND NEW YORK ENQUIRER, April 19, 1838.

1901 NEW YORK AMERICAN, April 21, 1838.

1902 NEW YORK COMMERCIAL ADVERTISER, May 25, 1838.

1903 NEW YORKER 5 (June 9, 1838):184.
        Recommended, although the reviewer finds the book "peculiar" and "inelegant."

1904 OASIS 1 (June 30, 1838):168-69.
        New and original.

Articles from Cooper's Death to the Present

1905 Davis, Leona King. "Literary Opinions on Slavery in American Literature from After the American Revolution to the Civil War." NEGRO HISTORY BULLETIN 23 (February 1960):99-101+.
        On C's. pro-slavery views.

1906 de Grazia, Sebastian. OF TIME, WORK AND LEISURE. New York: Twentieth Century Fund, 1962. Pp. 290-91.
        C. claimed that a nation's government affects its culture. A democracy, which accepts the will of the majority (a mediocrity), therefore finds it difficult to attain a high standard in literature, architecture, and the arts.

1907 Dekker, George and Larry Johnston, eds. "Introduction." THE AMERICAN DEMOCRAT. Baltimore: Penguin Books, 1969.

1908 Freimarck, Vincent and Bernard Rosenthal, eds. RACE AND THE AMERICAN ROMANTICS. New York: Schocken Books, 1971. Pp. 75-88.
        Letters by C. and a selection from THE AMERICAN DEMOCRAT. The editors conclude that C's. views on slavery were purely constitutional and not moral ones. While he often reflected the views of slavery apologists he also opposed the Missouri Compromise.

1909 Forgue, Guy J. "Mencken and Cooper." MENCKENIANA no. 14 (Summer 1965):1-3.
        Forgue, using examples from Mencken's 1931 preface to the second edition of THE AMERICAN DEMOCRAT (item no. 1912), argues that the two authors were surprising close in their political views.

1910 Hollis, C. Carroll. "Orestes Brown: Jacksonian Literary Critic." NO DIVIDED ALLEGIANCE: ESSAYS IN BROWNSON'S THOUGHT. Edited by Leonard Gilhooley. New York: Fordham University Press, 1980. Pp. 51-83.

On Brownson's BOSTON QUARTERLY REVIEW critique of THE AMERICAN DEMOCRAT (item no. 1897). The laudatory nature of this review resulted, not from friendship, but from Brownson's dissatisfaction with the tenor of C. criticism at this time.

1911 McWilliams, John P. "Cooper and the Conservative Democrat." AMERICAN QUARTERLY 22 (Fall 1970):665-77.

While C. did not promote the repression of civil liberties, his loss of faith in his fellow man allowed him to seek refuge in property rights, strong law enforcement, a limited franchise, curbs on majority rule, and a powerful executive.

1912 Mencken, Henry Louis. "Introduction To 'The American Democrat.'" THE AMERICAN SCENE: A READER. Edited by Huntington Cairns. New York: Alfred A. Knopf, 1931. Pp. 398-405.

Blames C's. unpopularity as a person on his anti-democratic attitudes. Credits him with extremely accurate observations and prophesies. As an aristocrat C. found himself devoted to social responsibility rather than to privilege. Reviews of this edition are found in the following sources: AMERICAN LITERATURE 4 (March 1932):71-73; BOOKLIST 28 (January 1932):211; CURRENT HISTORY 35 (December 1931):xii; NEW REPUBLIC 69 (December 16, 1931):143; OUTLOOK 158 (August 26, 1931):539; SATURDAY REVIEW OF LITERATURE 7 (August 15, 1931):59; and SPRINGFIELD REPUBLICAN November 7, 1931. p. 10.

7

MISCELLANEOUS PUBLICATIONS

PRECAUTION (1820)

Articles and Reviews Contemporary with Cooper

1913 BURTON'S GENTLEMAN'S MAGAZINE 5 (August 1839):117-18.
"Trash." Should not have been reissued.

1914 EXPOSITOR 1 (June 29, 1839):331.
A revised edition that is superior to most contemporary novels, although not equal to C's. other productions.

1915 GENTLEMAN'S MAGAZINE 91 (April 1821):345.
A good, entertaining novel, but unequal in quality. The characters, whose great number cause some confusion, are well drawn.

1916 GODEY'S LADY'S BOOK 19 (August 1839):96.
PRECAUTION lacked those traits that made C. a distinguished novelist.

1917 INDEPENDENT no. 14 (April 7, 1821):220-22.

1918 LADIES' COMPANION 11 (August 1839):197.
Deficient as are most first novels.

1919 LADIES' MONTHLY MUSEUM 18, imp. series (April 1821):217.
Good plot, admirable denoument.

1920 LITERARY AND SCIENTIFIC REPOSITORY AND CRITICAL RE-
VIEW 2 (April 1, 1821):364-75.
   A variety of well drawn characters, spirited dialogue, and possessed of proper religious principles and correct language. A truly American
novel.

1921 MONTHLY REVIEW 95 n.s. (June 1821):211.
   A good idea that is not developed. C. is attacked for his grammar
and the improbability of some of his incidents.

1922 NEW MONTHLY MAGAZINE 3 (March 1821):132.
   A promising novelist who, if he can rid himself of a certain for-
mality of style, will be read.

1923 NEW YORK LITERARY JOURNAL 4 (November 1820):38-41.
   Laudatory review. Praises C's. characterizations, including the
female ones. Complains of his wordiness.

Articles from Cooper's Death to the Present

1924 Cairns, William B. "British Republication of American Writings, 1783-
1833." Modern Language Association of America, PUBLICATIONS 43
(March 1928):303-10.
   PRECAUTION was printed in London in 1821 and reviewed by
several English periodicals. In neither case was there any reference to its
American origin.

1925 GRAHAMS AMERICAN MONTHLY MAGAZINE 41 (November
1852):553.
   On the new edition. PRECAUTION was not great art, but a
credible first novel. C. was America's greatest novelist, overcoming
deficiencies in style, plot, and composition.

1926 Hastings, George E. "How Cooper Became a Novelist." AMERICAN
LITERATURE 12 (March 1940):20-51.
   In PRECAUTION, C. attempted to imitate the plot and character
of Jane Austen's PERSUASION. He may also have been familiar with several
of her other novels, as well as those of Mrs. Opie and Mrs. Brunton's DIS-
CIPLINE.

1927 KNICKERBOCKER MAGAZINE 58 (November 1861):453.
   Described as "a fair and noble volume."

1928 Petter, Henri. THE EARLY AMERICAN NOVEL. Columbus: Ohio State University Press, 1971. Pp. 171-74, 249-50.

Petter suggests that C. was aware of the novels of Jane Austen, but was able to produce only poor imitations of them.

1929 Scudder, Harold H. "What Mr. Cooper Read to His Wife." SEWANEE REVIEW 36 (April 1928):177-94.

Presents evidence that it was Jane Austen's PRIDE AND PREJU-DICE that led C. to write PRECAUTION.

TALES FOR FIFTEEN (1823)

1930 Beard, James F. ed. "Introduction." TALES FOR FIFTEEN. Gainesville, Fla.: Scholar's Fascimile and Reprints, 1959.

Discusses why C., who had a reputation by 1823, would publish a book for young girls similar to those moral novels made popular by British female authors.

1931 THE CRITIC 12 (October 12, 1889):179.

Reprint of a newspaper clipping sent by Susan Cooper regarding TALES FOR FIFTEEN. The claim is made that the book was written to aid a financially embarrased friend.

AUTOBIOGRAPHY OF A POCKET HANDKERCHIEF (THE FRENCH GOVERNESS [ENGLISH TITLE]) (1843)

1932 Aldridge, A. Owen. "Fenimore Cooper and the Picaresque Tradition." NINETEENTH CENTURY FICTION 27 (December 1972): 283-92.

C's. selection of the picaresque as a means for promoting his social views was not an ideal one. This book, however, does serve as a good example (perhaps the only American one) of this style of literature.

1933 Brown, Walter Lee, ed. "Introduction." AUTOBIOGRAPHY OF A POCKET-HANDKERCHIEF. Evanston, Ill.: Golden-Book Press, 1897.

Although a failure in its attempt to reproduce the social life of New York, this novel effectively presents, in satirical form, some of C's ideas on society in the 1840s.

THE LAKE GUN (1850)

1934 Spiller, Robert E., ed. "Introduction." THE LAKE GUN. New York: William Farquhar Payson, 1932. Pp. 7-23.

An allegory, making use of Indian legend, that condemns the political system that C. believed was ruining the country. It favors neither the Whig nor the Democratic cause.

UPSIDE DOWN (1850)

Articles and Reviews Contemporary with Cooper

1935 THE ALBION 9, 4th series (June 22, 1850):296.

A meagre plot that could have been told in one act as easily as in three. The satire fails, the characters talk with little motivation, and the same incidents are repeated again and again.

1936 "Exit, Pursued By a Turkey." THE MONTH AT GOODSPEED'S BOOK SHOP 19 (May 1948):247-51.

Two letters to the actor James K. Hackett regarding the play.

Articles from Cooper's Death to the Present

1937 Kouwenhoven, John. "Cooper's 'Upside Down' Turns Up." COLOPHON 3 n.s. (Autumn 1938):524-30.

The surviving scene from C's. only play illustrates that he was a poor social critic, found comedy difficult, but handled dialogue skillfully.

1938 Odell, George C. D. ANNALS OF THE NEW YORK STAGE. Vol. 5. New York: Columbia University Press, 1931. Pp. 532.

First appeared June 18, 1848, at Burton's Theatre in New York City, running for only two or three performances. The main players in the cast are listed here.

NEW YORK; OR, THE TOWNS OF MANHATTAN

1939 Beard, James F. "The First History of Greater New York: Unknown Portions of Fenimore Cooper's Last Work." New York Historical Society, QUARTERLY 38 (April 1953):109-45.

Contains a history of events leading up to the publication of NEW

YORK in 1930, plus manuscript material and page proofs not published previously.

1940 "Fenimore Cooper and Manhattan." NEW YORK TIMES, "Book Review Section," September 1, 1900, p. 584.

        Accurate assessments of New York society, but made at a time when such criticism was poorly received.

1941 Fox, Dixon Ryan, ed. "Introduction." NEW YORK, BEING AN INTRODUCTION TO AN UNPUBLISHED MANUSCRIPT BY THE AUTHOR, ENTITLED "THE TOWNS OF MANHATTAN." New York: Printed for William Farquhar Payson, 1930.

        C. had been working on a piece entitled THE TOWNS OF MANHATTAN at his death. It was to be an essay on the growth of New York and speculation of what the future held. The "Introduction" had been sent to the publisher when the printing office burned. Except for the pages that had been set for printing, that portion represented here, the manuscript was lost. A review of this book is found in SATURDAY REVIEW OF LITERATURE 7 (February 7, 1931):585.

1942 "James Fenimore Cooper on Secession and State Rights." CONTINENTAL MONTHLY 6 (July 1864):79-83.

        Secession as dealt with in NEW YORK.

1943 Keese, G. Pomeroy. "Fenimore Cooper's Prophecy." NEW YORK TIMES, "Book Review Section," September 1, 1900, pp. 577-78.

        Composed largely of quotations from the manuscript.

AUTHOR AND EDITOR INDEX

References are to item numbers in the body of the text.

SUBJECT INDEX

References are to item numbers in the body of the text.